The Holy Spirit And His Gifts

Kenneth E. Hagin

15 14 13 12 11 10   18 24 23 22 21 20 19

The Holy Spirit and His Gifts Study Course
ISBN-13: 978-0-89276-085-5
ISBN-10: 0-89276-085-0

In the U.S. write:
Kenneth Hagin Ministries
P.O. Box 50126
Tulsa, OK 74150-0126
1-888-28-FAITH
www.rhema.org

In Canada write:
Kenneth Hagin Ministries
P.O. Box 335, Station D
Etobicoke (Toronto), Ontario
Canada, M9A 4X3
1-866-70-RHEMA
www.rhemacanada.org

Contents

Chapter 1

My Pentecostal Experience

Raised From the Bed of Sickness

I was born again on April 22, 1933, at twenty minutes to eight o'clock in the south bedroom of 405 North College Street in McKinney, Texas. I was raised up from the bed of sickness on the second Tuesday of August 1934, after spending sixteen long months flat on my back with two terminal organic heart conditions and an incurable blood disease. And my body was almost totally paralyzed.

When I first started reading the Word of God on the bed of sickness, Grandma would prop the Bible up in front of me as I lay there on my bed. I could only read for about ten minutes at a time — after that I could hardly see. Then that was all I could read for the day.

The next day I would read for another ten or fifteen minutes. After a few weeks of reading like that, I got so I could read for an hour at a time; eventually I could read for as long as I liked.

As a child, I had been brought up going to Sunday school; I can't remember the first time I went to church. Nor can I remember the first time I ever read the Bible. It seemed I had prayed all of my life, yet I had never been born again until April 22, 1933.

You see, you can be religious and yet not really be a born-again child of God. But when you are born again, the very same Bible that you have been reading looks different. The Bible becomes clear and easy to understand when you are born again. And as I read Grandma's Bible, I found that Jesus Christ is the same yesterday, today, and forever (Heb. 13:8).

The doctors had said I could die at any time, so when I began reading the Bible, I began reading in the New Testament. I reasoned, *I might not be alive ten minutes from now, so I will utilize this ten minutes, or whatever time I have, and I will start reading in the New Testament.*

I began reading in Matthew 1:1. When I got to Mark 11:24, I read, ". . . *What things soever ye desire, when ye pray, believe that ye receive them, and ye shall have them.*" From the first time I read that verse, I never forgot it. I didn't take time to memorize it; it just branded itself on my mind, so to speak, because Mark 11:24 was my answer for healing.

MARK 11:23,24
23 For verily I say unto you, That whosoever shall say unto this mountain, Be thou removed, and be thou cast into the sea; and shall not doubt in his heart, but shall believe that those things which he saith shall come to pass; he shall have whatsoever he saith.
24 Therefore I say unto you, What things soever ye desire, when ye pray, believe that ye receive them, and ye shall have them.

However, immediately after I read Mark 11:23 and 24, the devil hopped on my shoulder and said, "Yes, but divine healing has been done away with, you know."

I said, "Well, thank God, faith hasn't been done away with! This scripture says, '. . . *What things soever ye desire, when ye pray, believe . . .*' (Mark 11:24). I have never heard anyone say that believing and faith have been done away with."

"Yes, but healing has. You know all that healing business has been done away with."

I said to the devil, "What about Mark chapter 5? In Mark chapter 5, Jesus said to the woman with the issue of blood, '. . . *Daughter, thy faith hath made thee whole . . .*' [Mark 5:34]. Mr. Devil, if her faith made her whole, my faith will make me whole." And, thank God, it did!

At that time, I didn't know of anyone else in the whole world who believed in divine healing besides me. There was no Full Gospel church in my town at the time, and I had never heard healing preached. There weren't any Christian radio programs such as we have today; at least, if there were, I didn't know about them.

After my healing, I began my ministry just as a young Baptist boy preacher. When I heard that Full Gospel people preached on healing too, I began to fellowship with them because fellowshipping with those of like-precious faith was just like getting a spiritual shot in the arm. It built up my faith.

The Full Gospel folks preached some things I didn't quite understand or altogether agree with at that time, such as the baptism in the Holy Spirit, but I put up with that to have a little fellowship around the doctrine of healing!

God Is Not Nervous!

I wasn't used to church services where everyone would pray all together at one time, and this bothered me at first. I started to say something about it a time or two to straighten these Full Gospel folks out.

In fact, I once heard someone else tell them, "Now God's not hard of hearing, you know."

But the Full Gospel folks just replied, "He's not nervous either!"

When these Full Gospel folks invited Christians to come and pray at the altar, I would go forward to pray with them. But I would get as far away from them as I could because they bothered me all praying at the same time like that. I would get off in the corner somewhere and pray quietly.

However, after a while the thought occurred to me, *These folks knew about divine healing and my church didn't. They might know something more here in this area of praying than I do too.* So I decided I would read through the Book of Acts and see how the Early Church prayed.

As I read, I couldn't find one place where they called on "Deacon Brown" or "Sister Jones" to lead in prayer while everyone else remained silent. Instead, I found to my utter amazement that the Early Church all prayed at the same time!

ACTS 4:23,24
23 And being let go, they went to their own company, and reported all that the chief priests and elders had said unto them.
24 And when they heard that, they lifted up their voice to God WITH ONE ACCORD . . . .

The thing that cinched it with me was when I got down to Acts chapter 16 where it says that Paul and Silas were in jail. Their backs were bleeding; their feet were in stocks. Yet at midnight they prayed and sang praises to God. And the Bible says, ". . . *and the prisoners heard them*" (Acts 16:25). Until that time, I had believed in praying to God, but I believed in being quiet about it. But then I saw that Paul and Silas didn't pray quietly, not even in jail.

The next time I went to the Full Gospel service and they called us to the altar to pray, I got right in the middle of them and lifted my voice just like they did. When I did, I felt a release in my spirit. *The Word of God will set you free.* Jesus said, ". . . *ye shall know the truth, and the truth shall make you free*" (John 8:32). God's Word is truth, and it will set you free.

The Baptism in the Holy Spirit

These Full Gospel folks preached something else I couldn't quite accept — the baptism of the Holy Ghost with the evidence of speaking in other tongues. I believed in the Holy Ghost and in the baptism of the Holy Ghost. I knew I hadn't received the baptism in the Holy Ghost, but I believed in it. But that "tongues" business — that was a bitter pill for me to swallow.

I had been warned against speaking with tongues. But fellowshipping with Full Gospel people who did speak in tongues was kind of like one fellow down in East Texas said: "It's like a slippery creek bank. You keep fooling around it long enough and you'll slip in."

As a young boy preacher and pastor of a community church, I meditated and thought on the scriptures concerning the Holy Spirit, and I came to the conclusion that these Full Gospel folks were wrong about tongues. I concluded that tongues weren't necessary; they weren't for us today.

I decided that believers could receive this enduement of power — the baptism in the Holy Ghost — without speaking in tongues. That was my own opinion, of course. It certainly wasn't Scripture.

I said to the Lord in my heart, "Lord, I know these folks are good people. They are thoroughly saved — born again — and they knew about divine healing when my church didn't. I certainly do believe in the Holy Ghost. And I believe in the infilling of the Holy Ghost, the enduement of power from on High.

Then I said to the Lord, "I sense a lack of power in my own life, and I know I need the infilling of the Holy Ghost. And I expect to receive, all right. But I am of the opinion that tongues don't go along with the baptism in the Holy Ghost, and that they are not for us today."

Immediately the Lord spoke to my heart. I knew it was the Holy Spirit speaking through the Word of God. That same still small voice that had brought me off a bed of sickness and into divine healing asked me, "What does Acts 2:39 say?"

I quoted the scripture, "*For THE PROMISE is unto you, and to your children, and to all that are afar off, even as many as the Lord our God shall call*" (Acts 2:39).

Then the still small voice said, "What promise is that?"

I said, "The last part of Acts 2:38 says, '. . . *and ye shall receive the gift of the Holy Ghost.*' So the reference here is to the promise of the gift of the Holy Ghost." Then I hastened to add, "But, Lord, I believe in the Holy Ghost. It's tongues I am not sure about." (I had changed it a little bit this time to "*I'm not sure.*")

The Holy Spirit always leads us in line with the Word of God. The Word and the Spirit agree (1 John 5:7,8). I am not in favor of just following voices, because you can go wrong following voices; you can follow the wrong voice (1 Cor. 14:10). But you can never go wrong following the voice or the leading of the Holy Spirit because He will always lead you in line with the Word of God (John 16:13; 1 John 5:6-8).

Jesus said, ". . . *he* [the Holy Spirit] *shall receive of mine, and shall shew it unto you*" (John 16:14). And ". . . *he shall not speak of himself* [But, thank God, He does speak!]*; but whatsoever he shall hear, that shall he speak . . .*" (John 16:13).

Every born-again believer has the Holy Ghost in a measure through the new birth (John 3:5-8; John 4:14). But this is not the same as the baptism in the Holy Spirit — the enduement of power from on High that Jesus talked about in Luke 24:49, Acts 1:8, and John 7:38. Just because someone is born again doesn't mean he is *filled* with the Holy Spirit.

The Work of the Holy Spirit in the New Birth

There is the work of the Holy Spirit in the new birth, as we can see by the following scriptures.

JOHN 3:5-8
5 Jesus answered, Verily, verily, I say unto thee, Except a man be born of water and of THE SPIRIT, he cannot enter into the kingdom of God.
6 That which is born of the flesh is flesh; and that which is BORN OF THE SPIRIT is spirit.
7 Marvel not that I said unto thee, Ye must be BORN AGAIN.
8 The wind bloweth where it listeth, and thou hearest the sound thereof, but canst not tell whence it cometh, and whither it goeth: so is every one that is BORN OF THE SPIRIT.

ROMANS 8:16
16 THE SPIRIT itself [Himself] beareth witness with our spirit, that we are the children of God.

The Work of the Holy Spirit In the Baptism of the Holy Spirit

From these scriptures, we can see the work of the Holy Ghost in the new birth. But there is also a work of the Holy Spirit that God desires to perform in the life of every believer subsequent or following the new-birth experience, and that is called the infilling of the Holy Spirit or the baptism in the Holy Spirit. That is what Jesus was talking about in Luke 24:49 and Acts 1:8.

LUKE 24:49
49 And, behold, I send THE PROMISE OF MY FATHER upon you: but tarry ye in the city of Jerusalem, until ye be ENDUED WITH POWER FROM ON HIGH.

ACTS 1:8
8 But ye shall receive power, AFTER THAT THE HOLY GHOST IS COME UPON YOU: and ye shall be witnesses unto me both in Jerusalem, and in all Judaea, and in Samaria, and unto the uttermost part of the earth.

I had told the Lord that I believed in the baptism of the Holy Ghost, but that I wasn't sure about the *tongues* part. The Lord spoke to me again, "What does Acts 2:4 say?"

Of course, I could quote these scriptures from the Book of Acts, but just because you have the Word in your head does not mean that you really *know* what it means. In other words, you need to have the revelation of God's Word *in your spirit* to really know and understand what it means.

I quoted Acts 2:4: *"And they were all filled with the Holy Ghost, and began to speak with other tongues, as the Spirit gave them utterance."* I got that far and said again, *"And they were all filled with the Holy Ghost, and began to speak. . . ."*

Then I exclaimed, "Oh, I see it! I see it! It says, '. . . *they were all filled with the Holy Ghost, and began to speak WITH OTHER TONGUES*' [Acts 2:4]. And when I get filled with the Holy Ghost, I will begin to speak with other tongues too! Lord, that settles it. I am going right down to the Full Gospel preacher's house and receive the Holy Ghost."

'Tarrying' Is *Not* a Formula For Receiving the Holy Spirit

I then walked over to the parsonage and knocked on the door. The Full Gospel pastor came to the door. I said to him, "I've come to receive the Holy Ghost."

He said, "Son, you need to *wait*." (From that day until this I have never been able to figure out why anyone would ever tell someone to *wait* to receive the Holy Ghost!)

Someone may ask, "Haven't you ever read in the Bible where it says *to tarry*? And everyone knows that 'to tarry' means *to wait*." Yes, but that is not a formula for receiving the Holy Ghost, because Jesus actually said, ". . . *TARRY YE IN THE CITY OF JERUSALEM, until ye be endued with power from on high*" (Luke 24:49).

It was just as necessary for that group, the 120 who gathered in the Upper Room, to be in Jerusalem as it was that they *wait* or tarry. So if waiting were a formula for receiving the Holy Ghost, then why take the word "Jerusalem" out of this verse?

In other words, if it's still necessary for *us* today to wait or to tarry in order to receive the baptism in the Holy Spirit, then it must be necessary for us to go to Jerusalem to do it!

Also, the 120 people in the Upper Room weren't waiting in the sense that they were getting ready and preparing themselves to be filled with the Holy Ghost.

No, they were waiting for the Day of Pentecost to come. The Holy Ghost could not be given until then.

If they had been waiting and preparing themselves before they could receive the Holy Spirit, the Bible would have read, "When they were *ready*, they were all filled with the Holy Ghost." But it doesn't read that way.

In Acts 2:1 and 4, the Bible says, *"And when THE DAY OF PENTECOST WAS FULLY COME . . . they were all filled with the Holy Ghost. . . ."* (We will cover whether it is scriptural to tarry to receive the Holy Spirit in greater detail in Chapter 6 of this study course.)

Someone said, "But *waiting* gets you ready to receive the Holy Ghost." No, it doesn't. *Getting saved* gets you ready. The Bible mentions the *only* requirement for receiving the Holy Ghost. It says, *". . . the promise is unto you, and to your children, and to all that are afar off, even as many as the Lord our God shall call"* (Acts 2:39).

In other words, the promise of the baptism in the Holy Spirit is for as many as have received Jesus Christ as their Savior.

Any Believer Can Receive the Holy Spirit

By saying a person has to wait in order to receive the Holy Spirit, people are really saying a person has to clean himself up first. But you can't clean yourself up except through repentance of unconfessed sin (1 John 1:9). The blood of Jesus Christ is what cleanses believers from all sin (1 John 1:9). If you are blood washed, you are ready right now to receive the Holy Spirit. If a person who is saved is sincerely seeking the baptism in the Holy Spirit, he can receive.

LUKE 11:9-13
9   And I say unto you, Ask, and it shall be given you; seek, and ye shall find; knock, and it shall be opened unto you.
10   For every one that asketh receiveth; and he that seeketh findeth; and to him that knocketh it shall be opened.
11   If a son shall ask bread of any of you that is a father, will he give him a stone? or if he ask a fish, will he for a fish give him a serpent?
12   Or if he shall ask an egg, will he offer him a scorpion?
13   If ye then, being evil, know how to give good gifts unto your children: how much more shall your Heavenly Father give THE HOLY SPIRIT to them that ask him?

Biblical Example of Believers Receiving The Holy Spirit Without Tarrying

Any believer can ask the Father for the Holy Spirit and receive this precious Gift without tarrying or waiting. For instance, after Cornelius and those in his household were saved, they did not have to *wait* to receive the Holy Spirit.

In fact, they were not only saved but they were filled with the Holy Ghost almost at the same time (Acts 11:14,15). In other words, after salvation, they didn't have time to get "ready" to receive the Holy Spirit; they didn't wait or tarry for the Holy Ghost. They received the Holy Spirit immediately without having to get "ready" (Acts 10:30-48).

In recounting this experience to the apostles and brethren in Jerusalem, Peter explained that those in Cornelius' household received the Word that was preached to them and were saved. Then they were immediately filled with the Holy Spirit.

ACTS 11:11-15
11   And, behold, immediately there were three men already come unto the house where I was, sent from Caesarea unto me.
12   And the spirit bade me go with them, nothing doubting. Moreover these six brethren accompanied me, and we entered into the man's house. . . .
13   And he shewed us how he had seen an angel in his house, which stood and said unto him, Send men to Joppa, and call for Simon, whose surname is Peter;
14   Who shall tell thee words, whereby thou and all thy house shall be SAVED.
15   And as I [Peter] began to speak, THE HOLY GHOST FELL ON THEM, as on us at the beginning.

Also, there is something in Acts 10:45 and 46 that tells us that speaking in tongues goes hand in hand with the baptism in the Holy Ghost.

ACTS 10:45,46
45   And they of the circumcision which believed [the Jewish believers] were astonished, as many as came with Peter, because that on the Gentiles also was poured out THE GIFT OF THE HOLY GHOST.
46   FOR THEY HEARD THEM SPEAK WITH TONGUES, AND MAGNIFY GOD. . . .

You see, if it hadn't been for the evidence of speaking with tongues, the Jewish believers would never have accepted the Gentiles into the Church, because speaking in tongues is what convinced the Jews that the Holy Spirit had been poured out on the Gentiles! It was strictly a Jewish Church up until then.

Even Peter himself didn't know that the Gentiles could be saved until he had the vision which is recorded in Acts chapter 10. When the Holy Ghost was poured out upon the Gentiles, it astonished the Jewish believers who accompanied Peter to Cornelius' house.

Why Wait To Receive a Gift?

Thank God, God showed me His Word on the subject, so I knew I didn't have to wait or tarry before I could be filled with the Holy Spirit. I saw in God's Word that if believers in the Book of Acts didn't have to wait to receive the Holy Spirit, then I didn't have to wait either.

I also knew that when I received the Holy Spirit, I would speak in tongues. When I told this Full Gospel pastor, "I've come here to receive the Holy Ghost," and he said to wait, I blurted out, "But it won't take me long to receive!"

The church was having a revival service that night, and it was then already 6:00 in the evening, so he wanted me to wait and seek for the baptism of the Holy Ghost in the service.

But I knew I would have to wait until after 7:00 when the service started. Then I would have to wait until the preliminaries were over. And then I would have to wait until the preaching was over. In other words, it would have been about 9:00 that evening before I could have gotten to the altar. But why wait to receive a gift?

I have now been associated with Full Gospel folks for many years, and in all that time, I have never told anyone to wait to receive the Holy Spirit, or for that matter, to wait for *anything* that God freely offers us in His Word.

If someone says he wants to get saved, you don't say, "Wait and come to church Sunday and then seek salvation." If someone wanted you to pray for his healing, you wouldn't say, "Wait." No, sick people want to get healed immediately, especially if their bodies are in pain. Salvation is a gift; healing is a gift; and so is the baptism in the Holy Spirit.

Because of my obvious eagerness, the pastor said reluctantly, "Well, come on in then."

I stepped in the door and the pastor said to me, "I know you can receive the Holy Ghost right away because we read about it in the Acts of the Apostles. But when you have to wait a long time before you receive the Holy Spirit, the experience means so much more to you."

The pastor continued, "Take me, for instance. It took me three years and six months to receive the Holy Ghost. Oh, I waited and I waited; I tarried and I sought. Now that I've finally received, the Holy Ghost really means something to me."

I said, "Well, poor old Paul didn't know that. I wish you could have gotten to him and told him about waiting. He didn't know that, because he received the Holy Ghost immediately when Ananias laid hands on him [Acts 9:17,18]. Paul didn't wait or tarry or seek."

I continued, "But then, all Paul ever did was write about half the New Testament! Of course, *he* did more single-handedly in the years of his ministry than any *denomination* has done in five hundred years put together. But if you could have gotten to him and told him to wait for three years and six months to receive the baptism in the Holy Spirit, then maybe the Holy Ghost would have meant something to him too!"

I went into the living room and knelt down in front of a large chair. I just closed my eyes and shut out everything around me, and I lifted my hands to God. No one told me to do it, but I just lifted my hands (that's pretty good for a denominational boy).

I said, "Dear Lord, I've come here to receive the Holy Ghost." I repeated in my prayer what I had just learned from Acts 2:39 and Acts 2:4.

Then I said, "Your Word says that the Holy Ghost is a Gift. Therefore, I realize that the Holy Ghost is received by faith. I received the gift of salvation by faith. I received healing for my body by faith. Now I receive the gift of the Holy Spirit that You offer by faith too."

God Has Already Given the Holy Spirit: Believers Need Only To *Receive* This Gift

There is something here that folks need to see: The Holy Spirit was given on the Day of Pentecost, *and He has been here ever since!* God hasn't *given* Him to anyone since the Day of Pentecost. God gave the gift of the Holy Ghost once on the Day of Pentecost, and He never took back that gift. Now it is just a matter of folks *receiving* Him.

I can't find in the Acts of the Apostles where the disciples ever asked anyone, "Has God *given* you the Holy Ghost?" But I do read where Paul asked, "Have you *received* the Holy Ghost?" (Acts 19:2). In other words, the emphasis is not on God's *giving* because He has already done that. The emphasis is on man's *receiving*.

In the life of Jesus, we see an example of man *receiving* what God has already provided — the Holy Spirit: *"Therefore [Jesus Christ] being by the right hand of God exalted, and having RECEIVED of the Father the promise of the Holy Ghost . . ."* (Acts 2:33).

Jesus *received* of the Father *". . . the promise of the Holy Ghost. . . ."* And after Jesus received the promise of the Holy Ghost, the Bible says He *". . . hath shed forth this, which ye now see and hear"* (Acts 2:33).

The Ephesian Disciples

In Acts 19, we see another example of man *receiving* what God has already provided — the Holy Spirit.

ACTS 19:1,2
1 . . . Paul having passed through the upper coasts came to Ephesus: and finding certain disciples,
2 He said unto them, Have ye RECEIVED the Holy Ghost since ye believed? And they said unto him, We have not so much as heard whether there be any Holy Ghost.

When Paul came to Ephesus, he didn't ask the question, "Has God *given* you the Holy Ghost?" He asked, ". . . *Have ye RECEIVED the Holy Ghost since ye believed? . . .*" (Acts 19:2).

The Samaritan Christians

We see in the account in Acts chapter 8 that after the Samaritans were born again, it was only a matter of their *receiving* the Holy Spirit.

ACTS 8:14,15
14 Now when the apostles which were at Jerusalem heard that Samaria had received the word of God [concerning salvation], they sent unto them Peter and John:
15 Who, when they were come down, prayed for them, that they might RECEIVE the Holy Ghost.

Notice that it says ". . . *that they might receive the Holy Ghost*" (v. 15). Peter and John didn't pray that God would pour out the Holy Ghost on them. They prayed that the Samaritans might *receive* the Holy Ghost. Acts 8:17 says, "*Then laid they their hands on them, and they received the Holy Ghost.*"

Saul of Tarsus

Saul was born again on the road to Damascus (Acts 9:4-8). God sent Ananias to lay hands on Saul that Saul might receive his sight and be filled with the Holy Spirit.

ACTS 9:17
17 And Ananias went his way, and entered into the house; and putting his hands on him said, Brother Saul, the Lord, even Jesus, that appeared unto thee in the way as thou camest, hath sent me, THAT THOU MIGHTEST receive thy sight, and BE FILLED WITH THE HOLY GHOST.

Ananias didn't say, "God has sent me to pray for you that He would *give* you the Holy Ghost." And Ananias didn't say, "God has sent me to pray for you that He would pour His Holy Ghost out upon you." Ananias said, ". . . [Jesus] *hath sent me, that thou*

mightest . . . be filled with [receive] *the Holy Ghost*" (Acts 9:17).

You don't pray that God would send salvation and save someone; God has already done that through Jesus' death, burial, and resurrection. You pray for that person *to receive* salvation. You don't pray that God would send healing and heal someone. You pray for that person *to receive* healing. There is nothing wrong with the sending end. If people fail to receive something God offers, the problem is not with God; something is wrong on the receiving end.

The Sending End or the Receiving End?

A number of years ago, a minister friend of ours was going out West to visit a relative who was dying of cancer. She was the wife of another minister. My wife and I felt led to go out there with him to pray for her.

After we arrived, we all prayed for two days and nights for this minister's sick wife. We ate only one meal a day. We slept only three or four hours a night, getting up early in the morning to go into the room to pray where the woman was bedfast.

On the second night I said to my friend, "Something is wrong. I have been saved for sixteen years and healed for fifteen years, but never have I prayed this long for anything without getting an answer, and I hate to start now.

"Something is wrong with our praying," I said. "What I mean is this: In this little town there is only one radio station. If the radio in your car failed to pick up the local station, you wouldn't phone or write a letter to that station and say, 'You'd better have your radio station fixed. My radio won't pick up the broadcast.'

"Nothing would be wrong with the *sending* end. You would have to work on the *receiving* end. So in the morning when we go into that room, let's concentrate on the receiving end."

The next morning when we gathered at the woman's bedside for prayer again, I told everyone that we were missing it somewhere — that the fault was with us and certainly was not with God. The woman on the bed began to cry and said, "Oh, the trouble is with me. I have failed."

I said, "Wait a minute, Sister. Don't condemn yourself, because if you do, you can talk yourself right out of faith. Maybe you have failed. Who of us hasn't? But you asked the Lord to forgive you, didn't you? And First John 1:9 says, '*If we confess our sins, he is faithful and just to forgive us our sins, and to cleanse us from all unrighteousness.'* So if you've repented and have asked God to forgive you, He has forgiven you and cleansed you from all unrighteousness. You can stand in the Presence of God as though you have never done anything wrong."

I explained, "When I say something is wrong on the receiving end, I don't mean there is some terrible sin. I just mean that somehow we have not gotten in a receptive 'mood,' so to speak, for it is a matter of *receiving* the healing that is already yours.

"In other words," I continued, "your healing was already paid for on the Cross; therefore, we don't have to talk God into the notion of healing you." After explaining a little more about her redemptive rights in Christ, we began to pray.

The woman who was dying with cancer was saved, filled with the Holy Ghost, a pastor's wife, and a Sunday school teacher. But we discovered she had much doubt and fear. In fact, doubt and fear was hindering her from *receiving* the healing that God had already so graciously provided for her in redemption.

When we prayed and believed God and dealt with the real problem, we got results. In this case, God directed me to cast a spirit of doubt and fear out of the woman. (The evil spirit was not in her *spirit* because she was a believer, but it was affecting her mind — her thinking.)

When I cast that evil spirit out of her mind, the woman immediately raised up in bed and began to praise God. She got up and went into the living room and knelt down and praised and thanked God. That afternoon she ate dinner with us.

The Holy Spirit Gives the Utterance

I said all that to say that the problem is never on the sending end — with God. If there is a problem, it is always on the receiving end — with us. We must just learn to receive freely the blessings God has so graciously bestowed upon us in our redemption, which includes the infilling of the Holy Spirit.

So as I knelt in that Full Gospel parsonage in April 1937, I said to the Lord, "Lord, the Holy Ghost is a Gift. I received salvation by faith. I received healing for my body three years ago by faith. Now I receive the gift of the Holy Ghost by faith. And I want to thank You now, Heavenly Father, because I receive the Holy Spirit."

Then I said to the Lord, "By faith I have now received the Holy Ghost. Thank God, He is in me, because Jesus promised that in His Word. And I say it with my mouth because I believe in my heart that I have received the Holy Ghost. Now I expect to speak with tongues because believers spoke with tongues on the Day of Pentecost. And thank God, I will, too, as the Holy Ghost gives me utterance."

After I had prayed that, because I was grateful for the Holy Ghost that I had just received and for the speaking with tongues that God was going to give me, I said, "Hallelujah, hallelujah." But I had never felt so "dry" in all my life saying that word.

Feelings and faith are far removed from each other; in fact, sometimes when you *feel* as if you have the least faith, that is when you have the most faith because you do not base your faith on feelings. So I said, "Hallelujah" about seven or eight times, even though it seemed as if that word was going to choke me!

About the time I had said "Hallelujah" seven or eight times, way down inside of me, in my spirit, I heard these strange words. It seemed as if they were just going around and around in there. It seemed to me that I would know what they would sound like if they were spoken, so I just started speaking them out!

So about eight minutes from the time I first knocked on that pastor's door, I was speaking with tongues! The pastor had said, "Wait," but instead of waiting, I spent that hour and a half before the church service speaking in tongues! It is much better to wait *with* the Holy Ghost than to wait *without* the Holy Ghost!

I believe in waiting on God, of course. We should have tarrying meetings for people who are Spirit filled. It is more wonderful to tarry and wait in God's Presence *after* you've been filled with the Holy Ghost than it is to wait in God's Presence *before* being filled with the Holy Spirit.

Also, notice that you don't speak in tongues, and *then* know you *have* the Holy Ghost. No, you know you have the Holy Ghost *first*, and *then* you speak in tongues. Notice Acts 2:4: *"And they were all filled with the Holy Ghost. . . ."*

If we stop reading there, we would know that they were all filled with the Holy Spirit. But if we continue reading, we find, *". . . and [they] began to speak with other tongues, as the Spirit gave them utterance"* (Acts 2:4). Speaking with other tongues was a result of those believers having received the Holy Ghost. You receive the Holy Ghost first; *then* you speak in tongues.

During that hour and a half that I was speaking in tongues, I had a glorious time in the Lord. You see, speaking in tongues edifies you. First Corinthians 14:4 says, *"He that speaketh in an unknown tongue edifieth himself. . . .*" Therefore, speaking in tongues is a means of *spiritual* edification or building up.

Linguists tell us that there is a word in our modern vernacular that is closer to the meaning of the Greek word than "edify" and that is the word "charge." We charge a battery; we build it up.

JUDE 20
20 But ye, beloved, BUILDING UP YOURSELVES on your most holy faith, PRAYING IN THE HOLY GHOST.

In other words, when a person prays in the Holy Spirit, he charges himself up. He builds himself up like a battery that is charged or built up.

Edifying yourself by speaking in other tongues is just one of the many blessings that God has provided through the baptism in the Holy Ghost. And this wonderful blessing, this glorious gift of the Holy Ghost, is available to every born-again believer.

Questions for Study

1. What Scripture shows that the Early Church all prayed at the same time and lifted up their voice in one accord?

_____

_____

2. In Acts 2:38,39, what does "the promise" refer to?

_____

_____

3. Who will always lead you in line with the Word of God?

_____

_____

4. What does every born-again believer receive in a measure through the New Birth?

_____

_____

5. According to Acts 2:4, what did the 120 in the upper room begin to do when they were all filled with the Holy Ghost?

_____

_____

6. What were the 120 in the upper room waiting for and why?

_____

_____

7. If waiting doesn't get you ready to receive the Holy Spirit, what does get you ready?

_____

_____

8. What convinced the Jews that the Holy Spirit had been poured out on the Gentiles?

_____

_____

9. Complete the following statement: Salvation is a _____; healing is a _____; and so is the _____.

10. When a person prays in the Holy Spirit, what is he doing for himself?

_____

_____

Chapter 2

The Holy Spirit in the Denominational Church

In times past, it has been my privilege to speak on the subject of the infilling of the Holy Spirit, or the baptism of the Holy Spirit, to Full Gospel groups and to conduct special services all over the country. A great number of people have always been filled with the Holy Spirit in these services.

A move of God that we now call the Charismatic Movement took place during the '60s and '70s. That move of God was characterized by thousands of believers in denominational churches being filled with the Holy Spirit. In my own ministry, this was a time when I saw hundreds of denominational people receive the Holy Ghost.

For instance, in just three Bible classes I conducted once at a convention in Texas, more than one hundred people were filled with the Holy Spirit. In these classes, a denominational minister and his wife received the Holy Spirit and upon returning to their church in Florida, they sent me their church bulletin. In it they openly announced they had received the Holy Ghost and spoke with other tongues.

I also noticed in the bulletin that the chairman of the board of their church had also given his testimony about being filled with the Holy Ghost and speaking with tongues. There were more than five hundred people attending Sunday school in this church. And the people were telling the full-gospel story!

Another denominational minister and his wife also received the Holy Ghost at this convention. And a minister from Chicago from still another denomination also received the infilling of the Holy Spirit.

Two ministers from a very conservative denomination also attended that convention. There are several different branches of this particular denomination, just as there are in other denominations and among Pentecostals.

All of the different branches of this particular denomination were conservative, but some were *ultraconservative*. One of these two ministers attending the convention in Texas was from an ultraconservative branch. The one who was conservative received the baptism of the Holy Spirit right away, but the ultraconservative minister didn't receive until the last day of the meeting.

What bothered this ultraconservative minister and hindered him from receiving the baptism of the Holy Spirit was that he didn't believe in women preachers. And the first time he came forward to receive the Holy Ghost, two women preachers approached him to pray with him. (Many times it seems to work that way, doesn't it? God doesn't want us to be prejudiced about anything! He wants us to be in agreement with His Word.)

Because of this minister's preconceived ideas that women shouldn't be preachers, this took him aback and hindered him from receiving the Holy Spirit. He asked me, "Do I have to believe in women preachers before I can receive the Holy Ghost?"

I said, "No, you don't. At one time, I didn't believe in women being preachers either. But if you let it bother you, it can hinder your faith and therefore hinder you from receiving the Holy Spirit."

And we must remember, too, that when we do receive the Holy Spirit, that doesn't mean we know everything. In some of these areas, the Holy Spirit will change our thinking because the Bible says He will guide us into all truth (John 16:13).

For example, Peter and all of the apostles had been filled with the Holy Ghost for ten years, but they still didn't know the Gentiles could get saved. They didn't receive that revelation until Peter saw the vision while praying on the housetop, and God spoke to him and said, ". . . *what God hath cleansed, that call not common"* (Acts 10:15). Then Peter was sent to preach the gospel to Cornelius and his household, who were Gentiles (Acts 10:1-45).

So I said to this minister, "As long as you let women being preachers bother you, it will hinder you. The devil will use anything he can to get your mind off of God and on something else to try to bring you into confusion. Just stay open to God and let Him tell you whatever He wants to tell you. If you knew everything you should know and if you were everything you should be without the Holy Ghost, what would you need Him for?"

This minister finally received the baptism in the Holy Spirit. And, sure enough, when he was filled with the Holy Spirit, it was a woman preacher who prayed with him! After he was filled with the Holy Ghost, he said, "Now I believe in women preachers!" It didn't take him long to change his mind.

Actually, when you get filled with the Holy Ghost, you will see that a lot of things you thought were so important, aren't so important after all. And a lot of your prejudices and preconceived notions will fall away to the truth of God's Word as you get your mind renewed (Rom. 12:2).

This minister went back home and within one month's time he had gotten sixteen believers filled with the Holy Ghost. Particularly in the days of the Charismatic Movement, one saw denominational people get filled with the Holy Ghost. That number is still multiplying even today. For instance, with just this one man in a few days' time after he was filled with the Holy Spirit, the number of believers filled with the Holy Spirit was multiplied by sixteen. I rejoice in what God is doing in these days!

To be honest, as a young preacher I didn't believe I would live to see the supernatural in demonstration as I saw it during the Charismatic Movement of the '60s and '70s. If someone had told me years ago about what would be happening now, it would have been beyond my comprehension. Years ago, I never would have believed certain things to be possible that have happened even in my own ministry!

For example, a minister from the denomination I came from was filled with the Holy Ghost. He was the pastor of a church with two thousand members enrolled in the Sunday school program alone. This pastor's deacon was also filled with the Spirit.

In fact, this deacon was filled with the Holy Ghost first. Then the deacon kept talking to the pastor about it and finally got him to attend a Full Gospel meeting. The pastor saw what the Bible has to say about the Holy Ghost and was filled with the Holy Ghost and spoke with other tongues!

This deacon's brother was a member of a Pentecostal church and had been for nearly twenty years, but he had never received the Holy Ghost. The pastor and the deacon brought the deacon's brother to the meeting so he could be filled with the Holy Ghost too.

It used to be the other way around: Pentecostal people usually got denominational people filled with the Holy Ghost! But we have lived long enough to see things change because now sometimes denominational people are the ones getting Pentecostal church folks filled with the Holy Ghost!

I preached a meeting in a denominational church in Texas once where ninety-five percent of the church received the infilling of the Holy Ghost and spoke with other tongues. It was a glorious service filled with thrilling testimonies, and the service had that warm glow to it like Pentecostal services of years ago.

It was wonderful and refreshing to be a part of what God was doing during the Charismatic Movement. And I'm glad I am a part of what He is doing today!

Denominational Differences Don't Matter

We should share this wonderful experience of being filled with the Holy Spirit with everyone who is hungry for God. For example, if someone fell overboard and I had a lifesaver, I wouldn't ask him what church he belonged to before I threw him the lifesaver! And if he didn't belong to *my* church, I wouldn't refuse to throw him the lifesaver either!

If people are drowning, they need help. If people are lost, they need salvation. And if Christians are hungry for a deeper walk with God, they don't have to become a member of any particular church before they can be filled with the Holy Spirit!

The Holy Spirit is a Gift. We should just get believers who are hungry for more of God filled with the Spirit. And, thank God, we are doing that. Of course, we should always encourage believers who are not members of a local body to join a good church and become faithful members, so they can grow in their Christian walk. But joining a church is not a prerequisite to receiving the Holy Spirit.

In just four services of a local chapter of a Full Gospel group, I once saw 143 people filled with the Holy Ghost. That's a real revival in itself, isn't it? And some folks think God is not on the move! Thank God, He is. It is not what you *think* the Bible says that counts. And it's not what someone *told* you the Bible says. It is what you *know* for yourself about God's Word that counts. And God will confirm His Word with signs following.

The Holy Spirit: God's Promise to You

ACTS 1:5,8
5 For John truly baptized with water; but YE SHALL BE BAPTIZED WITH THE HOLY GHOST not many days hence....
8 But ye shall receive power, AFTER THAT THE HOLY GHOST IS COME UPON YOU: and ye shall be witnesses unto me both in Jerusalem, and in all Judea, and in Samaria, and unto the uttermost part of the earth.

ACTS 2:32,33
32 This Jesus hath God raised up, whereof we all are witnesses.
33 Therefore being by the right hand of God exalted, and having received of the Father THE PROMISE of the Holy Ghost, he hath shed forth this, which ye now see and hear.

Notice that in Acts 1:5 and 8 Jesus spoke of the promise of the Holy Ghost to the Church — the Body of Christ. He said, "*. . . ye shall be baptized with the Holy Ghost . . .*" (Acts 1:5). And in Acts chapter 2, we see the fulfillment of that promise: "*. . . he* [Jesus] *hath shed forth this, which ye now see and hear"* (Acts 2:33).

Then in Acts 2:38 and 39, Peter told the people that the promise of the Holy Spirit was given to as many as believed.

ACTS 2:38,39
38 Then Peter said unto them, Repent, and be baptized every one of you in the name of Jesus Christ for the remission of sins, and ye shall receive THE GIFT OF THE HOLY GHOST.
39 For THE PROMISE is unto you, and to your children, and to all that are afar off, even AS MANY as the Lord our God shall call [in other words, those who are born again].

The Holy Spirit Is a Person

Jesus refers to the Holy Spirit as a Person in John 14:16: *". . . I will pray the Father, and he* [the Father] *shall give you another Comforter, that HE* [the Comforter, the Holy Spirit] *may abide with you for ever."*

The Holy Spirit is a Person. In other words, when we receive the Holy Spirit, we receive *Him*, the third Person of the Godhead, not an "it." Jesus said, *". . . that HE may abide with you for ever"* (John 14:16).

Some people say it like this: "I received the baptism." But they didn't receive the baptism, they received the *Holy Spirit*. Sometimes folks say, "I am filled with the baptism." But they are not filled with the baptism; they are not even filled with the baptism of the Holy Spirit. That is not a scriptural statement. No, they are filled with *the Holy Spirit Himself* — the third Person of the Godhead.

Receiving the Holy Ghost is more than just an experience. When you receive the Holy Ghost, a Divine Personality, He comes to live in you, to dwell in you, and to make His home in you.

Receiving the Holy Spirit Is Just the Beginning

Also, we must not be so concerned with the outward initial *experience* that we miss the reality of the indwelling Presence of the Holy Ghost. If we have been filled with the Holy Ghost, we should be conscious of His indwelling Presence at every waking moment. We shouldn't have to look back to some experience that we had at an altar years ago as our only contact with this Divine Person — the Holy Spirit. The Holy Spirit should become more real to us every single day.

I received the infilling of the Holy Ghost more than fifty-five years ago. When I first received the Holy Spirit, I spoke in tongues for an hour and a half, and I sang three songs in tongues. But that experience was the *least* part of this fifty-five years of being filled with the Holy Spirit because that initial experience was just the beginning.

But to hear some people talk, the initial experience of receiving the Holy Spirit was the greatest thing that ever happened in their lives. Of course, in one sense that may be true, because that was the beginning. But some people haven't experienced anything since then!

However, if the Holy Ghost is living in you, you can have scriptural experiences with God and in His Word every day. You don't have just one experience and that's the end of it. No, when you receive the baptism in the Holy Spirit, a Divine Personality — the Holy Spirit — comes to live within you! Every day you can experience His indwelling Presence.

The infilling of the Holy Ghost is not for sinners; it is for believers. Referring to the infilling of the Holy Spirit, Jesus said, *"Even the Spirit of truth; WHOM THE WORLD CANNOT RECEIVE . . ."* (John 14:17).

The world cannot receive the promise of the Holy Spirit, the Spirit of Truth. The world *can* receive eternal life, however. The Bible says, *"For God so loved the world, that he gave his only begotten Son, that whosoever believeth in him should not perish, but have EVERLASTING LIFE"* (John 3:16).

Jesus Christ is God's Gift to the world. The world can receive Christ as Savior. A sinner *can* be born again. But a person has to be born again before he can receive the baptism of the Holy Ghost.

Extreme Teachings in the Church

There are some extreme teachings in the church today. When I speak of the church, I am not speaking of any particular group or denomination. I am speaking of the church world as a whole.

I began my ministry as a denominational preacher, and I know what that particular denomination teaches. And I have been among Full Gospel people for a great number of years now, and I know what they teach. I have found that we have extreme teaching that is unscriptural, even among Pentecostals.

Does One Receive the Fullness of the Holy Spirit in the New Birth?

The denominational church that I belonged to taught me that if you are born again, then you have the Holy Ghost — *and you have all the Holy Ghost there is to have.* They are partly right, but mostly wrong in that assertion.

They are right in that if you are born again, you *do* have the Holy Ghost because there is a work of the Holy Spirit in the new birth (John 3:5-8; Rom. 8:16).

It is the Holy Spirit who imparts eternal life to the unregenerated spirit of the sinner (Titus 3:5-7). It is the Holy Spirit who recreates the sinner's spirit and makes him a new creature in Christ Jesus (2 Cor. 5:17). It is the Holy Spirit who bears witness with the spirit of the born-again one that he is a child of God (Rom. 8:16).

But this is *not* the same as the infilling of the Holy Spirit (Acts 1:8), or the enduement of power from on High, even though the Holy Spirit is present in the life of the born-again believer.

Jesus illustrated the work of the Holy Spirit in salvation for us very beautifully in the Gospel of John. In chapter 4, Jesus was talking to the woman of Samaria at the well about salvation.

Salvation: The Well of Water

JOHN 4:13,14
**13 ... Whosoever drinketh of this water shall thirst again:
14 But whosoever drinketh of THE WATER that I shall give him shall never thirst; but THE WATER that I shall give him shall be in him A WELL OF WATER springing up into EVERLASTING LIFE.**

Here we see that Jesus was speaking of the *well* of water or the work of the Holy Spirit in *salvation.* Jesus referred to salvation as the *well* of water.

The Baptism in the Holy Spirit: Rivers of Living Waters

In the following verses, Jesus was talking about the *rivers* of living water which characterize the work of the Holy Spirit in the infilling or the baptism of the Holy Spirit.

JOHN 7:37-39
**37 In the last day, that great day of the feast, Jesus stood and cried, saying, If any man thirst, let him come unto me, and drink.
38 He that believeth on me, as the scripture hath said, out of his belly shall flow RIVERS OF LIVING WATER.
39 (But this spake he of THE SPIRIT, which they that believe on him should receive; for the Holy Ghost was not yet given; because that Jesus was not yet glorified.)**

The water in both John 4:13,14 and John 7:37-39 is a type of the Holy Ghost. But notice that two different experiences are mentioned: salvation and the infilling of the Holy Spirit.

First, to the woman at the well of Samaria, Jesus said, "... *the water that I shall give him shall be in him a WELL OF WATER springing up into EVERLASTING LIFE"* (John 4:14). This is referring to the work of the Holy Spirit in salvation or the new birth.

In John 7:37-39, the reference is to "rivers of living water." Jesus said, "... *out of his belly* [or innermost being] *shall flow rivers of living water"* (John 7:38). This is referring to the experience of the infilling of the Holy Ghost in the life of the born-again child of God.

The Same Holy Spirit in the New Birth As in the Baptism of the Holy Spirit

I was a member of a denomination and had been healed by the power of God. After that, I fellowshipped with Full Gospel people because they preached divine healing, and it stimulated my faith. You need to fellowship with people of like-precious faith in order to stay strong in faith.

However, these Full Gospel people also preached the baptism in the Holy Ghost and speaking with tongues. People in my denomination said, "Those Pentecostal folks are good people and they're all right in many ways. They preach a lot of good things, and much of what they preach is true." But I was warned by many who genuinely cared about me to be careful about that "tongues business" because they said that was of the devil.

However, in the course of time, I was filled with the Holy Ghost with the evidence of speaking with tongues. And I know from experience and from the Word of God that the baptism of the Holy Spirit is not of the devil. I didn't get some spirit that I didn't have before and didn't know anything about. It was the same Spirit — the Holy Spirit.

The same Holy Ghost whom I became acquainted with in the new birth — the same Spirit who bore witness with my spirit that I was a child of God — was the same Spirit that gave me utterance in tongues.

I told my denominational friends, "You said that speaking with tongues is of the devil. Well, if it is, then the new birth is of the devil too. For the same Holy Spirit who led me to Christ, and the same Holy Spirit who bore witness with my spirit that I am a child of God, gave me utterance in tongues."

You see, when you are born again, you don't have all the Holy Spirit there is to have. There is a further experience; an experience subsequent to the new birth that God desires every one of His children to experience. Jesus said, *". . . If any man thirst, let him come unto me, and drink"* (John 7:37). In the infilling of the Holy Spirit, one can drink of the rivers of living water until he gets full!

Someone asked, "How can you tell when you get full of the rivers of living water; that is, after you are filled with the Holy Ghost?"

Acts 2:4 tells us how we know when we are filled: *". . . they were all FILLED with the Holy Ghost, AND BEGAN TO SPEAK WITH OTHER TONGUES. . . ."* If you are a believer, it is just as simple as Jesus said it is in John 7:37. Just come and drink and keep on drinking until you get full. And when you get full, you will start speaking with other tongues. That is the initial sign or evidence that you are filled with the Holy Spirit.

Speaking in Tongues Is Not The Evidence of the New Birth

So you see, on one hand, an extreme teaching in many denominations is that when a person gets saved, that person has all the Holy Spirit there is to have. However, on the other hand, an extreme teaching and error in some Full Gospel circles is that no one is really *saved* unless he has spoken in tongues. But speaking in tongues is not an evidence of the new birth; it is an evidence of the *infilling* of the Holy Spirit.

We know that the baptism of the Holy Spirit with the evidence of speaking in tongues is *not* for the world — for unbelievers — because of something Jesus said in John 14:16,17.

JOHN 14:16,17
16 And I will pray the Father, and he shall give you another Comforter, that he may abide with you for ever;
17 Even the Spirit of truth [the Holy Spirit]; **WHOM THE WORLD CANNOT RECEIVE, because it seeth him not, neither knoweth him: but ye know him; for he dwelleth with you, and shall be IN you.**

Jesus said that the world cannot receive this experience of the baptism in the Holy Spirit. Now God does have a gift for the world, and that gift is salvation. The Heavenly Father has another gift for His children, and that is the gift of the Holy Ghost.

LUKE 11:13
13 If ye then, being evil, know how to give good gifts unto your children: how much more shall YOUR HEAVENLY FATHER give the Holy Spirit to them that ask him?

God isn't the Father of everyone. He is the Father of those who have been born again and recreated in His image and likeness (2 Cor. 5:17). We hear a lot about the Fatherhood of God and the brotherhood of man, and that God is the Father of all of us as humans and that we are all brothers. But that isn't true.

In John 8:44, Jesus said to the Pharisees, the strictest sect of the Jewish religion, *"Ye are of your father the devil. . . ."* So you see, God is only the Father of those who have been born again. And to those who have been born again, God the Father gives the gift of the Holy Ghost.

New Wine: A Type of the Holy Spirit

MARK 2:21,22
21 No man also seweth a piece of new cloth on an old garment: else the new piece that filled it up taketh away from the old, and the rent is made worse.
22 And no man putteth NEW WINE into old bottles: else the NEW WINE doth burst the bottles, and the wine is spilled, and the bottles will be marred: but NEW WINE must be put into new bottles.

Jesus said that no man puts new wine in old bottles. Back then, people used animal skins as bottles to hold wine, and they supposedly could use those skin bottles only once because if they let them lay longer than about a year, the skins would dry up and crack. Then if new wine was put in them, the skin bottles would burst.

In the Scriptures, wine is a type of the Holy Ghost. And God couldn't give the Holy Ghost in His fullness to a person unless he was made a new creature. (Thank God, through Jesus Christ, man can be made a new creature in Him!)

Jesus said if you put new wine in old wineskins, the wineskins will burst (Matt. 9:17; Mark 2:22; Luke 5:37). If He put the Holy Ghost into folks who had not been born again, they would burst; they would not be able to contain Him!

A person must become a new creature before he can be filled with the new wine — the Holy Spirit. *"Therefore if any man be in Christ, he is a new creature . . ."* (2 Cor. 5:17). When you have been made a new creature, you are ready to be filled with the new wine — the Holy Spirit.

Born-Again Samaritans Were Filled With the Holy Spirit

The scriptures that helped me see the truth of God's Word that the new birth and the baptism of the Holy Spirit are two separate experiences are found in Acts 8:5 and 12.

ACTS 8:5,12
5   Then Philip went down to the city of Samaria, and preached Christ unto them. . . .
12 But when they BELIEVED Philip preaching the things concerning the kingdom of God, and the name of Jesus Christ, they were baptized, both men and women.

Were these Samaritans saved? According to Jesus they were. He said, *". . . Go ye into all the world, and preach the gospel to every creature. He that believeth and is baptized shall be saved; but he that believeth not shall be damned"* (Mark 16:15,16).

Notice Acts 8:14: *"Now when the apostles which were at Jerusalem heard that Samaria had received the word of God, they sent unto them Peter and John."*

Then in the first Epistle of Peter, we read, *"Being born again, not of corruptible seed, but of incorruptible, by the word of God, which liveth and abideth forever"* (1 Peter 1:23). These Samaritans had received the Word of God, so according to Peter they were born again.

Paul said, *"For I am not ashamed of the gospel of Christ: for it is the power of God unto salvation to every one that believeth; to the Jew first, and also to the Greek"* (Rom. 1:16). Philip went down to Samaria and preached Christ to them. The Samaritans believed on Jesus and were baptized. They were saved.

As a denominational preacher years ago, these scriptures in Acts 8:5 and 12 helped me to see that if you were saved, you had experienced the working of the Holy Ghost in your life, but you had not actually received the *infilling* of the Holy Ghost. For in these scriptures, we see that the Early Church believed that receiving the Holy Ghost is an experience subsequent to or following salvation.

We know this because the Bible says, *". . . when they [Peter and John] were come down, prayed for them, that they might receive the Holy Ghost"* (Acts 8:15). The disciples didn't pray for the Samaritans to get saved. The Samaritans were already saved. Peter and John prayed that the Samaritans might *receive* the Holy Ghost.

The Holy Spirit: God's *Giving* vs. People's *Receiving*

As I discussed in Chapter 1, there has also been much misunderstanding in the Body of Christ on the question, Does God *give* the Holy Spirit to believers? Or do believers merely *receive* the Holy Spirit

because God has already given Him on the Day of Pentecost? Let me point out again that Peter and John did not pray that God would *give* the Samaritans the Holy Ghost. Peter and John prayed that the Samaritans might *receive* the Holy Ghost.

Very often we pray, "Dear Lord, save souls at this service tonight. Dear God, heal the sick at this service. Fill believers with the Holy Ghost." However, I can't find in the Acts of the Apostles that the New Testament Church ever prayed that way. We should pray according to the Word of God.

I pray for folks, not that God would save them, for He has already done something about saving them. He sent His Son to die for all mankind. God has already purchased salvation for everyone who has ever lived or who shall ever live on the earth.

But it is not going to do a person any good unless he *accepts* salvation. That is the reason He told us to tell people the good news of the gospel. Scripturally, we should pray that people will *receive* that which has already been purchased for them and freely offered to them.

I don't pray that God will heal people. I pray that people will *receive* the healing that God freely offers. I do not pray that God will fill people with the Holy Ghost. I pray, like Peter and John did, that believers might *receive* the gift that God offers — the precious Holy Spirit.

Notice in Acts 8:17, *"Then laid they their hands on them, and they received the Holy Ghost."* It doesn't say, "Then laid they their hands on them and God *filled* them with the Holy Ghost." It says, *". . . and they RECEIVED the Holy Ghost."*

The Ministry of Laying On of Hands

There are many in the Church today who do not understand the doctrine of laying on of hands which is taught in the Word of God (Heb. 6:2). But I believe that we are in good company with Peter and John, so I follow that same practice; I lay hands on people that they might *receive* the Holy Ghost.

We lay hands on people to receive the Holy Spirit in faith because it is scriptural. But some in the Body of Christ also have a ministry along this line. We saw that the apostles sent Peter and John to Samaria because they had a ministry along this line. Some have a ministry along lines that others do not. God anoints us to minister according to His calling on our lives.

Simon the sorcerer offered Peter and John money and said, *". . . Give me also THIS POWER [ability], that on whomsoever I lay hands, he may receive the Holy Ghost"* (Acts 8:19).

Some have thought that Simon tried to buy the Holy Ghost. He didn't. He tried to buy the ability to lay hands on people and have them receive the Holy Spirit. Peter said to him, *". . . Thy money perish with thee, because thou hast thought that the gift of God may be purchased with money"* (Acts 8:20).

There are at least four different Greek words translated "gift" in the New Testament. The particular Greek word used here in Acts 8:20 means *a gratuity*. In other words, the Holy Spirit is a free gift given to believers. The ministry of laying on of hands for the believer to receive the Holy Spirit cannot be purchased with money. Peter and John were endowed or gifted *by God* to lay hands on folks to receive the Holy Spirit.

Many years ago the Lord told me that He had given me that ministry. Immediately I started laying hands on people, and as I did, instantly I could also tell what was wrong with them — why they weren't receiving from God. That also goes along with the ministry of the prophet that He gave me.

Did the Baptism in the Holy Spirit 'Pass Away' With the Last Apostle?

Another extreme teaching in the Church is that the baptism of the Holy Spirit passed away and ceased when the last apostle died. Those who believe this say that the apostles received the Holy Ghost and consequently they were the only ones who could in turn pass on the Holy Ghost to others.

Supposedly then, as this "theory" goes, those folks who received the Holy Spirit by the laying on of the apostles' hands could *not* pass the Holy Ghost on to anyone else. People who teach this say that when the last apostle died, being filled with the Holy Spirit also ceased since there was no one else to "pass on" the Holy Spirit.

As this theory goes, that was why Philip didn't try to pass the Holy Ghost on to the Samaritans; he couldn't since he wasn't one of the original twelve apostles. People who believe this say that's why Philip had to call on Peter and John to lay hands on the Samaritan converts — because Peter and John were apostles and Philip was not an apostle.

This theory, however, could not be true because if we can find one layperson in the Bible who laid hands on another believer to receive the baptism in the Holy Spirit, we would know with a certainty that this theory is *not* true.

In Acts chapter 9, we find such an example of an ordinary believer — a layperson — who laid hands on another believer to receive the Holy Spirit. His name was Ananias. Ananias wasn't an apostle. He was just a disciple, a layman. Yet God used him to lay hands on Saul (later named Paul) to receive the Holy Spirit shortly after Saul's conversion on the Damascus road.

ACTS 9:10-12,17
10 And there was a certain disciple at Damascus, named Ananias; and to him said the Lord in a vision, Ananias. And he said, Behold, I am here, Lord.
11 And the Lord said unto him, Arise, and go into the street which is called Straight, and enquire in the house of Judas for one called Saul of Tarsus: for, behold, he prayeth.
12 And hath seen in a vision a man named Ananias coming in, and PUTTING HIS HAND ON HIM, that he might receive his sight. . . .
17 And Ananias went his way, and entered into the house; and putting his hands on him said, Brother Saul, the Lord, even Jesus, that appeared unto thee in the way as thou camest, hath sent me, that thou mightest receive thy sight, and BE FILLED WITH THE HOLY GHOST.

Ananias knew nothing at all about Saul's present spiritual condition and recent conversion other than what the Lord revealed to him supernaturally. The Lord spoke to Ananias supernaturally in a vision and told Ananias that Saul was praying, and that Saul had had a vision and had seen a man named Ananias coming to minister to him. In other words, Ananias was supernaturally directed by God to minister to Saul and lay hands on Saul to receive the baptism of the Holy Spirit.

As we've seen, the Scriptures declare that the gift of the Holy Spirit is for all who believe (Acts 2:39). The Holy Spirit is God's Gift to believers today as much as He was God's Gift to the believers in the Early Church.

And we have also seen that laying hands on believers to receive the Holy Spirit has not been done away with and is a biblical practice to this day as we observe how God is moving among His people regardless of denominational boundaries, we can understand more clearly God's desire that *all* of His children receive the promise of the Holy Spirit.

18

Questions for Study

1. What should we do for believers who are hungry for more of God?

   _____

   _____

2. What should believers who are not members of a local body be encouraged to do so they can grow in their Christian walk?

   _____

   _____

3. According to Acts 2:38 and 39, who was the promise of the Holy Spirit given to?

   _____

   _____

4. When you receive the Holy Ghost, what does He do?

   _____

   _____

5. The infilling of the Holy Ghost is not for sinners; it is for believers. What is it that the world cannot receive?

   _____

   _____

6. Who imparts eternal life to the unregenerated spirit of the sinner?

   _____

   _____

7. The _____ in both John 4:13,14 and John 7:37-39 is a type of the _____.

8. In Mark chapter 2, what type of the Holy Spirit is used ?

   _____

   _____

9. Complete these statements: Peter and John did not pray that God would _____ the Samaritans the Holy Ghost. Peter and John prayed that the Samaritans might _____ the Holy Ghost.

10. There are at least four different Greek words translated "gift" in the New Testament. What does the particular Greek word used in Acts 8:20 mean?

   _____

   _____

Chapter 3

Two Separate Experiences:
Salvation and the Baptism of the Holy Spirit

In Acts chapter 8, the ministry of Philip in Samaria is recorded. As we study this account, it becomes evident that salvation and the baptism of the Holy Spirit are two separate experiences.

ACTS 8:5-8,12-17
5 Then Philip went down to the city of Samaria, and PREACHED CHRIST unto them.
6 And the people with ONE ACCORD GAVE HEED UNTO THOSE THINGS which Philip spake, hearing and seeing the miracles which he did.
7 For unclean spirits, crying with loud voice, came out of many that were possessed with them: and many taken with palsies, and that were lame, were healed.
8 And there was great joy in that city. . . .
12 But when they BELIEVED Philip preaching THE THINGS CONCERNING THE KINGDOM OF GOD, and THE NAME OF JESUS CHRIST, they were baptized, both men and women.
13 Then Simon himself believed also: and when he was baptized, he continued with Philip, and wondered, beholding the miracles and signs which were done.
14 Now when the apostles which were at Jerusalem heard that Samaria had RECEIVED THE WORD OF GOD [concerning salvation], they sent unto them Peter and John:
15 Who, when they were come down, prayed for them, that they might RECEIVE THE HOLY GHOST:
16 (For as yet he was fallen upon none of them: only they were baptized IN THE NAME OF THE LORD JESUS.)
17 Then laid they their hands on them, and they RECEIVED THE HOLY GHOST.

Philip (who was later called Philip the evangelist in Acts 21:8) had a marvelous ministry in Samaria, as stated in verses 7 and 8: *"For unclean spirits, crying with loud voice, came out of many that were possessed with them: and many taken with palsies, and that were lame, were healed. And there was great joy in that city."*

Mighty miracles were constantly being manifested in Philip's ministry and many people were being saved. Yet notice that in Acts chapter 8, not one person received the Holy Spirit under Philip's ministry. Evidently, that was not a part of Philip's ministry, but getting folks saved and healed was.

However, the Bible says that when the apostles at Jerusalem heard about the wonderful things God had done through Philip's ministry in Samaria, they sent Peter and John to lay hands on the new Samaritan converts so that they might receive the Holy Ghost.

There is no record that any upon whom Peter and John laid their hands failed to receive the Holy Ghost because Peter and John had more of a ministry along this line. The Bible says, *"Then laid they [Peter and John] their hands on them, and they received the Holy Ghost"* (Acts 8:17).

These verses of Scripture helped me as a young minister in a denominational church to see that there is an experience subsequent to or following salvation, called the infilling or the baptism of the Holy Spirit. I had been taught that when you are saved, you have the Holy Spirit.

That is true in one sense because the Bible says that in the new birth we are born of the Spirit of God (John 3:3-8). But my denomination taught that when you are born again, you have all the Holy Ghost there is to have.

However, these Samaritans in Acts chapter 8 were saved or born again by the Spirit of God (vv. 12,14), as we will plainly see from the scriptures in a moment. But the apostles didn't seem to think they had all of the Holy Ghost there was to have because they sent Peter and John to them so the Samaritans could receive the baptism in the Holy Spirit. Therefore, salvation and receiving the infilling or the baptism of the Holy Spirit are two separate experiences.

The Samaritans Born Again Under Philip's Ministry

Now let's go back and look at the scriptures which prove conclusively that these Samaritans were born again under Philip's ministry, so we can see that being born again and receiving the Holy Spirit are two separate experiences.

We remember that Jesus told us in the Great Commission that salvation comes through the preaching of the gospel, the Word of God.

MARK 16:15,16
15 . . . Go ye into all the world, and PREACH THE GOSPEL to every creature.
16 He that BELIEVETH and is baptized shall be SAVED; but he that believeth not shall be damned.

First Scriptural Witness

ACTS 8:5
5 Then Philip went down to the city of Samaria, and PREACHED CHRIST unto them.

The Bible says that Philip preached Christ to the Samaritans. Preaching Christ is preaching the good news of the gospel of salvation through Jesus. Preaching Christ is obeying the Great Commission that Jesus gave to the Church.

These Samaritans believed the gospel message Philip preached: *"And the people with one accord GAVE HEED UNTO THOSE THINGS WHICH PHILIP SPAKE . . ."* (Acts 8:6). So according to what Jesus said in Mark 16:16, the Samaritans were saved.

The Bible says to let every truth be established in the mouth of two or three witnesses (2 Cor. 13:1), so let's look at another scriptural witness which proves these Samaritans were born again.

Second Scriptural Witness

The Bible says we are born again by the Word of God. The Book of Peter says we are born *". . . not of corruptible seed, but of incorruptible, BY THE WORD OF GOD, which liveth and abideth for ever"* (1 Peter 1:23).

Our scripture in Acts 8:14 says, *"Now when the apostles which were at Jerusalem heard that Samaria had RECEIVED THE WORD OF GOD. . . ."* Therefore, as our second scriptural witness, we have proof that the Samaritans were genuinely saved because they had received the incorruptible Word of God preached by Philip.

Third Scriptural Witness

The third scriptural witness is that the apostles recognized that the Samaritans were saved: *"Now when the apostles . . . heard that Samaria had RECEIVED THE WORD OF GOD"* (Acts 8:14). So we see that the Samaritans were saved under Philip's ministry.

These Samaritans had received the Word of God concerning salvation, but the Bible says they had yet to be filled with or baptized in the Holy Spirit: *"For as yet he was fallen upon none of them: only they were baptized in the name of the Lord Jesus"* (Acts 8:16).

There is a work of the Holy Spirit that takes place in the new birth, but that is not called the baptism in the Holy Spirit or receiving the Holy Spirit. That is called being born again, being born of the Spirit of God, receiving salvation, or receiving eternal life (John 3:3-8).

Then there is an experience following salvation called the baptism in the Holy Spirit (Acts 1:5). It is also referred to as *receiving* the Holy Spirit (Acts 8:15), or *being filled with* the Holy Spirit (Acts 2:4), or being endued with power from on High (Luke 24:49).

The Samaritans Received the Holy Spirit

Peter and John were sent down to Samaria for the specific purpose of praying for the Samaritan believers to receive the baptism in the Holy Spirit.

ACTS 8:14-17
14 Now when the apostles which were at Jerusalem heard that Samaria had received the word of God [that they were born again], **they sent unto them Peter and John:**
15 Who, when they were come down, prayed for them, that they might RECEIVE THE HOLY GHOST:
16 (For as yet he was fallen upon none of them: only they were baptized in the name of the Lord Jesus.)
17 Then laid they their hands on them, and they RECEIVED THE HOLY GHOST.

Some might ask why Peter and John had to go pray for the Samaritans to receive the Holy Ghost? Why couldn't Philip have prayed for them just as well? But we must remember that we each have our place in God's plan. We must each find that place and do what God wants us to do. God has special ministries. He didn't call all of us to minister the same, and He didn't give all of us the same gifts or ministry.

Philip had a mighty ministry, but it was in the Lord's plan to send Peter and John to lay hands on the new converts so they could receive the Holy Ghost. As I said previously, while it is true any Christian can lay hands on another believer *in faith* to receive the baptism of the Holy Spirit, it is also true that some members of the Body of Christ have more of a ministry and more of an anointing along this line.

Philip, for example, had more of a ministry of bringing people into salvation and of ministering healing. As we saw in Acts 8:12, when Philip preached the good news of salvation through Jesus Christ, people were saved. And there were also many healings under Philip's ministry (Acts 8:6,7).

Peter and John, on the other hand, had a ministry more along the line of bringing believers into the baptism of the Holy Spirit; when they laid their hands upon the Samaritans, these new converts received the Holy Ghost.

ACTS 8:17-19
17 Then laid they [Peter and John] **their hands on them, and they received the Holy Ghost.**
18 And when Simon SAW that through laying on of the apostles' hands the Holy Ghost was given, he offered them money,
19 Saying, Give me also this power, that on whomsoever I lay hands, he may receive the Holy Ghost.

Evidence the Samaritans Received the Holy Spirit

Some who object to speaking with tongues say, "It's true the Samaritans received the Holy Ghost, but they didn't speak with tongues." There isn't any proof, however, that the Samaritans did not speak with tongues. In fact, Church historians agree that all of the Early Church fathers concur that the Samaritans *did* speak with tongues.

It is apparent that the Samaritans must have spoken in tongues, for the Bible says, "*. . . Simon SAW that through the laying on of the apostles' hands THE HOLY GHOST WAS GIVEN . . .*" (Acts 8:18). What did Simon *see*? You certainly can't see the Holy Ghost, for He is a Spirit and cannot be seen with the physical eye.

Therefore, there had to be some kind of physical sign or evidence whereby Simon would know that the Samaritans had *received* the Holy Ghost. There had to be something that would register on Simon's physical senses whereby he could tell that the Samaritans had received the Holy Ghost. Simon didn't receive the Holy Ghost himself, but he could see that these others had received Him.

One minister said to me, "It may have been that Simon just saw that the Samaritans were full of joy." This couldn't explain it, however, and joy couldn't be the sign that Simon had seen, because the believers were *already* filled with joy when Philip preached Christ unto them.

ACTS 8:5,8
5 Then Philip went down to the city of Samaria, and PREACHED CHRIST unto them. . . .
8 And THERE WAS GREAT JOY IN THAT CITY.

Therefore, the Samaritans already had great joy, so that could not have been the sign or evidence which Simon saw that indicated the Samaritans had been filled with the Spirit.

As I said, since the Holy Ghost can't be seen with the physical eye, there had to be some kind of sign that would cause Simon to know that these Samaritans had received the Holy Ghost when Peter and John laid hands on them.

All evidence indicates that the sign that was manifested was speaking in tongues. Speaking in tongues was the sign that convinced Simon beyond a shadow of a doubt that the Samaritans had received the Holy Ghost (we discuss the Bible evidence for receiving the Holy Spirit in Chapter 9).

Two Separate Experiences: Saul's Conversion And Baptism in the Holy Spirit

The passage in Acts chapter 9 which records Saul's baptism in the Holy Spirit also shows us that receiving salvation and receiving the baptism in the Holy Spirit are two separate experiences.

We know that Saul was already born again when Ananias came to lay hands on him, but Saul had not yet received the baptism in the Holy Spirit.

Saul's Conversion

We know Saul had already been converted or born again on the Damascus Road (Acts 9:1-9) for three reasons. First, in Acts 9:15,16, Jesus, speaking to Ananias in a vision, called Saul *His* chosen vessel.

ACTS 9:15,16
15 But the Lord said unto him [Ananias], Go thy way: for he [Saul] is a CHOSEN VESSEL UNTO ME, to bear MY NAME before the Gentiles, and kings, and the children of Israel:
16 For I will shew him how great things he must suffer for MY NAME'S SAKE.

Second, we know Saul was saved because when Ananias entered the house where Saul was staying, Ananias greeted Saul by calling him *"Brother Saul."*

ACTS 9:17
17 And Ananias went his way, and entered into the house; and putting his hands on him [Saul] said, BROTHER SAUL, the Lord, even Jesus, that appeared unto thee in the way as thou camest, hath sent me, that thou mightest receive thy sight, and be filled with the Holy Ghost.

Ananias recognized that Saul was already a Christian brother in the faith.

Third, we also know Saul was already saved when Ananias came to lay hands on him to receive the Holy Spirit because the Bible says in Romans 10:13, *"For whosoever shall call upon the name of the Lord shall be saved."* Saul called Jesus, *"Lord"* in his conversion on the Damascus Road.

ACTS 9:3-6
3 And as he [Saul] journeyed, he came near Damascus: and suddenly there shined round about him a light from heaven:
4 And he fell to the earth, and heard a voice saying unto him, Saul, Saul, why persecutest thou me?
5 And he said, Who art thou, LORD? And the Lord said, I am Jesus whom thou persecutest: it is hard for thee to kick against the pricks.
6 And he trembling and astonished said, LORD, what wilt thou have me to do? And the Lord said unto him, Arise, and go into the city, and it shall be told thee what

thou must do.

However, even though Saul had received Jesus as his Lord, Saul was not yet baptized in the Holy Spirit. As we have seen, Saul was not baptized in the Holy Spirit until Ananias came and laid hands on him to receive the Holy Spirit.

Saul's Baptism in the Holy Spirit

ACTS 9:17
17 And Ananias went his way, and entered into the house: and putting his hands on him said, Brother Saul, the Lord, even Jesus, that appeared unto thee in the way as thou camest, hath sent me, that thou mightest receive thy sight, and BE FILLED WITH THE HOLY GHOST.

So we see that salvation and the baptism in the Holy Ghost are two separate experiences.

The Gentiles of Cornelius' Household: Salvation and the Baptism of the Holy Spirit

We also have other scriptural accounts of those who were saved and then immediately following salvation, they received the baptism of the Holy Spirit.

We find one such example in the very next chapter, Acts 10, where the Bible gives us Peter's account of his visit to Cornelius' household. The men of Cornelius' household were all Gentiles, and they were not saved until Peter came and preached the gospel to them.

In Acts chapter 11, Peter recounts his visit to Cornelius' household to the brethren in Jerusalem.

ACTS 11:13-15
13 And he [Cornelius] shewed us [Peter and the six Jewish brethren] how he had seen an angel in his house, which stood and said unto him, Send men to Joppa, and call for Simon, whose surname is Peter;
14 Who shall tell thee words, whereby thou and all thy house shall be SAVED.
15 And as I began to speak, THE HOLY GHOST fell on them as on us at the beginning.

According to Peter's account, these Gentiles received salvation and the baptism of the Holy Spirit almost simultaneously. (Actually, the best time for someone to receive the baptism in the Holy Spirit is when he is first saved.) Notice that no one in Cornelius' household failed to receive the Holy Spirit.

Notice, no one laid hands on these Gentiles. They all received the Holy Spirit about the same time. And, again, not one person failed to receive the Holy Spirit.

Actually, speaking with tongues is what fully convinced Peter's company — the Jewish believers who accompanied Peter — that these Gentiles had received the Holy Spirit. The Jewish believers were astonished

that the Holy Ghost was poured out on the Gentiles.
ACTS 10:45,46
45 And they of the circumcision which believed were astonished, as many as came with Peter, because that on the Gentiles also was poured out the GIFT OF THE HOLY SPIRIT.
46 For they heard them speak with TONGUES, and magnify God . . . .

Also, as we mentioned earlier, there is no suggestion of waiting in order to be filled with the Holy Spirit.

The Ephesian Disciples: Salvation and the Baptism of the Holy Spirit

We find another example in the Bible showing that salvation and the baptism in the Holy Spirit are two separate experiences.

ACTS 19:1-7
1 And it came to pass, that, while Apollos was at Corinth, Paul having passed through the upper coasts came to Ephesus: and finding certain disciples,
2 He said unto them, Have ye received the Holy Ghost since ye believed? And they said unto him, We have not so much as heard whether there be any Holy Ghost.
3 And he said unto them, Unto what then were ye baptized? And they said, Unto John's baptism.
4 Then said Paul, John verily baptized with the baptism of repentance, saying unto the people, that they should believe on him which should come after him, that is, on Christ Jesus.
5 When they heard this, they were baptized IN THE NAME OF THE LORD JESUS.
6 And when Paul had laid his hands upon them, THE HOLY GHOST CAME ON THEM; and THEY SPAKE WITH TONGUES, and prophesied.
7 And all the men were about twelve.

These Ephesian disciples were also all Gentiles. They had all been followers of John the Baptist, but they hadn't heard that Jesus had come, and therefore they had never been saved and baptized in the Name of the Lord Jesus. They had been baptized in the Name of the Father according to John's baptism.

We must understand that news didn't travel then like it does now. Back then, you could live your entire life and die, and something newsworthy could have taken place a hundred miles from you, and you would probably have never known about it because in that day news only traveled by word of mouth.

These folks had heard John the Baptist preach and tell that One was coming who would save them from their sins and baptize them in His Holy Spirit. They believed John's message and were baptized by John. But they had never heard that Jesus had come.

They were walking in all the light they had, of course.

Then here in Acts chapter 19, we see that Paul came to Ephesus and told these disciples that Jesus the Promised One, had come and that Jesus had died on the Cross and had risen again.

Paul explained to these believers in Ephesus that the One whom John said would come after him had come, and that now they should believe on Jesus, and be saved. So when Paul came to these Ephesian disciples, he then baptized them in the Name of the Lord Jesus, and they were born again (Acts 19:5; Gal. 3:27).

But Paul didn't stop there. He also wanted them to be filled with the Holy Spirit, so he laid hands on them to receive the Holy Spirit. When he did this, the Holy Ghost came upon them, "... *and they spake with tongues* ..." (Acts 19:6).

These Ephesians, who were brand-new converts, received the Holy Spirit when Paul laid hands on them. All of them received the Holy Spirit without exception. Again, there is not one suggestion of tarrying or waiting to receive the Holy Spirit.

In conclusion, let us sum up two important thoughts. First, as we have seen, salvation and the baptism in the Holy Spirit are two separate experiences, although the Holy Spirit is involved in both supernatural events.

Second, in all of these scriptures we have examined, there is no suggestion that the people in the Early Church were ever taught to tarry or to wait before they could be filled with the Holy Ghost.

Let's find out what the *Bible* says about the baptism of the Holy Spirit. The Bible should be our example in everything we do; not tradition, nor the opinion of men. Believers can receive this wonderful experi-

Questions for Study

1. Which two men did the apostles at Jerusalem send to lay hands on the new Samaritan converts that they might receive the baptism in the Holy Spirit?

   _____

   _____

2. What experience is subsequent to or following salvation?

   _____

   _____

3. What are three scriptures which prove conclusively that the Samaritans were born again under Philip's ministry?

   _____

   _____

4. There is an experience following salvation called the baptism in the Holy Spirit. It is also referred to as _____ the Holy Spirit (Acts 8:15), or being _____ with the Spirit (Acts 2:4), or being _____ with power from on High (Luke 24:49).

5. Can any believer lay hands on another believer _in faith_ to receive the baptism in the Holy Spirit?

   _____

   _____

6. What happened when Philip preached the good news of salvation through Jesus Christ?

   _____

   _____

7. Why couldn't joy be the sign that Simon had seen to indicate that the Samaritans had been filled with the Spirit?

   _____

   _____

8. What was the sign that convinced Simon that the Samaritans had received the Holy Ghost?

   _____

   _____

9. Name three reasons why we know Saul had already been converted or born again on the Damascus Road.

   _____

   _____

10. Give two scriptural accounts of those who were saved and then immediately received the baptism in the Holy Spirit.

   _____

   _____

Chapter 4

The Holy Spirit Within: His Indwelling Presence

In this lesson we will deal with the subject of the indwelling Presence of the Holy Spirit in the life of the believer in the new birth.

JOHN 14:16,17
16 And I will pray the Father, and HE SHALL GIVE YOU ANOTHER COMFORTER, that he may abide with you for ever;
17 Even the Spirit of truth; whom the world cannot receive, because it seeth him not, neither knoweth him: but ye know him; for he dwelleth with you, and SHALL BE IN YOU.

In this lesson I want to focus our attention on that last phrase of John 14:17: *". . . for he dwelleth with you, and shall be IN you."* Being born again is not just an experience; rather, it is receiving the *indwelling* Presence of the Holy Spirit, a Divine Personality, who comes to make His home in us.

There is no need for any believer ever to feel comfortless, bereaved, or forlorn. Christ's purpose in sending the Holy Spirit was so that the Holy Spirit, a Divine Personality, might come to *live* in us and be *in* us.

God *For* Us, *With* Us, and *In* Us

The New Testament gives us three relations that God sustains toward man. First, God is *for* us. Second, God is *with* us. And third, God is *in* us.

To have God be *for* us guarantees our success: *". . . If God be for us, who can be against us?"* (Rom. 8:31). If God is on our side, we are sure to win in life. If God is for you, and you *know* that He is for you, you become utterly fearless in life.

No matter how difficult the situation may be, no matter how dark the clouds that hang upon the horizon of your life may be, you are calmly assured that you must win in every circumstance because God is for you.

There can be no defeat if the Lord is for us. And, thank God, He is for us. If God be for us, who can be against us?

You can also have the assurance that not only is God *for* you, but in every place in life and in every situation, God is *with* you. No matter what the circumstances may be, if you are a Christian, the Lord is *with* you.

The knowledge of the Word of God along this line should certainly cause our hearts to leap for joy within us, and buoy our spirits up in faith and confidence.

Under the New Testament or New Covenant, the Bible says we have a better covenant established on better promises (Heb. 8:6). Under the covenant in the Old Testament, God was *for* Israel and *with* Israel, but He was not *in* Israel.

However, in the New Testament, God is with us and for us, but we also have something better — God is *in* us. God is actually making His home in our bodies as His temple (1 Cor. 6:19).

Believers Are the Temple of the Holy Spirit

Of all the mighty truths in connection with our redemption, this is the apex of the reality of our redemption: that after God Himself recreated us and made us new creatures in Christ and made us His own, then He, in the Person of the Holy Ghost, makes our bodies His home!

1 CORINTHIANS 3:16
16 Know ye not that ye are the temple of God, and that THE SPIRIT OF GOD DWELLETH IN YOU?

1 CORINTHIANS 3:16 (Amplified)
16 Do you not discern and understand that you [the whole church at Corinth] are God's temple (His sanctuary), and that God's Spirit has His permanent dwelling in you — to be at home in you [collectively as a church and also individually]?

1 CORINTHIANS 6:19
19 What? know ye not that your body is THE TEMPLE OF THE HOLY GHOST which is IN YOU, which ye have of God, and ye are not your own?

1 CORINTHIANS 6:19 (Amplified)
19 Do you not know that your body is the temple — the very sanctuary — of the Holy Spirit who lives within you, whom you have received [as a Gift] from God? You are not your own?

2 CORINTHIANS 6:16
16 And what agreement hath the temple of God with idols? for YE ARE THE TEMPLE OF THE LIVING GOD; as God hath said, I will dwell IN THEM, and walk IN THEM; and I will be their God, and they shall be my people.

2 CORINTHIANS 6:16 (Amplified)
16 What agreement (can there be between) a temple of God and idols? For we are the temple of the living God; even as God said, I will dwell in and with and among them and will walk in and with and among them, and I will be their God, and they shall be my people.

Through the Holy Ghost, the third Person of the Godhead, God Himself indwells the believer through the new birth experience. No longer does God dwell in the earth-made Holy of Holies. Our *bodies* have become His temple.

You see, in the Old Testament, under the Old Covenant, God's Presence was kept enclosed in the Holy of Holies. No one dared approach the Holy of Holies except the high priest, and he did so only with great precaution. If anyone else dared to intrude into the Holy of Holies, that person would fall dead.

Also, it was necessary that every male in all of Israel present himself at least once a year at Jerusalem, because that was where God's Presence was in the Holy of Holies. And the high priest was designated by God to go into the Holy of Holies to offer sacrifices and to make atonement for the sins of the people.

But on the Cross just before Jesus died, He said, "It is finished" (John 19:30). He was not referring to the New Covenant when He said, "It is finished." He was talking about the Old Covenant being finished.

The New Covenant wasn't instituted and ratified until Jesus was raised from the dead ascended on High and entered into the heavenly Holy of Holies with His own blood (Heb. 1:3; 10:12). Once Jesus obtained eternal redemption for us, as Hebrews declares, then and only then were the terms of the New Covenant consummated and ratified.

Hanging on that rugged Cross on Golgotha's rugged brow, Jesus said, "It is finished." The Word tells us that at that moment the curtain that partitioned off the Holy of Holies in the Temple was rent in two from top to bottom (Matt. 27:51).

Jewish historians tell us that curtain was forty feet wide, twenty feet high, and four inches thick. When Jesus Christ was crucified on the Cross of Calvary, God sent His messenger to rend that curtain in the Holy of Holies from top to bottom, signifying that the Old Covenant was finished and that God's Presence would no longer be kept shut up in the man-made Holy of Holies. Under the New Covenant, God would dwell *in* the believer (Jer. 31:33,34; Heb. 8:6-13; 10:1-17).

Notice that the curtain was not ripped from the bottom to the top as might happen if that curtain were ripped by some human agency. No, the curtain was ripped from *top to bottom*, indicating that it was not of human agency.

When that happened, God's Presence which had been kept in the Holy of Holies, moved out of that earth-made Holy of Holies and God has never dwelt in an earth-made Holy of Holies since.

Because God now makes His abode in believers, when we call a building the house of God, we are partly correct and partly incorrect, according to what we mean by that statement.

If we mean the building is the house of God because God lives and dwells there, we are wrong. God does not dwell in a building. But if we mean that the building is God's house because it is dedicated to the service of the Lord, then we are right — it is a house of God. But God doesn't live in a building made with hands. He lives and dwells in us through the power of the Holy Spirit!

Relatively few Christians are really conscious of God *in* them — dwelling in their hearts and bodies as His temple. If men and women were conscious of God in them as His temple, they wouldn't talk and act as they sometimes do. Some Christians constantly talk about their *lack* of power, and their *lack* of ability. But if they realized that God is *in* them, they would know that there is nothing impossible to them.

Instead of believing what the Bible says, too many believers believe only what they feel. For example, when people are born again, they feel wonderful. But many times, later they will say, "I had a marvelous experience when I was saved, but God must have left me because I don't feel now as I did then."

However, Jesus said, "*. . . that he* [the Holy Spirit] *may abide with you FOR EVER*" (John 14:16). The Holy Spirit didn't come as a guest to stay for just a few days. He didn't come on a vacation to dwell inside of you for just a short time. He came *to dwell* in you *to be at home* in you forever. The Holy Spirit's home in this life is in your body — God's temple.

The Bible says, "*. . . all things are possible to him that believeth*" (Mark 9:23). The reason that all things are possible to him who believes is that God our Father planned that the believing one should have God Himself living in him through the indwelling Presence of the Holy Ghost. And with God *in* the believer, *nothing* is impossible!

Greater Is He That Is *in* You

First John 4:4 says, "*Ye are of God, little children, and have overcome them: because GREATER IS HE THAT IS IN YOU, THAN HE THAT IS IN THE WORLD.*" Who is the "he" that is in the world? That is Satan, the god of this world.

2 CORINTHIANS 4:4
4 In whom THE GOD OF THIS WORLD hath blinded the minds of them which believe not, lest the light of the glorious gospel of Christ, who is the image of God, should shine unto them.

But He who is in you — the Holy Ghost — is greater! The Greater One is in you if you are born again. God Himself in the Person of the Holy Spirit lives in the born-again believer. All that God could possibly be to you and do for you, the Holy Ghost through His indwelling Presence is *to* you and *for* you and *in* you.

If we were really conscious of the Greater One in us, then we would have no fear of the devil. We would have no fear of "he that is in the world" because "He that is *in us* is greater than he that is in the world."

John said, "*. . . greater is he that is IN YOU . . .*" (1 John 4:4). Going back to John 14:16, we hear Jesus say, "*And I will pray the Father, and he shall give you another Comforter, that he may abide with you for ever.*"

Then in the last part of verse 17, Jesus said, "*. . . he . . . shall be IN YOU.*" That is exactly what John was saying in First John 4:4 too: "*. . . greater is he that is IN YOU, than he that is in the world.*"

Some people say, "I have a poor memory and just can't remember things well. I can't remember scriptures."

I tell them, "Why don't you quit trying to remember scriptures, and look to the Comforter, the Holy Spirit, and expect Him to bring whatever you need to your remembrance."

You see, it's one thing to try to do something mentally yourself; it's another thing to trust Him — the Greater One — who is in you.

He is everything *in* us that the Scriptures say He is. He'll do everything *in* us the Word says He will do. And He will be everything *in* us the Word says He will be.

A Thousand Times Bigger on the Inside!

Smith Wigglesworth, a man of God who was used mightily of the Lord to preach faith and perform miracles of healings, said in his book, *Ever Increasing Faith*, "I am a thousand times bigger on the inside than I am on the outside." [1]

I hadn't been in Pentecost very long when I read this, and this statement was hard for me to understand because my mind wasn't renewed sufficiently with the Word.

I knew there was an outward man and an inward man, of course. The inward man is our spirit — the man that is on the inside. After I read that statement by Wigglesworth, I laid the book down and wondered how in the world a man could be a thousand times bigger on the inside than he is on the outside. I thought, for example, *How could you put a big pot in a little pot?*

For example, if your foot were ten times bigger than your shoe, how could you put your foot in your shoe? *If a man were a thousand times bigger on the inside than on the outside, the outside would just burst wide open.*

In the nighttime this statement Wigglesworth had made would come to me, rolling over and over in my mind. The Holy Ghost was bringing it to my remembrance. So I determined to read that chapter in Wigglesworth's book again, asking the Holy Spirit to give me insight into what Wigglesworth was saying.

In the book, I came upon the scripture, "*. . . greater is he that is in you, than he that is in the world*" (1 John 4:4). I began to see it then. With this enlightened understanding I felt Wigglesworth should have said, "I am a *million* times bigger on the inside." That still wouldn't have done it justice because God is infinitely bigger than we can think or imagine.

Someone asked Wigglesworth, "What is your secret to the great place of spirituality you have attained?"

His answer was, "All I ever did was to remember that greater is He who is in me than he who is in the world."

Dare to act on that scripture!

This doesn't belong only to preachers. It is not just preachers who are a thousand times bigger on the inside than they are on the outside. It is not just preachers who have the Holy Ghost in them.

John was writing to lay members when he said, "*Ye are of God, little children, and have overcome them: because GREATER is he that is in you, than he that is in the world*" (1 John 4:4). You are not left helpless in this life. The Greater One is in you.

The Role of the Holy Spirit Within

We saw how the Holy Spirit came to dwell in us. Let's look now at *what* He is going to do *in us.*

The Holy Spirit *Within* Results in the Fruit of the Recreated Spirit

It is significant to notice in the Scriptures that there are two groups of nine in connection with the work of the Holy Spirit in the life of the believer:

1. The nine *fruit* of the Spirit, which are a result of the Holy Spirit's *indwelling* Presence.

2. The nine *gifts* of the Spirit, which are a result of the Holy Spirit's *infilling* power.

We will discuss the nine gifts of the Spirit in the baptism or the *infilling* of the Holy Spirit in Chapter 5. But let's look first of all at the ninefold manifestation of the fruit of the born-again human spirit that is a result of the Holy Spirit's indwelling Presence. Paul lists them in Galatians 5.

GALATIANS 5:22,23
22 But the fruit of the Spirit is LOVE, JOY, PEACE, LONG-SUFFERING, GENTLENESS, GOODNESS, FAITH,
23 MEEKNESS, TEMPERANCE: against such there is no law.

In John 15:5, Jesus told the disciples, *"I am the vine, ye are the branches. . . ."* Now where does the fruit grow? It grows out on the branches!

This fruit, then, that Paul is talking about in Galatians 5 is the fruit of the recreated, born-again human spirit, growing within the believer's life as a result of the life of the Holy Spirit *within*.

We see a biblical example of the *fruit* of the born-again human spirit in Luke 24:51-53 before the Day of Pentecost when the disciples were filled with the Holy Spirit.

LUKE 24:51-53
51 And it came to pass, while he blessed them, he was parted from them, and carried up into heaven.
52 And they worshipped him, and returned to Jerusalem WITH GREAT JOY:
53 And were continually in the temple, praising and blessing God. Amen.

According to Galatians 5:22, joy is a fruit of the born-again, recreated human spirit. We see in this passage in Luke 24 that the disciples had great joy, but they were not yet filled with the Holy Spirit. Therefore, the fruit of the spirit could not be a result of the baptism in the Holy Spirit, for the Day of Pentecost had not yet come.

This scripture shows that the disciples already had one of the fruit of the spirit, joy, *before* they were endued with power from on High. In fact, they had *great* fruit because the Bible says they had great joy (v. 52)!

As we yield to God and obey His Word, the life of the Holy Spirit within us causes us to grow continually in love, joy, and peace, as well as the other fruit of the spirit. So we can see that one of the main purposes of the indwelling Presence of the Holy Spirit in the life of the believer is for *fruit bearing*.

The Holy Spirit Within: Our Helper and Comforter

We notice in *The Amplified* version of John 14:16-18 that the Holy Spirit is a Comforter, a Counselor, a Helper, an Intercessor, an Advocate, a Strengthener, and a Standby.

JOHN 14:16-18 (*Amplified*)
16 And I will ask the Father, and He will give you another COMFORTER (COUNSELOR, HELPER, INTERCESSOR, ADVOCATE, STRENGTHENER and STANDBY) that He may remain with you forever,
17 The Spirit of Truth, Whom the world cannot receive (welcome, take to its heart), because it does not see Him, nor know and recognize Him. But you know and recognize Him, for He lives with you [constantly] and will be in you.
18 I will not leave you orphans — comfortless, desolate, bereaved, forlorn, helpless — I will come [back] to you.

Notice Jesus said the Holy Spirit would be a Comforter, Counselor, Helper, Intercessor, Advocate, Strengthener, and a Standby. We don't need anything more than that. Many believers have missed the reality of what the Holy Spirit came to do in us on a continual basis.

Too often when some people need help, they just run around frantically — almost in a frenzy — just trying to find someone to pray for them. They cry first on one person's shoulder and then on another's, shed a few "crocodile" tears, and quote a few scriptures. But when they are alone, they are in just about the same mess they were in to begin with. They forget that on the inside of them, they have a Helper. They don't have to pray for a Helper: they already have the Helper *in* them.

Jesus said in John 16:7 that the Holy Spirit would be our Comforter. Jesus also said, *". . . It is expedient for you that I go away: for if I go not away, the Comforter will not come unto you; but if I depart, I will send him to you"* (John 16:7).

The Holy Spirit Within: Our Guide in the Affairs of Life

The Holy Spirit is also our Guide. *"Howbeit when he, the Spirit of truth, is come, he will guide you into all truth . . ."* (John 16:13). Not only will He guide us into all truth, but Jesus said speaking to God the Father, *". . . Thy word is truth"* (John 17:17). The Holy Spirit will also guide us into the truth of God's Word.

The Holy Spirit will guide us in all the affairs of life. *"For as many AS ARE LED by the Spirit of God, they are the sons of God"* (Rom. 8:14). No one can be guided or led, however, without placing themselves in the hands of the Guide.

In other words, it is useless to pray to God, "Lord, guide me. Give me directions," unless you are going to allow yourself to be guided.

By way of illustration, when we go some place and a guide is there to escort us, if we don't follow the guide, there would be much that we wouldn't understand and we might even get lost. The guide is there to explain certain things to us and to show us the way to go.

Certainly no one would want to go through Carlsbad Caverns, for instance, without a guide. It is pitch black inside those caverns. We would never get out of the Carlsbad Caverns if we failed to follow the guide. But the guide knows right where to turn on the lights. (Thank God, the Holy Ghost knows right where to turn on the lights!)

That is the reason many folks have gotten into such a mess in life — they were not following the Guide. The Holy Spirit will guide us, but in order to be guided in life, we have to put ourselves into His hands.

When you have guidance, you can be prepared ahead of time, for the Bible says the Holy Spirit will show you things to come (John 16:13). He will guide you into all truth, and He will also guide you and lead you in all the affairs of life.

During the many years I have traveled on the evangelistic field leaving my wife and small children at home, I have depended upon my Guide, the Holy Spirit. And He has always warned me ahead of time of a need in my family. Although many times I had no communication with my family, I always knew by the Spirit of God when a member of the family was sick.

The Holy Spirit is not in me to help me just because I am a preacher. If you are a believer, He is in you to help you too. And if you will learn to listen to Him and look to Him, He will guide you.

Knowing on the Inside of You What To Do

Under the Old Covenant in Jeremiah 31:33, God speaks of the New Covenant that He would be establishing with His people. This verse gives us a clue as to how believers are to be guided under the New Covenant.

JEREMIAH 31:33
33 But this shall be the covenant that I will make with the house of Israel: After those days, saith the Lord, I WILL PUT MY LAW IN THEIR INWARD PARTS, and WRITE IT IN THEIR HEARTS; and will be their God, and they shall be my people.

This Old Covenant promise was fulfilled in the new birth — in the recreation of man's spirit.

2 CORINTHIANS 5:17
17 Therefore if any man be in Christ, he is a NEW CREA-TURE: old things are passed away; behold, all things are become new.

Where does God make us a new creature? In our *hearts* or *spirits* by the regeneration of the Holy Spirit (Titus 3:5).

God said He would put His law in our "inward parts" — in our hearts or spirits. It is by the Holy Spirit that God's laws are written in our hearts (2 Cor. 3:3).

Also, because you are born again, you will know by the Holy Spirit living on the inside of you what to do in every situation in life, for He is our Guide into all truth (John 16:13). Just look on the inside; check to see what the Holy Spirit within your human spirit is leading you to do (Rom. 8:14).

The trouble with many folks is that instead of looking to the Holy Ghost within them to guide and lead them, they are looking on the *outside* for their answer. They are running around looking for another person to give them the answer they need.

Let me give you an example of someone who just needed to "look on the inside" to the Holy Spirit who dwells within. We were holding a Faith Seminar in Ohio, and after one of the morning services, a man came up to me and said, "Brother Hagin, I want you to pray for me."

The man explained his prayer request. "For several years," he said, "I was a member of a church here in town.

"I had a disagreement with the pastor," the man continued, "and ended up leaving the church. Since then we've gotten our disagreement all straightened out and we're good friends. But for seven years now I've been going to another church."

The man said, "Recently there have been some developments at the church where I have been attending. The pastor has left and I have felt like leaving too.

"So I don't know what to do," this man concluded. "I don't know whether I should stay at this church I've been attending, find a new church, or go back to the church I left seven years ago. I want you to pray that the Lord would guide me."

I said, "All right, we'll just agree together that you will understand what God is saying to you because John 16:13 says the Holy Spirit is our Guide, and Romans 8:14 says that as many as are led by the Spirit, they are the sons of God."

And so I laid my hand on his forehead, and began to pray. I had only prayed a few words when the Spirit of God on the inside of me said, "Ask him what he's got in his heart."

You see, that is where the Holy Spirit is, in your heart or your spirit. That is where you are going to find the guidance you need. The Bible says, *"The spirit of man is the candle of the Lord . . ."* (Prov. 20:27).

I stopped praying and I said to the man, "Open your eyes and look at me."

He opened his eyes and I said, "Dear brother, look right down in your heart, your spirit. Don't look at me. Don't look up to your head. Look right down on the inside of you."

You see, when the Bible talks about your heart, it is not talking about the physical organ that pumps blood through your body and keeps you alive.

Romans 10:10 says, *". . . with the HEART man BELIEVETH unto righteousness. . . ."* Well, you couldn't believe with your physical heart any more than you could believe with your physical nose or your physical foot! No, the heart is used as an illustration of the heart of man, the spirit of man.

"Look down in your spirit," I told him. "What does your spirit tell you?"

When I said that, he responded, "I'm going to have to go back to the church I used to attend."

I answered, "That's the answer. Go on back to that church then." That man knew the answer in his heart all the time.

Many times things will happen in your life, some good and some bad, and afterwards you will say, "I knew what to do all the time."

Where did you know it? You knew it on the inside of you. Why didn't you listen? It would save you many problems if you would learn to listen to your spirit. For the spirit of man is the candle of the Lord (Prov. 20:27). The Holy Spirit is dwelling in our spirits, and He is our Guide.

The Holy Spirit Within: Testifies of Jesus

In the Book of John, Jesus spoke of another role of the Holy Spirit as He dwells *within* believers. The Holy Spirit always lifts up the Word of God and the Name of Jesus and testifies of Jesus.

JOHN 15:26
26 But when the Comforter is come, whom I will send unto you from the Father, even the Spirit of truth, which proceedeth from the Father, HE SHALL TESTIFY OF ME.

Now notice John 16:14: *"HE SHALL GLORIFY ME: for he shall receive of mine, and shall SHEW IT unto you."* And in John 14:26, Jesus said the Holy Spirit would be our Teacher.

JOHN 14:26
26 But the Comforter, which is the Holy Ghost, whom the Father will send in my name, HE SHALL TEACH YOU ALL THINGS, and bring all things to your remembrance, WHATSOEVER I HAVE SAID UNTO YOU.

In other words, the Holy Spirit will make Jesus and the things of God real to you. And when you need it, He will bring to your remembrance the Word of God that you have hidden in your heart (Ps. 119:11).

The Holy Spirit, our Helper, has made His home in us as believers. All that we could ever need Him to be *for* us, He is. He is our Comforter, our Guide, our Counselor, and our Teacher. He is the Greater One in us who puts us over in life.

If we are conscious of Him who dwells *within* us and if we believe God's Word, then no matter what or whom we face in life, we will have no fear. The Greater One who lives in us is greater than he who is in the world! He will put us over in life!

------

[1] Smith Wigglesworth, *Ever Increasing Faith* (1924; Springfield, Missouri: Gospel Publishing House, 1971), p. 95.

Questions for Study

1. What was Christ's purpose in sending the Holy Spirit?

   _____

   _____

2. What three relations does the New Testament give us that God sustains toward man?

   _____

   _____

3. When were the terms of the New Covenant consummated and ratified?

   _____

   _____

4. Under the New Covenant where does God dwell?

   _____

   _____

5. In First John 4:4, who is the "he" that is in the world?

   _____

   _____

6. In the Scriptures, there are two groups of nine in connection with the work of the Holy Spirit in the life of the believer. What are they?

   _____

   _____

7. What fruit is Paul talking about in Galatians 5?

   _____

   _____

8. What is one of the main purposes of the indwelling Presence of the Holy Spirit in the life of the believer?

   _____

   _____

9. _The Amplified_ version of John 14:16-18 it says that the Holy Spirit is a _____, a _____, a _____, an _____, an _____, a _____, and a _____.

10. According to Proverbs 20:23, what is spirit of man?

    _____

    _____

Chapter 5

The Holy Spirit Upon: His *Infilling* Power

In Chapter 4 we discussed the *indwelling* Presence of the Holy Spirit. But there should be a twofold work of God in the life of the individual believer. God desires for every one of His children to experience this dual working of the Spirit of God in their lives: The Holy Spirit within (*indwelling*) in the new birth. And the Holy Spirit upon (*infilling*) in the baptism of the Holy Spirit.

In John 14:16,17, we saw that Jesus promised the *indwelling* Presence of the Holy Spirit when He said, "*. . . I will pray the Father, and he shall give you another Comforter. . . . he dwelleth WITH you, and shall be IN you.*"

At the time Jesus was saying this, the Holy Ghost was not yet *in* the disciples, nor in any of the followers of Jesus. But Jesus' promise in John 14:16,17 was that under the New Covenant, the Holy Spirit is to be *in* all believers. Jesus said to His disciples, "*. . . he [the Holy Spirit] dwelleth WITH you, and shall be IN you*" (v. 17).

Jesus' promise to the disciples of the indwelling Presence of the Holy Spirit was fulfilled in John 20:21,22 when the resurrected Savior breathed on them and said, "*. . . Receive ye the Holy Ghost.*"

When Jesus said that, He was referring to receiving the Holy Spirit in the new-birth experience. That was when the disciples were born again; that was when they were regenerated by the Holy Ghost (Titus 3:5).

The Promise of the Holy Spirit

However, then as a separate and subsequent experience, Jesus promised His disciples and all believers the enduement of power from on High.

LUKE 24:49
49 And, behold, I send the PROMISE OF MY FATHER upon you: but tarry ye in the city of Jerusalem, until YE BE ENDUED WITH POWER FROM ON HIGH.

In this passage, Jesus is referring to a different working of the Holy Spirit in the lives of believers — the outpouring of the Holy Spirit *upon* believers to receive an enduement of *power* from on High.

ACTS 1:5,8
5 For John truly baptized with water; but ye shall be BAPTIZED WITH THE HOLY GHOST not many days hence. . . .
8 But ye shall receive POWER, AFTER THAT THE HOLY GHOST IS COME UPON YOU: and ye shall be witnesses unto me both in Jerusalem, and in all Judaea, and in Samaria, and unto the uttermost part of the earth.

The Holy Spirit Upon

Notice the use of the word "upon" in both Luke 24:49 and Acts 1:8, referring to the baptism in the Holy Spirit: "*. . . I send the promise of my father UPON you. . . ,*" and "*. . . ye shall receive power, after that the Holy Ghost is come UPON you. . . .*"

There is a work of the Holy Spirit that God desires in the lives of *believers*: This is the Holy Spirit coming *upon* believers to endue them with power from on High.

Just as the Spirit *within* in the new birth is a definite experience, so there is also a genuine *infilling* of the Holy Spirit which believers can receive today, which is also a definite experience. On the Day of Pentecost, God gave this outpouring of the Holy Spirit not only to the 120 who were gathered in the Upper Room (Acts 2:1-4), but to the Church — to all who would believe in Jesus.

As I pointed out in the previous lesson, it is not a matter of the Father's *giving* believers the Holy Ghost. God has already given the Holy Ghost to the Church on the Day of Pentecost. No, it is a matter now of believers' *receiving* the Holy Ghost.

The world — unregenerated sinners — cannot receive the Holy Spirit, the Spirit of truth. The world *can* receive the new birth, however. Sinners can receive Jesus Christ as their Lord and Savior and be born again. But the experience of the infilling of the Holy Ghost is only for believers.

Jesus called the outpouring of the Holy Ghost "the promise of my Father" (Luke 24:49; Acts 1:4). Peter also spoke of the outpouring of the Holy Spirit in Acts 2, using the phrase "the promise of the Holy Ghost," and "the gift of the Holy Ghost."

ACTS 2:32,33
32 This Jesus hath God raised up, whereof we all are witnesses.
33 Therefore being by the right hand of God exalted, and having received of the Father THE PROMISE of the HOLY GHOST, he hath shed forth this, which ye now see and hear.

ACTS 2:38,39
38 Then Peter said unto them, Repent, and be baptized every one of you in the name of Jesus Christ for the remission of sins, and ye shall receive the GIFT OF THE HOLY GHOST.

39 For THE PROMISE is unto you, and to your children, and to all that are afar off, even as many as the Lord our God shall call.

Jesus promised in Luke 24:49 and Acts 1:5,8 that the Holy Ghost would be given that believers might be "endued with power from on High." Then on the Day of Pentecost, God shed forth the Holy Spirit as He came *upon* believers (Acts 2:33). And the Holy Spirit has been here ever since for believers to receive.

When the Church Began

Some people have said, "The Church began on the Day of Pentecost." But the Bible doesn't teach that. The Church actually began when Jesus breathed on the disciples and said, "Receive ye the Holy Ghost" (John 20:22). This is when the Holy Spirit indwelt the disciples and did His work of recreating their spirits and making them new creatures on the inside (2 Cor. 5:17).

Before Jesus breathed on His disciples, the disciples had a promissory note on salvation (John 14:16,17,23), but they weren't born again. Until Jesus breathed on the disciples, the Holy Spirit had not yet been given to bring people into the new-birth experience, because Jesus had not yet redeemed mankind through His death, burial, and resurrection (John 7:39).

But then in John 20:22, the resurrected Jesus breathed on the disciples and said, ". . . *Receive ye the Holy Ghost.*" As you study the Scriptures it becomes evident that something transpired *within* the disciples at that time.

The disciples had just watched their Master die on a cross and they had buried Him. They were a confused, mystified group of people. But after meeting with the risen Christ and having the Holy Spirit imparted to them in the work of the new birth, the disciples were changed.

We know that something happened to the disciples when Jesus breathed on them because after Jesus ascended, even before the Day of Pentecost, the Bible says that the disciples returned to Jerusalem with ". . . *GREAT JOY: And were continually in the temple, praising and blessing God*" (Luke 24:52,53). They were a changed group of people because they had been born again.

Therefore, John 20:22 records the beginning of the Church, for that is when the disciples were born again.

Born Again, but Waiting for the Outpouring

These same men that received the Holy Spirit when Jesus breathed on them were all there in the Upper Room on the Day of Pentecost, along with the rest of the 120 mentioned (Acts 1:13-15). These same disciples were waiting in the Upper Room to receive the *outpouring* of the Holy Ghost; to be *baptized* with the Holy Ghost; to be *endued with power* by the Holy Ghost (Acts 1:8; Luke 24:49). These are all describing the same New Testament experience — the infilling of the Holy Spirit.

There Is More To Receive of the Holy Spirit After the New Birth

If the disciples had heard some of these modern-day theologians and preachers who say that a believer receives all of the Holy Spirit at the new birth, then the disciples never would have gone to wait in the Upper Room for the promise of the Holy Spirit and the enduement of power from on High.

They would have said, "Jesus breathed on me and I received the Holy Ghost, so I've got Him! Therefore, I've got all of the Holy Spirit there is to get. That's all there is to it, *period!*" But as we will see, that *isn't* all there is to it, praise God!

'Are You Hungry for More of God?'

A number of years ago, I was speaking at a Full Gospel Businessmen's Convention. One of the other speakers, a Spirit-filled Episcopal priest, related an experience he had with a denominational minister who believed that a person receives all of the Holy Spirit there is to receive in the new-birth experience.

This Episcopal priest was speaking at a meeting about this experience of being baptized with the Holy Ghost and speaking with other tongues. In the middle of the sermon, the denominational minister jumped up and ran down the aisle to where the priest stood.

The denominational minister said to the priest, "I want you to know that I'm just as much filled and baptized with the Holy Ghost as you are, and I don't speak with tongues. I don't plan to ever speak in tongues either!"

The Episcopal priest smiled and said kindly, "Well, fine, Brother. If you're satisfied with your Christian walk, then I'm satisfied. But may I ask you a question?"

The denominational minister said yes and the priest said, "On the inside of you, do you have all of

God you could ever want to have? Do you have all you need? Are you hungry for any more of God?"

The minister said, "Well, yes, I'm hungry for more of God."

The Episcopal priest said, "If you will just kneel down right here, I will lay my hand on you and pray that God will satisfy your hunger."

The denominational minister knelt down and the priest laid his hand on him and said, "God, satisfy his hunger." And the minister immediately began speaking in tongues! Hallelujah! There is more of God to receive through the baptism of the Holy Spirit!

Wigglesworth's Testimony of Being Filled With the Holy Spirit

Over the years I've read in various accounts of Smith Wigglesworth's baptism in the Holy Spirit. Before Wigglesworth was baptized in the Holy Ghost, he wanted to argue with anyone who said he needed to receive more of the Holy Ghost. He told them, "I've got the Holy Ghost; it's these tongues I want."

People would tell him, "No, you need the fullness of the Holy Spirit, and then you'll speak in tongues." But Wigglesworth didn't want to accept the possibility that there was more of the Holy Spirit to receive than he already had by being born again.

However, Wigglesworth was determined to "receive those tongues." He was at the end of some meetings and preparing to get on the train to go back to his home. He decided to visit a Spirit-filled Episcopal priest's home before he left.

The priest was out making a pastoral call when Wigglesworth got there. But the priest's wife told Wigglesworth, "Come on in and I'll pray for you."

Wigglesworth said, "I want you to pray that I will receive those tongues."

The priest's wife said, "You don't want tongues; you want the Holy Ghost! You receive this experience of the baptism of the Holy Ghost, and the tongues will be a part of that experience. But don't seek tongues. Seek the Holy Ghost. Seek Jesus who is the Baptizer in the Holy Ghost."

"But I already have the Holy Ghost!" Wigglesworth argued. "I know what I want!"

"Be quiet, shut your eyes, and I'll pray for you!" the priest's wife said. So she laid her hands on Wigglesworth's head as he knelt there and she prayed, "Oh Lord, help this poor fellow. Forgive him and baptize him in the Holy Ghost."

About that time someone knocked at the door and the priest's wife went to answer it. While she was gone and Wigglesworth was kneeling there alone, suddenly with his eyes shut he had a vision.

In the vision, Wigglesworth saw the empty cross and the glorified Savior. He was conscious of the cleansing of Jesus' precious blood, and he began to cry out, "Clean! Clean! Clean! I'm clean through the blood! Through the blood, I'm clean!"

About that time Wigglesworth realized he wasn't saying "clean" anymore; he was talking in some kind of strange language! And he traveled back home speaking with other tongues.[1]

After Wigglesworth was baptized in the Holy Ghost, he would tell people, "I used to have an argument, but now I have an experience inside the Bible and outside the realm of argument!" He found out there was more to receive of the Holy Spirit after being born again.

Speaking in Tongues Is Not Evidence of the New Birth

As I said, one extreme is believing a person has all of the Holy Spirit there is to have in the new birth. On the other extreme, some people think that a person doesn't have the Holy Ghost in his life at all *until* he speaks in tongues. These people would say the disciples did not receive the Holy Ghost at all in the new birth when Jesus breathed on them. They believe the disciples didn't have the Holy Ghost *until* they spoke in tongues.

But speaking in tongues is not the Bible evidence for *the new birth*. It is the Bible evidence for *the baptism of the Holy Spirit*, as we will later discuss in detail. Only *believers* can receive the infilling of the Holy Spirit. Therefore, the disciples *had* to be born again before they could have been baptized with the Holy Spirit with the evidence of speaking in tongues (Acts 2:4).

So did the disciples receive the Holy Ghost in the new birth as recorded in John 20:22, or not? If they didn't, then Jesus sure did pull a funny trick on them. He sure did fool them when He said that to them! No, when Jesus said, "Receive ye the Holy Ghost," He meant what He said!

The disciples received the Holy Spirit in the new-birth experience at that moment. This is when the disciples were born again, yet fifty days later they gathered with other believers in the Upper Room to be endued with power from on High by the same Holy Spirit.

It Is the Same Holy Spirit in the New Birth and In the Baptism of the Holy Spirit

I knew as a young Baptist boy preacher that I had been born of the Spirit when I was born again (Rom. 8:16). But I didn't know the Bible that well back then, and I didn't understand that there was also the promise of a dual working of the Holy Spirit in the believer's life (Luke 24:49).

Some Pentecostal folks I knew made it sound like you didn't have the Holy Ghost in any measure until you spoke with tongues. So from listening to them, I thought that I was going to receive another "Spirit" when I got baptized in the Holy Ghost.

When I was baptized in the Holy Ghost and began to speak in other tongues, I said, "Why, this is the same Spirit I've had all the time. It's the same Holy Ghost! There aren't two Holy Ghosts — there's just *one*! He's not twins!"

Before I got baptized in the Holy Spirit, some of my Baptist colleagues would warn me about associating with Pentecostal people. They would say, "Now those are good people all right. They live better lives than people do in our church. But that speaking in tongues is of the devil!"

I wouldn't say much when they said that, but I would think, *Isn't it strange that people can get something from the devil that will help them live better lives!*

One man in particular, a graduate of a Baptist seminary, had warned me again and again about Pentecostal people and speaking in tongues. After I had been baptized in the Holy Spirit, I rushed over to see him.

He gave me the same warning that he had given me many times before: "I want to warn you, Kenneth, about going around with those Full Gospel people. That speaking in tongues is of the devil!"

I told him, "Well, if it is, then the whole Southern Baptist movement is of the devil!"

"What are you talking about?" he asked, surprised.

I said, "I got baptized with the Holy Ghost in the Full Gospel pastor's house. I didn't get any new Spirit. The same Holy Spirit that I received in the new birth in the Baptist church is the same Holy Spirit that gave me utterance in other tongues!"

I had just discovered what the Bible had taught all along. Just like the disciples in Acts 2:1-4, I had received an enduement of power from on High from the same Holy Spirit who had recreated my spirit when I was born again.

The Holy Spirit Upon: The Gateway Into the Supernatural

As we discussed in Chapter 4, the Bible teaches that there are two groups of nine in connection with the work of the Holy Spirit in the life of the believer. First, there is the ninefold manifestation of the fruit of the born-again human spirit that Paul lists in Galatians 5:22,23. The fruit of the spirit is the result of the Holy Spirit's *indwelling* Presence.

We find a second ninefold group in connection with the Holy Spirit in First Corinthians 12:7-11. These are the nine manifestations of the Holy Spirit known as the gifts of the Spirit. The gateway into these nine supernatural manifestations of the Holy Spirit is the baptism of the Holy Spirit with the evidence of speaking with tongues.

1 CORINTHIANS 12:7-11
7 But the MANIFESTATION OF THE SPIRIT is given to every man to profit withal.
8 For to one is given by the Spirit THE WORD OF WISDOM; to another THE WORD OF KNOWLEDGE by the same Spirit;
9 To another FAITH by the same Spirit; to another the GIFTS OF HEALING by the same Spirit;
10 To another THE WORKING OF MIRACLES; to another PROPHECY; to another DISCERNING OF SPIRITS; to another DIVERS KINDS OF TONGUES; to another THE INTERPRETATION OF TONGUES;
11 But all these worketh that one and the selfsame Spirit, dividing to every man severally as he will.

These nine gifts of the Spirit are given ". . . *to profit withal . . .*" (1 Cor. 12:7). In other words, the gifts of the Spirit are given so that believers can bless others.

We can draw a conclusion as we study these two ninefold groups of the Holy Spirit's working in the life of the believer:

The *indwelling* of the Holy Spirit is for *fruit bearing.*

The *infilling* of the Holy Spirit is for *service.*

The Holy Spirit Upon: Being Filled With the Fullness of God

As we have already seen, when a person is born again, he receives a measure of the Holy Spirit as the Holy Spirit comes to dwell within him. The Holy Spirit lives within the believer to help him, comfort him, guide him, and cause him to bear fruit in his life.

But the believer can experience more of God! There is more of the Holy Spirit to receive! There is a deep Pentecostal experience that is not to be despised, but rather coveted. God has given us the gift of the Holy Spirit *upon* us through the baptism of the Holy Spirit so that believers might enter into *all of the fullness of God.*

EPHESIANS 3:19,20
19 . . . to know the love of Christ, which passeth knowledge, that YE MIGHT BE FILLED WITH ALL THE FULNESS OF GOD.
20 Now unto him that is able to do exceeding abundantly above all that we ask or think, ACCORDING TO THE POWER THAT WORKETH IN US. . . .

When Paul said, *". . . that ye might be filled with all the fulness of God"* (Eph. 3:19), he was talking to Spirit-filled believers.

As we study Paul's epistles, we must always bear in mind that they were written to churches. In other words, he wrote to people who had not only received eternal life in the new-birth experience, but had also received the baptism of the Holy Spirit.

In the New Testament Church it was the rule or standard for everyone not only to be born again, but also to be filled with the Holy Ghost and to speak with other tongues. Those who were not filled with the Spirit were the exception rather than the rule.

We have a different situation in the Church in these modern times. Today in the church world (I am not speaking of just Full Gospel churches, but the church world as a whole), there are many who are born again. However, because of a lack of knowledge, many believers have not entered into their full inheritance of being filled with the Holy Ghost.

There is a greater measure of the Holy Spirit for believers to receive in the baptism of the Holy Spirit. Just as being born again and having the Holy Spirit dwell *within* is the entrance into the ninefold *fruit* of the spirit, so being *filled* with the Spirit is the doorway into the ninefold supernatural manifestations of the *gifts* of the Spirit. There is no other way to get into the supernatural manifestations of the Holy Spirit than through the baptism of the Holy Spirit.

The Holy Spirit Upon: Power To Put Us Over in Life

Paul said in Ephesians 5:20 that we would be filled with the fullness of God *". . . according to the POWER that worketh in us"* (Eph. 3:20). Jesus told the disciples *". . . ye shall receive POWER, after that the Holy Ghost is come upon you . . ."* (Acts 1:8).

I maintain that every Spirit-filled believer has in him, on account and ready for use, all the power that he will ever need to put him over in this life. Why?

Because of the infilling Presence of the Greater One, the Holy Spirit.

To illustrate this point, I can relate an experience that Wigglesworth, who was a mighty Spirit-filled man of faith, once had in England when he was asked to pray for the daughter of an elderly couple.

The parents of the girl led Wigglesworth to an upstairs room, pushed open the door, and stepped back motioning for him to enter. Inside was a woman lying on the floor. She was so violently insane, she had to be held down by five grown men.

When the door was opened, the insane woman looked at Wigglesworth, her eyes ablaze. She arose from off the floor and tore herself loose from the men. They couldn't hold her. The evil spirit in that woman screamed at Wigglesworth, "We are many. You can't cast us out!"

Quietly Wigglesworth said, "Jesus can." He remembered that the Bible said, *". . . greater is he that is in you . . ."* (1 John 4:4) and that he was a thousand times bigger on the inside than he was on the outside. He dared to believe that God was inside him.

He said to the woman, "Jesus can. And out you come in the Name of the Lord Jesus Christ." Thirty-seven devils came out, giving their names. That young woman's mind was completely restored. She dressed and came downstairs to eat the evening meal with them that same day. [2]

The same power of God that Wigglesworth operated in to cast out those demons in the Name of Jesus is made available to every believer through the baptism of the Holy Spirit!

The Holy Spirit Upon: Supernatural Praying

We discussed in Chapter 4 the role of the Holy Spirit as our Guide in life. Remember, in John 16:13 Jesus said, *". . . he [the Holy Spirit] shall not speak of himself; but whatsoever he shall hear, that shall he speak. . . ."* What shall He speak? What He hears God say. And not only will He speak whatever He hears, but *". . . he will shew you things to come"* (John 16:13).

We also saw in *The Amplified Bible* that the Holy Spirit is our Intercessor.

JOHN 14:16 (Amplified)
16 And I will ask the Father, and He will give you another Comforter (Counselor, Helper, INTERCESSOR, Advocate, Strengthener and Standby) that He may remain with you forever.

While it is true that the number one way the Holy Spirit guides us is through the inward witness in our spirits, it is also true that the Holy Spirit will help us and give us guidance in our prayer life (Rom. 8:26,27). And when we receive the infilling of the Holy Spirit, a new dimension is made available in our private prayer life through speaking in tongues.

My Own Experiences in Prayer

I have had many experiences in prayer in which the Holy Spirit has guided me and shown me "things to come." For example, one night while in a meeting in Oregon, I was very burdened in prayer. The Holy Spirit showed me that my oldest brother was having physical difficulty, but that he would be all right.

I told my wife, "The doctors will think that his condition is very serious, and from the natural standpoint, it is serious. But he is coming out of it all right. The Lord said so."

In just a few hours we got a long distance call from my sister. She was almost in hysterics as she said, "Our brother has had an accident and has broken his back. His condition is very serious. What are we going to do?"

Thank God, I was able to tell her, "I already have inside information on this. He is not as bad off as they think he is. He will be all right. Don't fret about it."

Later the doctors said to my brother, "We don't understand it. The X rays show that your spine is completely broken. The bone is severed in two. Why you aren't paralyzed we don't know."

I knew why, however. My brother was in Iowa, but there was an Intercessor inside of me in Oregon — the Holy Spirit who had already taken care of the situation.

Another time I was traveling alone to minister in St. Louis, while my wife stayed at home to take care of our children. Late one night I suddenly sensed a need to pray.

I began to pray in tongues, and I continued to pray, knowing that something was wrong at home. I sensed that someone's physical life was in danger.

The Holy Spirit showed me that it was my mother. I continued to pray, saying, "You are my Helper. You are my Intercessor. Help me to pray for her."

While I was praying, the phone rang. My wife was calling to say that they had just taken my mother to the hospital.

"She has had a very serious heart attack," my wife said. "They don't know if she will live or not."

I said, "I know it. And I have already been praying. The Holy Spirit showed me that she will be all right." And she was, praise God!

If space permitted, I could tell of experience after experience along this line. In 1959 my wife and I were in California preaching. At that time our daughter was expecting her first child. One Friday night I was awakened during the night. Very often I would wake up and pray. I would just lay there quietly and do most of my praying in tongues, the Holy Ghost giving me utterance.

That night I lay there and prayed for about an hour or more in tongues, never disturbing my wife sleeping by my side. After praying in tongues, I started prophesying. Sometimes I prophesy to myself as well as to others as the Spirit leads.

As I continued to prophesy the Lord said, "I'll be with Pat, and she will come through safely. The baby shall be born. You need have no worry or fear."

I wondered why He was saying that to me because I knew Pat was all right. We were expecting to be home before the baby was born. I didn't know that she was having great difficulty at that very moment. I thought that the Lord was just reassuring me that everything would be all right and that she would carry the baby the full length of time.

The Lord said to me, "You have obeyed me. You did what I asked you to do. You left your family and your children and were away from them eighty-five percent of the time for eight years as they were growing up. Since you did what I asked you to do, I am going to do this for your sake because you obeyed me."

You see, what we do affects not only our lives but the lives of our children and our family as well.

A week later we received a call from our pastor back home while we were still on the road. He said that Pat had just been rushed to the hospital in an ambulance. Our pastor related to us that the baby was going to be born prematurely.

He said, "There are serious symptoms. I'm going to be honest with you, Brother Hagin. Her condition is terribly serious. It looks as if there is very little hope for the baby and little hope for her."

I said immediately with joy, "Oh, Brother, don't bother about it. I already have the answer! I've had it for a week. Last Friday night about this time the Lord was speaking to me. He said the baby would be born. The Lord said He would see Pat through. She will come through splendidly, and everything will be all right. I am not going to pray. Just rejoice with me because everything is going to be all right."

A short time later the Holy Spirit spoke to me and said, "The baby is being born right this minute." I looked at the clock and told my wife, "The Holy Spirit just said to me that the baby is being born and is all right. The baby is being born right this minute and is alive." So we began to praise the Lord.

The next morning my son-in-law called and said, "I just wanted to call and tell you everything is fine. Pat is fine. The baby is fine. Everything is lovely."

I asked, "When was the child born?" He told me the very minute the baby had been born. It was the very minute the Holy Ghost told me she was born.

The Holy Spirit is our Intercessor and our Guide, and as we yield to Him in our prayer life, He will help us and at times show us things to come, as He wills (John 14:16 *Amp.*; Rom. 8:26; John 16:13).

Cooperating With the Holy Spirit, the Power Source

We have discussed how the baptism of the Holy Spirit is the gateway into the supernatural manifestations of the gifts of the Holy Spirit and the power of God. Yet the truth is so many believers who have received the infilling of the Holy Spirit do not reach their full potential in learning to cooperate with the Holy Spirit, who is the Source of all power.

I believe that often we have been so concerned with receiving the Holy Spirit as an outward experience or with some feeling of ecstasy from the natural standpoint, that we have missed the reality of what the Holy Spirit came to do *in* us and *through* us on a continual basis through the baptism of the Holy Spirit.

When the baptism of the Holy Spirit is just an experience with believers, they talk about "it," the outward manifestation and miss the reality of the Holy Spirit on the inside of them. We should be conscious of the Holy Spirit's indwelling Presence every waking moment.

'Something More'

At the close of one of my services once, a man came to me and said, "Brother Hagin, I want you to pray for me. I need something more than what I have."

I said, "First, let's find out why you need this 'something more.'"

"Well," he replied, "to put me over in life."

I said, "Oh, then you want me to pray that God would give you something more than what you have to put you over in life, to make you a successful Christian, to give you power, and to help you when you meet the tests and trials of life?"

"Yes, yes, yes! That's it!" he exclaimed.

"Well, let's find out what you *do* have and we will see what we need to pray for that you *don't* have. Are you saved?"

"Yes, Brother Hagin, I was born again eight years ago."

"All right," I said. "I will accept your testimony. Don't let the devil talk you out of it."

I continued, "Have you ever read where Jesus said, '. . . we [My Father and I] *will come . . . and make our abode with him*'?" (John 14:23).

"Yes, I have," he answered.

"And have you received the baptism of the Holy Ghost? Are you filled with the Holy Ghost?" I asked.

"Oh yes, I was filled with the Holy Ghost just one year after I was saved."

Then I quoted the scriptures to him: *"Ye are of God, little children, and have overcome them: because greater is he that is in you, than he that is in the world"* (1 John 4:4) and *"What? know ye not that your body is the temple of the Holy Ghost which is in you, which ye have of God. . . ?"* (1 Cor. 6:19). Then I asked him if he had ever read these scriptures.

"Yes," he said, "I have read them."

"Well, if you are born again and Spirit-filled, you have God the Father, God the Son, in the person of the Holy Spirit dwelling in you and living in you [Col. 2:9,10 *Amp.*]. And, Brother, there isn't anything more to get that will put you over in life. If God the Father, God the Son, and God the Holy Ghost can't put you over, then you will never get over!"

"Well, I know that. But I need *power*."

"I thought you said you had the Holy Ghost," I said. "Jesus said, *'But ye shall receive power, after that the Holy Ghost is come upon you . . .'* [Acts 1:8]. In fact, the Holy Ghost is the Source of all power."

I continued, "If you are filled with the Holy Ghost, you have the potential in you for all the power there is. What you need to do is to learn *to cooperate* with Him — the Power Source. You need to learn to walk in the light of what you have. You need to learn to put Him who is in you to work for you."

He said, "But I don't *feel* like I have any power."

I quoted Acts 1:8 to him again: *" 'But ye shall receive power, after that the Holy Ghost is come upon you. . . .'* Jesus didn't say a word here about your *feeling* like it."

Then I said, "Acts 2:4 says, *'And they were all filled with the Holy Ghost, and began to speak with other tongues. . . .'* It doesn't say that they *felt* like speaking with other tongues. It just says they did it."

I told him, "By way of illustration, I would rather have a million dollars any time, rather than just to feel like I had it, because you can't spend what you feel. But you *can spend* what you *have*!"

The same principle works in the spiritual realm. I have had some of the greatest supernatural things happen when I felt no anointing or unction at all. I have had the greatest miracles of healing happen in my ministry when I felt nothing.

Why is that so? Because I knew how to put the Greater One to work for me and to stand on God's Word regardless of feelings.

Basing Our Faith on the Word, Not on Our Feelings

Every believer has the Holy Spirit dwelling within him, and if he has received the infilling of the Holy Spirit he has also received the enduement of power from on High. These truths are a reality, whether we feel like they are or not. The Bible says, *"For we walk by faith, not by sight"* (2 Cor. 5:7). We must believe what the Word of God says, regardless of what our feelings tell us.

I learned the lesson of faith on the bed of sickness more than fifty-five years ago. I acted on God's Word even though I didn't feel anything.

My paralysis disappeared in ten minutes' time when I leaned on the Greater One on the inside and acted on God's Word in simple faith. My heart symptoms disappeared, and I was raised up from an incurable, terminal heart disease, perfectly healed.

Since then I have never paid a bit of attention to my physical feelings, because they haven't got a thing in the world to do with the Christian walk. *"For we walk by faith, not by sight"* (2 Cor. 5:7)!

Feelings are the voice of the flesh. If you are walking by feelings, you are being dominated by the flesh. But the Bible tells us to crucify the flesh. If the flesh is crucified, the *voice* of the flesh is also to be crucified.

You can't walk by feelings and be a successful Christian, for if you are walking by feelings, then your flesh, not your spirit, is dominating you.

And you can't walk by *reason* and be a successful Christian either, because reason is the voice of your mind. But you *can* walk by faith and be a successful Christian, because faith is of the Spirit.

Walking by faith is letting your spirit man dominate you. Walking by faith is listening to the Voice of the Greater One on the inside of you and walking in line with the Word of God.

How do we walk by faith and not by sight? We walk by faith by putting faith in what God has said in His Word. It never pays to walk by sight. It never pays to walk by feelings when God has spoken to us by His Word.

We must listen to what God has to say in His Word and act on that. It always pays to walk by faith — to simply take God at His Word — because He is faithful who promised (Heb. 10:23).

As we learn to lean on the Greater One who dwells within us, and as we are filled with the Holy Spirit, then the power of God is made available to us and the supernatural manifestations of the Holy Spirit can operate through us as the Spirit wills.

We need to learn how to put the Greater One who *indwells* us and who has *infilled* us to work *for* us. When we do, we will have no need to walk by sight, to look at circumstances, or to be ruled by our feelings. We can rise above our physical limitations and natural circumstances and enter into the realm of the supernatural through the power of the Holy Spirit!

---

[1] Smith Wigglesworth, *Ever Increasing Faith* (1924; Springfield, Missouri: Gospel Publishing House, 1971), pp. 112,113.
[2] *Ever Increasing Faith*, pp. 65,66.

Questions for Study

1. When was Jesus' promise to the disciples of the indwelling Presence of the Holy Spirit fulfilled?

   _____

   _____

2. When did God give the outpouring of the Holy Spirit and to whom did He give it?

   _____

   _____

3. The *outpouring* of the Holy Ghost, to be *baptized* with the Holy Ghost, and to be *endued with power* are all describing what New Testament experience?

   _____

   _____

4. Speaking in tongues is the Bible evidence for _____ _____ _____

   _____ _____ _____.

5. What is the gateway into the nine supernatural manifestations of the Holy Spirit?

   _____

   _____

6. Why has God given us the gift of the Holy Spirit upon us through the baptism in the Holy Spirit?

   _____

   _____

7. Every Spirit-filled believer has in him, on account and ready for use, all the power that he will ever need to put him over in life. Why?

   _____

   _____

8. What is the number one way that the Holy Spirit guides us?

   _____

   _____

9. What should we be conscious of every waking moment?

   _____

   _____

10. We must believe what the Word of God says, regardless of what?

    _____

    _____

Chapter 6

How Important Is Speaking in Tongues?

There is more to being filled with the Holy Ghost than speaking in tongues, but tongues are an integral and an important part of receiving the Holy Ghost, since they are the initial evidence of the infilling of the Holy Spirit (Acts 2:4). Also, speaking in tongues is an integral part of the believer's devotional prayer life, for as the Apostle Paul said, *"I thank my God, I speak with tongues . . ."* (1 Cor. 14:18). I, too, can say with Paul, "I thank my God I speak with tongues."

Have Tongues Been Done Away With?

In the church world today many people say, "Tongues have been done away with, because the Bible says that tongues will cease." The Bible does say that one day tongues will cease, but that is not referring to this present church age. However, to try to prove that tongues have already ceased, these folks usually refer to First Corinthians 13:8-12:

1 CORINTHIANS 13:8-12
8 Charity [love] never faileth: but whether there be prophecies, they shall fail; WHETHER THERE BE TONGUES, THEY SHALL CEASE; whether there be knowledge, it shall vanish away.
9 For we know in part, and we prophesy in part.
10 But when THAT WHICH IS PERFECT is come, then THAT WHICH IS IN PART shall be done away.
11 When I was a child, I spake as a child, I understood as a child, I thought as a child: but when I became a man, I put away childish things.
12 For NOW we SEE THROUGH A GLASS, darkly; but THEN FACE TO FACE: NOW I KNOW IN PART; but THEN SHALL I KNOW even as also I am known.

These folks use verse 10 to try to prove that tongues have ceased, because they say the Bible is "that which is perfect" which has already come. They say that since we have the Bible in its complete form now, we no longer need "that which is in part" — which includes supernatural gifts (1 Cor. 13:10).

Of course, the Bible is perfect, but our understanding of the Bible certainly is not perfect. Therefore, until that which is perfect has come, we still "see through a glass darkly" in this life (1 Cor. 13:12). Hence, "that which is in part" (1 Cor. 13:10) has not ceased.

1 CORINTHIANS 13:8
8 Charity never faileth: but whether there be prophecies, they shall fail; whether there be tongues, they shall cease; whether there be KNOWLEDGE, it SHALL VANISH AWAY.

These folks who say tongues have ceased don't say anything about *knowledge* having vanished away (1 Cor. 13:8)! But if they are going to quote that verse, they need to quote *the whole verse* because it also says, *". . . whether there be tongues, they shall cease; whether there be KNOWLEDGE, it shall VANISH AWAY"* (1 Cor. 13:8).

Verse 10 says that when that which is perfect has come, we shall see face to face and not through a glass darkly. *That's* when prophecies, tongues, and knowledge shall "vanish away" and cease to exist; however, as I said, that is not in this Church Age.

However, since it is quite evident that we still see through a glass darkly, it is also obvious that that which is perfect has not yet come. Hence, prophecies, tongues, and knowledge have not passed away or ceased to exist.

Knowledge has not vanished away. Prophecies have not failed or ceased to exist, and, therefore, tongues have not ceased. However, one of these days, tongues will cease. In heaven there will be no necessity for tongues because that which is perfect will have come (1 Cor. 13:10).

1 CORINTHIANS 14:2
2 For he that speaketh in an unknown tongue speaketh not unto men, but unto God: for no man understandeth him; howbeit in the spirit he speaketh mysteries.

Let's look at *Moffatt's* translation of First Corinthians 14:2.

1 CORINTHIANS 14:2 (Moffatt)
2 . . . For he who speaks in a 'tongue' addresses God, not man; no one understands him; he is talking of divine secrets in the Spirit.

When we get to heaven, there won't be any more mysteries or secrets, so it won't be necessary to speak with tongues. As long as we are this side of heaven, however, tongues will not cease.

Are Tongues Available for All Believers?

As we said before, there is more to being filled with the Holy Spirit than speaking in tongues; but speaking in tongues is the initial evidence of being filled with the Holy Spirit.

There are those who purport to believe in speaking in tongues but do not feel that tongues are necessary for all believers. However, the baptism in the

Holy Spirit is for all those who believe (Acts 2:38,39); therefore, speaking in tongues as an evidence of the Spirit's infilling is also for all those who believe.

These who say that speaking in tongues is not necessary for all believers use the scripture in First Corinthians 12:30 which says, "*. . . do all speak with tongues? . . .*" to prove their argument.

However, one could take a part of a verse of Scripture, or even one entire verse of Scripture out of its setting and try to prove anything with it. But we have to read the entire context to see what the writer is talking about.

To learn what Paul is talking about in First Corinthians 12:30, "*. . . do all speak with tongues? . . .*" we must read the entire context in First Corinthians chapter 12.

Having done that, then let's look specifically at verses 27 through 30.

1 CORINTHIANS 12:27-30
27 Now ye are the body of Christ, and members in particular.
28 And God hath set some in the church, first APOSTLES, secondarily PROPHETS, thirdly TEACHERS, after that MIRACLES, then GIFTS OF HEALINGS, HELPS, GOVERNMENTS, DIVERSITIES OF TONGUES.
29 Are all apostles? are all prophets? are all teachers? are all workers of miracles?
30 Have all the gifts of healing? do all speak with tongues? do all interpret?

Ministry Gifts vs. Spiritual Gifts

What is Paul talking about in this passage of Scripture? He is talking about *ministry gifts*, not *spiritual gifts*. Ministry gifts are those people in the Body of Christ who are called by God to stand in the fivefold ministry (Eph. 4:11,12).

These apostles, prophets, teachers, and so forth, listed here in First Corinthians 12:27 and 28 are ministry gifts that God has set in the Church.

For example, first, "apostles" is not a spiritual gift, but it is an *office* or a *ministry gift*.

Second, "prophets" is not a spiritual gift, but it is a ministry gift. Third, "teachers," the office of a teacher, is not a spiritual gift, but a ministry gift, or one called to minister to the Body of Christ.

Therefore, in this passage of Scripture in First Corinthians 12:27-30, Paul is talking about ministry gifts, or those called to the fivefold ministry, not about spiritual gifts.

In order to see the difference between ministry gifts and spiritual gifts, let's look at the nine spiritual gifts, or gifts of the Spirit. Paul lists them in the first part of this chapter.

1 CORINTHIANS 12:8-10
8 For to one is given by the Spirit the WORD OF WISDOM; to another the WORD OF KNOWLEDGE by the same Spirit;
9 To another FAITH [special faith] by the same Spirit; to another the GIFTS OF HEALING by the same Spirit;
10 To another the WORKING OF MIRACLES; to another PROPHECY; to another DISCERNING OF SPIRITS; to another DIVERS KINDS OF TONGUES; to another the INTERPRETATION OF TONGUES.

It is certainly true that gifts of the Spirit may be manifested through the laity, not just through ministry gifts or those called to the fivefold ministry, because the Bible does say, "*But the manifestation of the Spirit is given TO EVERY MAN to profit withal*" (1 Cor. 12:7).

However, there are those in the fivefold ministry who are especially equipped with certain gifts of the Spirit in order to fulfill their office or function in the Body of Christ. We do not call those *people* spiritual gifts or gifts of the Spirit; they are *ministries* or *ministry gifts* that God has set in the Church.

Paul talks about ministry gifts in writing to the Church at Ephesus. Paul said that when Jesus ascended on High, "*. . . he led captivity captive, and gave GIFTS unto men*" (Eph. 4:8).

What were those gifts? Paul goes on to list them. They are ministry gifts Jesus set in the Church.

EPHESIANS 4:11,12
11 And he gave some, APOSTLES; and some, PROPHETS; and some, EVANGELISTS; and some, PASTORS and TEACHERS;
12 For the perfecting of the saints, for the work of the ministry, for the edifying of the body of Christ.

There are five ministry gifts or offices. They are people in the Body of Christ who are called by God to stand in the fivefold ministry.

Now let's look at First Corinthians 12:28 *in context* so we can understand what Paul meant when he said, "*. . . do all speak with tongues? . . .*" (1 Cor. 12:30).

In First Corinthians 12:28, Paul is also listing *ministry gifts*, but he lists them in a little different way.

1 CORINTHIANS 12:28
28 And God hath set some in the church, first APOSTLES, secondarily PROPHETS, thirdly TEACHERS, after that MIRACLES, then GIFTS OF HEALINGS, HELPS, GOVERNMENTS, DIVERSITIES OF TONGUES.

Now let's look at each one of these ministry gifts, so we can understand the phrase "do all speak with tongues?"

As we said, "apostle," "prophet," and "teacher," which are also mentioned in First Corinthians 12:28, indicate those in the fivefold ministry offices.

Then Paul also includes the ministry of helps because those in the ministry of helps assist those called to the fivefold ministry. But what about "miracles" and "gifts of healings" (1 Cor. 12:28)?

Miracles and Gifts of Healings

Those gifts of "miracles" and "gifts of healings" indicate a ministry gift — the office of the evangelist. The ministry of an evangelist is not listed at all here, except as "miracles" and "gifts of healings," indicating the office of the evangelist.

Philip is our only example of a New Testament evangelist. We can see the working of miracles and gifts of healings operating in his ministry which indicate the ministry of an evangelist.

ACTS 8:5-7
5 Then Philip went down to the city of Samaria, and preached Christ unto them.
6 And the people with one accord gave heed unto those things which Philip spake, HEARING AND SEEING THE MIRACLES WHICH HE DID.
7 For unclean spirits, crying with loud voice, came out of many that were possessed with them: and many taken with palsies, and that were lame, were healed.

Later on Philip was called an evangelist.

ACTS 21:8
8 And the next day we that were of Paul's company departed, and came unto Caesarea: and we entered into the house of PHILIP THE EVANGELIST, which was one of the seven; and abode with him.

If a person is a New Testament evangelist, he will be equipped with supernatural gifts such as working of miracles and gifts of healings. In fact, it takes at least those two gifts to constitute the office of the evangelist.

Many times we call people evangelists who are really exhorters. In other words, they just exhort sinners to get saved, but they are not really New Testament evangelists; they are *exhorters*.

Exhorters do *not* have the gifts of healings or the gift of the working of miracles operating in their ministries. They are exhorters; that is their function in the Body of Christ. And they can exhort people to get saved, but there is no manifestation of supernatural gifts operating in their lives or ministries on a continual basis. Paul speaks of exhorters in the Book of Romans (Rom. 12:8).

Helps

The ministry of helps is included in this passage in First Corinthians 12:27-30 too. These are people in the Body of Christ who are divinely called and anointed by God to help those in the fivefold ministry. Verse 28 calls this ministry, "helps." Their function is as a supportive role to those called to the ministry.

Governments

Also, the ministry or the office of the pastor is not listed in this verse either, as such. However, the office of *governments* is listed which indicates the pastoral office because the pastor is the head of a church. He "governs" or shepherds the local body.

Diversities of Tongues

Another ministry gift we see listed in First Corinthians 12:28 is diversities of tongues. Paul has not changed his subject in this verse. He is still talking about ministry gifts, or fivefold ministry offices, not gifts of the Spirit.

In other words, in this passage, Paul isn't talking about being filled with the Holy Ghost and speaking with tongues as a devotional gift because he said, *"Are all apostles? [No!] are all prophets? [No!] are all teachers? [No!] are all workers of miracles? [No!] Have all the gifts of healing? . . ."* The answer is no (1 Cor. 12:29,30).

Then Paul said, *". . . do all speak with tongues? do all interpret?"* (1 Cor. 12:30). The answer is no, all do not speak with tongues as a *ministry gift*. Paul was not talking about believers being filled with the Holy Ghost and speaking with tongues in their private devotional prayer lives. However, all believers are encouraged to speak in tongues to themselves and to God (1 Cor. 14:2,4).

Paul was talking about ministering in tongues in a public assembly with interpretation as a ministry gift, and not everyone does that. Ministering in tongues in public assembly with interpretation on more of a continual basis denotes the ministry gift of diversities of tongues most closely related to the office of the prophet, and not every believer has that gift. This is not referring to a believer who is used in tongues or interpretation of tongues on an occasional basis.

Of course, every believer can have the gift of speaking in other tongues for private devotion. The gifts of the Spirit are for all believers. But ministry gifts only refer to those who are called to the fivefold ministry.

It is true that the laity are sometimes used in the manifestation of the gift of tongues and interpretation of tongues — the gift of the Spirit listed in First Corinthians 12:10. But, actually, diversities of tongues listed here in First Corinthians 12:28 is not referring to lay members speaking in tongues; it is referring to an office — a fivefold ministry gift.

1 CORINTHIANS 12:28
28 And God hath set some in the church, first apostles, secondarily prophets, thirdly teachers, after that miracles, then gifts of healings, helps, governments, DIVERSITIES OF TONGUES.

1 CORINTHIANS 14:27,28
27 If any man speak in an unknown tongue, let it be by two, or at the most by three, and that by course; and let one interpret.
28 But if there be no interpreter, let him keep silence in the church; and let him speak to himself, and to God.

Paul was speaking here about one of the fivefold ministry gifts which is equipped with tongues and interpretation of tongues. This spiritual equipment of diversities of tongues is manifested on a consistent basis through one who is called to the fivefold ministry in the office of the prophet.

Tongues and Interpretation in Public Ministry

For years I have ministered to people through the gift of tongues and interpretation. Now I do the same thing in prophecy. It is important to note that a person doesn't always necessarily have just one gift operating at a time. Many times spiritual gifts operate together. Like the colors of a rainbow, they sometimes come together and overflow one into another.

For example, I have ministered healing to people through tongues and interpretation. I have seen them get up from a deathbed, and they are still well and alive today. In a case such as that, the gifts of healings operate in conjunction with tongues and interpretation.

Also, many times through tongues and interpretation the Holy Spirit will make manifest the secrets of men's hearts. And at times through tongues and interpretation, the Spirit of God through me has told ministers their very need and the desire of their hearts.

The Value of Speaking in Tongues

Many have been robbed of the blessings God intended them to have by believing that speaking in tongues isn't for everyone, or that speaking in tongues is one of the lesser gifts of the Spirit.

Before I was baptized in the Holy Spirit, I used to say, "We've got wisdom and knowledge, and those are the greater gifts of the Spirit."

(The Bible never said a thing in the world about wisdom and knowledge being spiritual gifts or gifts of the Spirit in and of themselves, but I didn't have enough sense to know that!)

What the scripture says is, *"For to one is given by the Spirit the WORD of wisdom; to another the WORD of knowledge . . ."* (1 Cor. 12:8). But the Bible isn't speaking here of wisdom and knowledge at all. It is speaking about the spiritual gifts of the *word of wisdom* and the *word of knowledge*.

As I already said, before I received the infilling of the Holy Ghost, I used to say, "We have wisdom and knowledge and those are the important gifts." I also said, "Now a few of those Pentecostals might have that little ole gift mentioned down toward the end of First Corinthians 12:8-10, the gift of *tongues*. But that gift really isn't very important, so we don't need it."

To my utter astonishment, the Spirit of God began to show me from His Word that I *needed* this valuable spiritual gift; I needed to be filled with the Holy Ghost with the evidence of speaking in tongues. The Lord showed me from the Word that when I got filled with the Holy Ghost, I would speak with tongues (Acts 2:4).

The Spirit of God revealed to me from the Word that speaking with tongues is an initial evidence or sign of the infilling of the Holy Spirit. Acts 2:4 says, *"And they were all filled with the Holy Ghost, and BEGAN TO SPEAK WITH OTHER TONGUES, as the Spirit gave them utterance."*

However, speaking with tongues does not occur as just one initial experience of being filled with the Holy Ghost, and then it ceases. Speaking with tongues is a continual experience for the rest of one's life to assist in the worship of God. As Howard Carter said, "It is a flowing stream that should never dry up, but will [continually] enrich the life spiritually."[1]

Notice that in writing to the Church at Corinth, Paul very definitely encouraged the Corinthian Christians to follow the practice of speaking with tongues in their own private prayer lives. And he gives a number of reasons for it.

Paul said, *"He that speaketh in an unknown tongue edifieth himself . . ."* (1 Cor. 14:4). The word "unknown" is italicized in the *King James* translation. When a word in the Bible is italicized in the *King James* translation, that means the word isn't in the original Scriptures. It was added by the translators to clarify the meaning.

Therefore, in one sense of the word, there isn't any such thing as an unknown tongue. For instance, the translators of the *King James Version* added the word "unknown" in order to convey the idea to readers that tongues are unknown to *the speaker*. However, tongues aren't necessarily *always* unknown to *everyone*, and they are *never* unknown to *God*.

For example, as I have spoken in tongues publicly on different occasions, I have spoken in a number of different languages that I have never learned, such as Hebrew and Chinese. And some folks who were present have understood what I said. But if I were asked now to speak these languages, I couldn't say one word in any of them. So in that sense, the tongues were unknown to me, but they weren't unknown to everyone, and they are certainly never unknown to God.

A Jewish man was present in one of my services in Texas. He didn't believe in Christ as the Messiah, nor did he believe in the New Testament. At the close of my sermon I spoke in tongues and then interpreted.

This Jewish man came to me after the service and said, "Sir, you made a statement tonight in Aramaic that I never heard anyone make. In fact, no Jewish person would ever make such a statement. I wondered what you were going to do when you began to translate it."

I said, "Well, how did I do?"

"Oh, you did splendidly."

"Good. I didn't know what I was saying."

He said, "What? You mean you don't know the Aramaic language?"

"No, I don't. I didn't know what I was saying," I answered. "I was speaking with other tongues and interpreting the tongues as the New Testament tells us in First Corinthians chapter 14."

"Oh, I don't believe in the New Testament," he said.

"Well, I cannot talk to you about it then, because what you heard me do tonight — speak in tongues and interpret — is found in the New Testament. You see, in the Old Testament, all the gifts of the Spirit were in operation except tongues and interpretation. Tongues and interpretation are distinctive of this New Testament dispensation."

He said, "You mean, what you did tonight is found in the New Testament?"

"Yes, it is in there. You know your Old Testament, don't you?" I asked.

"Oh, yes," he said. "But I don't accept Jesus. In fact, this is the first time I've ever spoken His Name. He is not the Messiah."

"Well," I said, "you know your Old Testament. In the Old Testament the prophets of God were anointed with the Holy Ghost or Holy Spirit. We can see a word of wisdom being given to one. And we can see a word of knowledge, discerning of spirits, the gift of faith, or special faith in operation being given to others."

I continued, "And we see gifts of healings and working of miracles and prophecy. All of the gifts of the Spirit listed in First Corinthians 12:8-10 were in operation at different times in the Old Testament except one: tongues and interpretation. No one in the Old Testament spoke with tongues and no one interpreted, because tongues and interpretation are distinctive to this New Testament dispensation."

He said, "If that is in the New Testament, then show it to me. I have never read that, but let's see it."

I opened my Bible and read to him out of First Corinthians chapter 14. Then he said, "Well, I could be wrong, you know. I am going to say His Name again for the second time in my life without using it as cursing. Jesus may be the Messiah. I will come back to your services."

Praise God, tongues and interpretation of tongues aren't just for the benefit of the believer. Tongues and interpretation of tongues can also minister to the unbeliever (1 Cor. 14:22)!

Some people believe that all speaking in tongues is prayer, and that those who speak with tongues are just praying to God and that God is the only one who understands what is being said. However, if I had been praying, that Jewish man would have known I was praying.

However, I wasn't praying. I was addressing the congregation in tongues, and then the interpretation came. The interpretation of those tongues ministered to that man.

All tongues are not prayer. For instance, there is the gift of the Spirit called tongues and interpretation of tongues, which is manifested for the benefit of others.

Then there is the devotional use of tongues (1 Cor. 14:2). *"For he that speaketh in an unknown tongue speaketh not unto men, but UNTO GOD: for no man understandeth him . . ."* (1 Cor. 14:2). Here Paul is not talking about diversities of tongues: that is, ministering tongues in a public assembly as a ministry gift.

Paul is talking about the individual Spirit-filled believer employing the use of tongues in his prayer life. First Corinthians 14:2 says, *". . . howbeit in the spirit he speaketh mysteries."* Moffatt's translation says, *". . . he is talking divine secrets in the Spirit."*

For the believer who is filled with the Holy Ghost, his tongues are given to him to use constantly in his worship and devotion to God. And worshipping God is a form of prayer.

The Bible says in Acts 10:46 concerning Cornelius and his household when they began to speak with tongues, *"For they heard them speak with tongues, and magnify God. . . ."* Speaking with tongues is a supernatural way to magnify God.

Tongues are also used as a means of spiritual edification. The Bible says, *"He that speaketh in an unknown tongue edifieth himself . . ."* (1 Cor. 14:4). The word "edifieth" means *to build up.*

Greek language scholars tell us there is a word in our modern vernacular that is closer to the meaning of the original Greek than the word "edifieth," and that is the word "charge." We use the word "charge" in connection with charging a battery.

A more literal translation of First Corinthians 14:4 would be, "He that speaketh in an unknown tongue edifies, or builds up, or charges himself like a battery being charged." And that isn't just for a few of God's children; it is for every one of us. I appreciate this wonderful, supernatural means of spiritual edification.

Notice that praying in tongues is not mental edification, nor is it physical edification, but it is *spiritual* edification. Paul said, *"For if I pray in an unknown tongue, MY SPIRIT prayeth . . ."* (1 Cor. 14:14).

The Amplified Bible reads, ". . . my spirit [by the Holy Spirit within me] prays, but my mind is unproductive . . ." (1 Cor. 14:14). So praying in tongues is not for *mental* edification, but for *spiritual* edification.

"For he that speaketh in an unknown tongue speaketh not unto men, but unto God: for no man understandeth him . . ." (1 Cor. 14:2). Here Paul is not talking about diversities of tongues: that is, ministering tongues in a public assembly as a ministry gift.

Paul is talking about the individual Spirit-filled believer employing the use of tongues in his prayer life. *". . . howbeit in the spirit he speaketh mysteries"* (1 Cor. 14:2). *Moffatt's* translation says, ". . . he is talking of divine secrets in the Spirit."

The Bible says in Acts 10:46 concerning Cornelius and his household when they began to speak with tongues, *"For they heard them speak with tongues, and magnify God. . . ."* Speaking with tongues is a supernatural way to magnify God.

Speaking in Tongues: The Door Into the Supernatural

I have found in my own life over a period of more than fifty-five years that the more I speak in tongues — the more I pray and worship God in tongues — the more manifestation of the other gifts of the Spirit I have in my life too. And the less I speak in tongues, the less manifestation of the supernatural gifts of the Holy Spirit I have operating in my life.

Speaking with tongues is the door into all the other spiritual gifts. Some people like to jump in and get all the gifts of the Spirit at once, but you have to go through the door to get into the supernatural. Also, it is as the Spirit of God wills, not as we will (1 Cor. 12:11). In other words, you can't force or "put on" a manifestation of the gifts of the Spirit.

The Bible teaches us to desire spiritual gifts (1 Cor. 14:1). The Bible also teaches us to earnestly covet the best gifts (1 Cor. 12:31). But remember that those words were written to people who already spoke in tongues. They weren't written to people who did not speak with tongues.

In fact, the Corinthians had a superabundance of speaking with tongues in the public assembly. It seemed that when these Corinthians came to church, all of them wanted to speak in tongues at the same time. It is interesting to note, however, if everyone is speaking in tongues all at one time, the entire church congregation cannot be edified or built up, for no one would understand what is being said (1 Cor. 14:2-19).

Therefore, Paul instructed the Corinthians that in public meetings only two or three people should speak, and another should interpret (1 Cor. 14:27). Also, if there wasn't an interpreter present, they should keep silent in the church (1 Cor. 14:28).

Paul didn't say that the Corinthians had received the wrong gift. They had received the right gift, but they were just so thrilled and exuberant that they wanted to talk in tongues all at once. They needed instruction on how to use this gift.

You see, if we are all praising God, it is fine for all of us to praise God in tongues altogether and all at the same time. But it would certainly be wrong if everyone started talking in tongues while the preacher was trying to preach or teach. And it would not be right for someone to spend an hour speaking in tongues without any interpretation. The speaker would be edified, but the listener wouldn't get anything out of it.

That's why the Bible said it is better to speak a few words with our own understanding so we can *teach* others than it is to speak ten thousand words in tongues, unless we speak with tongues and interpret what we've said so that *all* may be edified.

1 CORINTHIANS 14:18,19
18 I thank my God, I speak with tongues more than ye all:
19 YET IN THE CHURCH I had rather speak five words with my understanding, that by my voice I might TEACH others also, than ten thousand words in an unknown tongue.

Some folks, however, have made a mountain out of a molehill, so to speak, in this area. They claim that Paul was trying to tell the Corinthians not to speak with tongues at all. This couldn't have been his intention, however, for notice what he said in verse 18: *"I thank my God, I speak with tongues more than ye all"* (1 Cor. 14:18).

Paul was saying that it would be better for him to stand before the congregation and speak five words in his own language so people could understand him and he could *teach* others, than it would be to speak ten thousand words in tongues that were uninterpreted.

But to correct one error, Paul would not suggest we make another by abandoning speaking in tongues altogether. We are just to get instruction regarding the public use of this gift. We are told to covet earnestly the best gifts.

And as we do this, we will walk in more power and be more effective in our Christian life. We will go through the door of the baptism of the Holy Spirit to receive the glorious spiritual gifts that God has promised those who believe His Word.

I am thoroughly convinced that if we would be sensitive and responsive to the Holy Spirit, He knows what is coming in the future, and He will show us things to come (John 16:13). He will equip each of us for that which lies ahead in life, if we will yield to Him. Praying and speaking with tongues is one way to do that. It is one way to be built up spiritually in order to prepare and be ready for whatever may come in the future.

It is wonderful what the Lord is doing these days. Are you as a Spirit-filled believer taking full advantage of the gift of tongues? God has given each of us a supernatural means of edifying ourselves or building ourselves up spiritually. God has given to us a supernatural means of communication with Him. Are you taking full advantage of this gift of the Spirit, speaking in tongues, that God has made available to each one of His children?

---

[1] Howard Carter, *Questions and Answers on Spiritual Gifts* (Tulsa, Oklahoma: Harrison House, Inc., 1976), p. 120.

Questions for Study

1. What two things are produced when people are taught to tarry for the baptism in the Holy Spirit?

   _____

   _____

2. In Acts 8:5-8, joy isn't necessarily a characteristic of being filled with the Holy Spirit. Why?

   _____

   _____

3. What happened in every single New Testament instance where a company of believers sought the Holy Spirit?

   _____

   _____

4. If you do your part — receive the Holy Spirit, what will the Holy Spirit do on His part?

   _____

   _____

5. If you are born again, what are you ready to receive right away?

   _____

   _____

6. Who said "Come and drink and get filled with the Holy Spirit"?

   _____

   _____

7. What is Canaan a type of?

   _____

   _____

8. What is Egypt a type of?

   _____

   _____

9. What is going through the Red Sea a type of?

   _____

   _____

10. What must you do to receive the Holy Spirit?

    _____

    _____

Chapter 7

Is It Scriptural To Tarry for the Holy Ghost?

In Chapter 1, we said there are some who believe that candidates must wait or tarry in order to receive the baptism of the Holy Spirit and to be endued with power from on High. They use Luke 24:49 and Acts 1:4 to support this claim. Some have supposed this is the Bible formula for receiving the Holy Spirit.

LUKE 24:49
49 And, behold, I send the promise of my Father upon you: but TARRY ye in the city of Jerusalem, until ye be endued with power from on high.

ACTS 1:4,5
4 And, being assembled together with them, commanded them that they should not depart from Jerusalem, but WAIT for the promise of the Father, which, saith he, ye have heard of me.
5 For John truly baptized with water; but ye shall be BAPTIZED WITH THE HOLY GHOST not many days hence.

Tarrying Is Not a Formula For Receiving the Holy Spirit

It is true that Jesus made both of these statements to His disciples before the Day of Pentecost. However, if these verses were a formula for receiving the Holy Ghost, we would not have any right to take the word "Jerusalem" out of the text. Jesus told the disciples not only to wait, or "tarry," but He said to wait *in Jerusalem*. Why didn't He say to tarry in Bethlehem? Why didn't He say to tarry in Jericho? Because it was necessary that they wait in Jerusalem in order for the Church to have its beginning there.

What were the disciples waiting or tarrying for? They were waiting for the Day of Pentecost to come, for that is when the Holy Spirit was poured out upon the Church. They were not waiting or tarrying in order to get ready or to prepare themselves to be filled with the Holy Ghost.

If that had been true, the Bible would have said, "When they were *fully ready*, the Holy Ghost came." But it doesn't say that. Acts 2:1 says, *"And when the DAY OF PENTECOST was fully come. . . ."* That is what they were waiting for — the Day of Pentecost.

ACTS 2:1-4
1 And WHEN THE DAY OF PENTECOST WAS FULLY COME, they were all with one accord in one place.
2 And suddenly there came a sound from heaven as of a rushing mighty wind, and it filled all the house where they were sitting.
3 And there appeared unto them cloven tongues like as of fire, and it sat upon each of them.
4 And they were all FILLED WITH THE HOLY GHOST, and began to SPEAK WITH OTHER TONGUES, as the Spirit gave them utterance.

Then reading in Acts chapter 8, notice that when Peter and John went down to pray for the Samaritans to receive the Holy Spirit, there is not the slightest hint or suggestion that Peter and John taught the Samaritans to tarry or to wait before they could be filled with the Holy Spirit.

ACTS 8:14-17
14 Now when the apostles which were at Jerusalem heard that Samaria had received the word of God, they sent unto them Peter and John:
15 Who, when they were come down, prayed for them, that they might receive the Holy Ghost:
16 (For as yet he was fallen upon none of them: only they were baptized in the name of the Lord Jesus.)
17 Then laid they their hands on them, and they received the Holy Ghost.

The infilling or the baptism of the Holy Spirit has already been given to the Church on the Day of Pentecost as a free gift. To teach people to tarry for the baptism of the Holy Spirit only produces doubt and confusion in those candidates who desire to receive this gift.

Rev. Howard Carter was the general supervisor of the Assemblies of God in Great Britain for nineteen years and the founder of the oldest Pentecostal Bible school in the world. He was also a leading teacher in Full Gospel circles worldwide. Rev. Carter has said that to teach people to wait or to tarry for the Holy Ghost is nothing in the world but a combination of works and unbelief. How true that is.

I am not saying that tarrying before the Lord is always unscriptural. Certainly I believe in tarrying before the Lord and waiting on the Lord in prayer, praise, and worship. Many times in prayer meetings we have waited up to five and six hours on the Lord in prayer.

So I believe in praying long and waiting earnestly before God. Yet when I see people waiting and praying, crying out and agonizing to receive the Holy Ghost, it breaks my heart because I know it isn't necessary.

In my Bible I have not been able to find any record where anyone ever waited, cried, agonized, struggled, or tarried to be filled with the Holy Ghost. Someone said, "But I believe in receiving the Holy Ghost the old-time way."

Well, I do too. You can't get any more old-time or any more scriptural than the way the Early Church received the Holy Spirit in the Book of the Acts of the Apostles. I propose that we look at the Acts of the Apostles, see how they did it, and follow their example in getting people filled with the Holy Ghost.

Bible Examples of Receiving the Holy Ghost

In reading through the 28 chapters of the Book of Acts, one might suppose that the events recorded occurred over a period of a few days, a few weeks, or just a very few years. However, the events in the Book of Acts cover a number of years. The first account we'll examine occurred at Samaria.

The Samaritan Believers

ACTS 8:5-8
5   Then Philip went down to the city of Samaria, and preached Christ unto them.
6   And the people with one accord gave heed unto those things which Philip spake, hearing and seeing the miracles which he did.
7   For unclean spirits, crying with loud voice, came out of many that were possessed with them: and many taken with palsies, and that were lame, were healed.
8   And there was great joy in that city.

This passage in verse 8 says, ". . . there was great joy in that city." Joy is not necessarily a characteristic of being filled with the Holy Ghost, because these Samaritans who heard the Word preached had great joy before they were filled with the Spirit.

You can have joy before you get filled with the Holy Spirit and you can have joy afterwards. It is joyous to be saved. It is joyous to be healed and to enjoy the blessings of God.

ACTS 8:12-15,17-20
12   But when they believed Philip preaching the things concerning the kingdom of God, and the name of Jesus Christ, they were baptized, both men and women.
13   Then Simon [the sorcerer] himself believed also: and when he was baptized, he continued with Philip, and wondered, beholding the miracles and signs which were done.
14   Now when the apostles which were at Jerusalem heard that Samaria had received the word of God, they sent unto them Peter and John:
15   Who, when they were come down, prayed for them, that they might receive the Holy Ghost. . . .
17   Then laid they their hands on them, and they received the Holy Ghost.
18   And when Simon saw that through laying on of the apostles' hands the Holy Ghost was given, he offered them money,

19   Saying, Give me also this power, that on whomsoever I lay hands, he may receive the Holy Ghost.
20   But Peter said unto him, Thy money perish with thee, because thou hast thought that the gift of God may be purchased with money.

It seems that Philip had a glorious revival in Samaria. Hundreds of people must have been saved, and scores healed. And all of these folks received the Holy Ghost: "Then laid they their hands on them, and they received the Holy Ghost" (Acts 8:17). Notice that all of these Samaritans received the Holy Ghost without waiting, praying, or agonizing — and they received without exception or disappointment.

Cornelius and His Household

The Word gives us another account of people getting saved and filled with the Holy Spirit without tarrying or waiting.

Reading Acts chapters 10 and 11, we see how an angel appeared to Cornelius and told him to send to Joppa, and to inquire in the house of a certain individual for Simon Peter "Who shall tell thee words, whereby thou and all thy house shall be SAVED" (Acts 11:14).

Neither Cornelius nor his household was saved. They were Gentiles who had become Jewish proselytes. A person can't be saved without hearing the gospel. Those of Cornelius' household didn't know that Jesus had died for the sins of mankind and was raised from the dead for our justification.

Therefore, Peter preached to them about Jesus' death, burial, and resurrection (Acts 10:34-43). They believed the gospel message (Rom. 10:9,10), and they were born again while Peter was preaching (Acts 11:14). Then they received the Holy Ghost and spoke in tongues before Peter even finished his message.

ACTS 10:44,45
44   While Peter yet spake these words, the Holy Ghost fell on all them which heard the word.
45   And they of the circumcision which believed [the Jewish Christians] were astonished, as many as came with Peter, because that ON THE GENTILES ALSO WAS POURED OUT THE GIFT OF THE HOLY GHOST.

Notice that while Peter was still speaking, Cornelius and his household were not only saved, but were filled with the Holy Ghost and spoke with tongues — without waiting, agonizing, or struggling.

How did the Jewish believers know the gift of the Holy Ghost was poured out on the Gentiles? "For they heard them SPEAK WITH TONGUES, and magnify God . . ." (Acts 10:46).

We make a mistake by thinking that things have to be done a certain cut-and-dried way. God doesn't have any cut-and-dried methods. While Peter was yet preaching, these Gentiles received the Holy Ghost.

In ministering the baptism in the Holy Ghost to believers, many Pentecostal or Charismatic church people want everyone to follow the same formula. They want to cut everyone's experience out with the same cookie cutter, so to speak.

Saul of Tarsus

Paul, who laid hands on these folks in Acts chapter 19, was previously known as Saul of Tarsus. The account of his experience of receiving the Holy Ghost is found in Acts chapter 9.

ACTS 9:11,12
11 And the Lord said unto him, Arise, and go into the street which is called Straight, and enquire in the house of Judas for one called Saul of Tarsus: for, behold, he prayeth,
12 And hath seen in a vision a man named Ananias coming in, and putting his hand on him, that he might receive his sight.

Ananias said to Saul, ". . . [Jesus] *hath sent me, that thou mightest receive thy sight, and BE FILLED WITH THE HOLY GHOST*" (Acts 9:17). And Saul received the Holy Spirit right then. We know that Paul received the Holy Spirit because he later said, "*I thank my God, I SPEAK WITH TONGUES more than ye all*" (1 Cor. 14:18).

Notice in this passage of Scripture that there was no suggestion of the need for Saul to tarry or wait to be filled with the Holy Ghost; Saul was immediately filled with the Holy Spirit when Ananias laid hands on him. It is most probable that Saul didn't know a thing in the world about the Holy Ghost until Ananias came in and laid hands on him. But Ananias obeyed the Lord and Saul was *immediately* filled with the Holy Spirit.

The Ephesian Disciples

The following incident occurred at Ephesus.

ACTS 19:1-3
1   And it came to pass, that, while Apollos was at Corinth, Paul having passed through the upper coasts came to Ephesus: and finding certain disciples,
2   He said unto them, Have ye received the Holy Ghost since ye believed? And they said unto him, We have not so much as heard whether there be any Holy Ghost.
3   And he said unto them, Unto what then were ye baptized? And they said, Unto John's baptism.

Then in Acts 19:6 we read, "*And when Paul had laid his hands upon them, the Holy Ghost came on them; and they spake with tongues, and prophesied.*"

These folks at Ephesus had not heard about being filled with the Spirit and speaking in tongues. But as soon as Paul laid his hands on them, the Holy Ghost came upon them, and they spoke with tongues. Every one of them was filled with the Holy Ghost and spoke with other tongues as the Spirit of God gave them the utterance — without waiting, agonizing, struggling, or tarrying.

We have read from the New Testament every instance where people received the Holy Ghost over a twenty-year period, and there has been absolutely nothing at all in the Scriptures that even resemble what we call "a tarrying meeting" in order to be filled with the Holy Ghost.

In every single instance where a company of believers sought the Holy Spirit, everyone received right away. Not one went away disappointed because of failing to receive the Holy Spirit.

If we taught this to our people today, they would receive the Holy Spirit in the same way — the Acts of the Apostles way — the New Testament way. I have had the baptism of the Holy Ghost more than fifty-five years, and I have never told anyone to wait or to tarry to receive the Holy Spirit. I have always told people, "Come and receive the Holy Ghost." And I have seen people receive Him everywhere I go to minister.

Come and Drink of the Holy Spirit

In John chapter 7, Jesus talks about receiving the Holy Ghost.

JOHN 7:37-39
37 In the last day, that great day of the feast, Jesus stood and cried, saying, If any man thirst, let him come unto me, and drink.
38 He that believeth on me, as the scripture hath said, out of his belly shall flow RIVERS OF LIVING WATER.
39 (But this spake he of the Spirit, which they that believe on him should receive: for the Holy Ghost was not yet given; because that Jesus was not yet glorified.)

Jesus was not talking here about salvation, because He said speaking of salvation to the woman of Samaria in John 4:14, ". . . *the water that I shall give him shall be in him A WELL of water springing up into everlasting life.*" John 4:14 refers to a *well*, and John 7:39 refers to a *river*.

What was the "river" Jesus was talking about in John 7:37-39? He was talking about receiving or being filled with the Holy Ghost. Also, notice Jesus said, "Come and drink" (John 7:37), not come and *shout*; not come and *pray*; not come and *praise*; not come and *sing* and then go away empty. No, Jesus said, "Come and *drink* and out of your belly will flow rivers of living water" (John 7:37,38).

We make a mistake a lot of times by not just taking Jesus at His Word. Jesus said, "Come and drink" (John 7:37). Also, how many people can drink and talk at the same time?

Have you ever tried to drink water, for example, and talk at the same time? Or can you drink and sing, or drink and praise God at the same time? Of course, the Holy Ghost is present to give the utterance in other tongues. But you can't "come and drink" and speak your native language at the same time.

When Jesus said, "Come and drink," that implies that you don't have to wait or tarry to drink. How long does it take you to drink? Jesus said it is just as easy to drink of the Spirit, that is, to be filled with the Spirit, as it is to drink water or to be filled with water. In other words, if you're saved, you don't have to wait at all!

Notice another aspect of drinking water and being filled with water is that it is something that *you* do, not something the water does. Likewise, drinking of the Holy Ghost and being filled with the Holy Ghost is something *you* do, not something the Holy Ghost does.

In other words, if you do your part — *receive* Him, the Holy Spirit will do His part — fill you up to overflowing, and you will speak in tongues.

So quit talking and start drinking! Just drink in of the Holy Spirit. Drink until you get full. When you get full of the Holy Spirit, He will give you utterance in other tongues. Then you will speak in your new, heavenly prayer language!

Someone might ask, "Do you mean to insinuate that there is no need to tarry anymore?" No, I don't mean to insinuate it. I mean *to state* it! There isn't any need to tarry anymore!

"Do you mean to insinuate that there is no need to say, 'Oh, Lord, send the power right now'?" No, I don't mean to insinuate it. I mean to state it! There is no need to say, "Oh, Lord, send the power right now."

Jesus said, "*You* come and drink." And when *you* drink of the Holy Spirit until you get full, out of your belly will flow rivers of living water — the Holy Spirit.

And Jesus promises that we would receive *power* after we receive the Holy Spirit.

ACTS 1:8
8 But ye shall receive POWER, after that the Holy Ghost is come upon you: and ye shall be witnesses unto me both in Jerusalem, and in all Judaea, and in Samaria, and unto the uttermost part of the earth.

ACTS 1:8 (Amplified)
8 But you shall receive POWER — ABILITY, EFFI-CIENCY and MIGHT — when the Holy Spirit has come upon you; and you shall be My witnesses in Jerusalem and all Judaea and Samaria and to the ends — the very bounds — of the earth.

God doesn't need to send the power *"right now."* If you have received the Holy Spirit, according to Acts 1:8, the power is already resident within you.

The Holy Spirit Is a Gift

Remember, Paul said to the Ephesians, "Have you *received* the Holy Spirit?" (Acts 19:2). He didn't say, "I have come down here to pray that God would pour the Holy Ghost out upon you." And the apostles in Jerusalem sent Peter and John down to Samaria so that they might lay their hands on the Samaritan Christians to receive the Holy Ghost (Acts 8:14-17). Notice also that they didn't send them down there to pray that the Lord would send the power to the Samaritans.

You can't buy the gift of the Holy Spirit any more than you can buy salvation. You don't do anything to merit the infilling of the Holy Spirit. In other words, babes in Christ can receive the infilling of the Holy Spirit just as well as more mature Christians can.

You don't get the Holy Ghost just because you have graduated to some marvelous degree of spirituality beyond everyone else, and, therefore, God puts a seal on you saying you are perfect.

The Holy Ghost is a Gift. The Bible says, "*. . . ye shall receive THE GIFT of the Holy Ghost*" (Acts 2:38). And if you are born again, you are ready to receive the gift of the Holy Spirit right away. If you had to do one more thing after the new birth to receive the Holy Spirit, then the baptism of the Holy Spirit ceases to be a gift and becomes a reward. The Holy Ghost is not a reward; He is a Gift.

Some say that I make it too easy for folks to receive the Holy Ghost. But it's not me who has made it easy to receive Him. It was God who made it easy to receive this gift. It wasn't me who said, "Come and drink and get filled with the Holy Spirit." It was Jesus. I wasn't the one who put receiving the Holy Spirit on a gift basis, it was God.

Someone else said, "Yes, but I don't believe in 'railroading' people through to receiving the Holy Ghost." Well, if "railroading" people through means getting them filled quickly, then that same person no doubt doesn't believe in "railroading" people through to salvation. But that is ridiculous!

Actually, it isn't a matter of "railroading" people at all. But we should be getting people saved as quickly as we can, because they might die and go to hell tomorrow. And if someone is sick, we should believe in getting them healed quickly.

Salvation is a gift. Healing is a gift. And the Holy Ghost is a Gift. You can receive one of these gifts just as quickly as you can the other.

Reading in the Acts of the Apostles, we see that the Early Church believed in getting folks filled with the Holy Ghost as quickly as they did getting them saved or healed, as we have already studied in this lesson. I not only believe in "railroading" people through to receiving the Holy Spirit, I believe in "jet planing" them through!

Possessing What Is Yours

Canaan's land is a type of the baptism of the Holy Ghost and of all of our rights and privileges in Christ. Some have thought it was a type of heaven. But Canaan's land couldn't be a type of heaven, because there were enemies to overcome in Canaan and there were battles that the children of Israel had to fight.

But there won't be any enemies to overcome or battles to fight when we get to heaven. The last enemy shall have been conquered. There won't be any enemies to overcome in the land over there.

Canaan is a type of the baptism of the Holy Ghost and our rights and privileges in Christ. The children of Israel came out of Egypt, and Egypt is a type of the world. Then the children of Israel were all baptized, because going through the Red Sea was a type of water baptism.

They also all drank of Christ; that rock out of which the water flowed was a type and shadow of Christ (Exod. 17:6; 1 Cor. 10:4).

The children of Israel could have gone directly into Canaan's land, but because of unbelief and disobedience, they wandered in the wilderness for forty years. Their descendants did eventually enter in, but the unbelieving Israelites took quite a detour.

If you want to detour and take the long way into the baptism in the Holy Ghost, you can. For example, you can detour by tarrying unnecessarily at the altar in order to receive the Holy Ghost. You can detour a lot of ways. But you can also come directly in and receive Him immediately if you are born again. That's God's best! The door is open to receive this precious Gift.

Take the Direct Route!

By way of illustration, if you wanted to go from Oklahoma City to Dallas, for example, you could go directly down the highway to get there. Or if you wanted to, you could go by way of St. Louis, down to Memphis, over to Atlanta, down to New Orleans, over to Houston, and then up to Dallas. You wouldn't have to, but you could.

It is the same way with receiving the baptism of the Holy Spirit. You can detour if you want to and take the long way to receiving the Holy Spirit, but why not take the direct route?

Someone said, "But I remember those wonderful times of seeking God for several years before I was filled."

"Well, have you stopped seeking God since you got filled?" I asked. "Because I remember the wonderful time I spent *last week* seeking God. In fact, I remember the wonderful time I spent *today* seeking God. I believe in seeking God and tarrying before God, but not to receive the Holy Ghost, or anything else God offers, for that matter."

Spirit-filled believers need to seek God just as much as folks who are not filled. But seek God *with* the Holy Spirit, not without Him.

"Yes," someone said to me, "but I learned many lessons in those many years of seeking God for the baptism in the Holy Spirit."

I replied, "You could have learned those same lessons a whole lot faster with the Holy Ghost than you did without Him! And I will tell you something else: The thing you should have learned when you did get the baptism was that you didn't have to do all of that waiting and tarrying in order to receive the Holy Spirit."

This person I was talking to started laughing and patted me on the back, saying, "Oh, you have me pegged. You are exactly right. That is the first thing I said after I received — if only someone would have told me, I could have received years before I finally did. If you had just been there to tell me, Brother Hagin, I could have received years before."

As I said, in more than fifty-five years of having the Holy Ghost myself, I have never told anyone to wait or tarry to receive Him.

Someone else said, "More people have received the Holy Ghost after the midnight hour than at any other time." My answer to that is if they received the Holy Ghost *after* midnight, it's because they didn't believe God *before* midnight! God is not any different after midnight than He is before midnight!

Then there are those who warn, "Be careful about getting in the flesh." In one sense I understand what they mean by the words, "in the flesh." However, in another sense of the expression, you can't get the Holy Ghost any other way but in the flesh! Every person who ever got the Holy Ghost was in the flesh, because we are all still clothed in mortal bodies — the flesh.

On the Day of Pentecost, Peter quoted Joel's prophecy saying, *"And it shall come to pass in the last days, saith God, I will pour out of my Spirit upon all FLESH . . ."* (Acts 2:17). And the Apostle Paul said, *". . . know ye not that your body* [flesh] *is the temple of the Holy Ghost?"* (1 Cor. 6:19).

Let's look at what Jesus had to say in John chapter 14 on this subject.

JOHN 14:17,23
17 Even the Spirit of truth; whom the world cannot receive, because it seeth him not, neither knoweth him: but ye know him; for he dwelleth with you, and SHALL BE IN YOU [your body or your flesh]. . . .

23 . . . If a man love me, he will keep my words: and my Father will love him, and we will come unto him, and MAKE OUR ABODE WITH HIM [in his body or his flesh].

The Holy Spirit comes to dwell in us in the new birth; our bodies become His temple. So in that sense, we will receive the Holy Spirit in the flesh too!

To receive the Holy Spirit, open your entire being to God with a strong desire toward Him. In simple faith, receive the gift of the Holy Ghost that God freely offers, breathe in or drink in of the Spirit of God, and you will be filled with the precious Holy Spirit.

Then as a sign or evidence that you have been filled, utterance in other tongues will be given to you. If you are simple enough in faith and strong enough in courage, you can speak that utterance out immediately.

If you can drink water, you can drink of the Spirit *right now*. I am quoting good authority — the Word of the Lord Jesus Christ (John 7:37-39).

Questions for Study

1. Why are tongues an integral and an important part of receiving the Holy Ghost?

   _____

   _____

2. According to First Corinthians 13:10, when that which is perfect comes, what will "vanish away" and cease to exist?

   _____

   _____

3. Why won't there be a need for tongues in Heaven?

   _____

   _____

4. According to Acts 2:38 and 39, who is the baptism of the Holy Spirit for?

   _____

   _____

5. What is Paul talking about in First Corinthians 12:27-30?

   _____

   _____

6. Ministry gifts are those people in the Body of Christ who are called by God to stand in the _____ ministry.

7. As listed in Ephesians 4:11,12, what are the ministry gifts that Jesus set in the Church ?

   _____

   _____

8. If a person is a New Testament evangelist, what will he be equipped with?

   _____

   _____

9. What is the gift of the Spirit called tongues and interpretation manifested for?

   _____

   _____

10. In addition to the devotional use of tongues, tongues are also used as a means of _____ _____.

Chapter 8

The Bible Evidence of the Baptism Of the Holy Spirit

In order to determine the Bible evidence of the baptism of the Holy Spirit, let's look at five recorded instances in the Book of Acts of believers receiving the Holy Ghost.

Scriptural Witnesses for Tongues as the Evidence of The Baptism of the Holy Spirit

The Bible says, *". . . in the mouth of two or three witnesses every word may be established"* (Matt. 18:16). As we study these accounts, notice the Bible gives us three scripture "witnesses" to *specifically* show that speaking with tongues is the initial evidence or sign that a person is filled with the Holy Spirit, and two "witnesses" which *infer* that speaking in tongues is the evidence of the infilling of the Holy Spirit.

Let's look first at the three Biblical accounts which specifically show that speaking in tongues is the evidence of receiving the Holy Spirit.

First Witness: The One Hundred and Twenty

First of all, in Acts 2:4, we read that on the Day of Pentecost the 120 who were gathered in the upper room were all filled with the Holy Ghost.

ACTS 2:1-4
1 And when the day of Pentecost was fully come, they were all with one accord in one place.
2 And suddenly there came a sound from heaven as of a rushing mighty wind, and it filled all the house where they were sitting.
3 And there appeared unto them cloven tongues like as of fire, and it sat upon each of them.
4 And THEY WERE ALL FILLED WITH THE HOLY GHOST, AND BEGAN TO SPEAK WITH OTHER TONGUES, AS THE SPIRIT GAVE THEM UTTERANCE.

It wasn't just Jesus' disciples, who were filled with the Holy Spirit that day. There were 120 who gathered in the upper room and were filled with the Holy Spirit (Acts 1:14,15; Acts 2:1-4)). Women as well as men were in that company. Even Mary the mother of Jesus was there (Acts 1:14). And they were all filled with the Holy Ghost and *". . . began to speak with other tongues, as the Spirit gave them utterance"* (Acts 2:4).

Second Witness: Cornelius and His Household

Second, in Acts chapter 10, we find that speaking in tongues was the same sign or evidence that convinced the Hebrew Christians who went with Peter to Cornelius' house that the Gentiles had received the Holy Spirit.

ACTS 10:44-46
44 While Peter yet spake these words, THE HOLY GHOST FELL ON ALL THEM which heard the word.
45 And they of the circumcision which believed were astonished, as many as came with Peter, because that on the Gentiles also was poured out the GIFT OF THE HOLY GHOST.
46 For they heard them SPEAK WITH TONGUES, and magnify God. . . .

These brethren of the circumcision were astonished because the gift of the Holy Ghost was poured out on the Gentiles. How did they know that the Gentiles had received the Holy Spirit? *"For they heard them speak with tongues, and magnify God . . ."* (Acts 10:46).

Third Witness: The Ephesian Disciples

The third instance of believers receiving the Holy Spirit and speaking in other tongues is recorded in Acts 19:1-7. This is the account of Paul ministering to the Ephesian disciples, which occurred years after the Day of Pentecost.

ACTS 19:1-7
1 And it came to pass, that, while Apollos was at Corinth, Paul having passed through the upper coasts came to Ephesus: and finding certain disciples,
2 He said unto them, Have ye received the Holy Ghost since ye believed? And they said unto him, We have not so much as heard whether there be any Holy Ghost.
3 And he said unto them, Unto what then were ye baptized? And they said, Unto John's baptism.
4 Then said Paul, John verily baptized with the baptism of repentance, saying unto the people, that they should believe on him which should come after him, that is, on Christ Jesus.
5 When they heard this, they were baptized in the name of the Lord Jesus.
6 And when Paul had laid his hands upon them, THE HOLY GHOST CAME ON THEM; and THEY SPAKE WITH TONGUES, and prophesied.
7 And all the men were about twelve.

Fourth Witness: The Samaritan Believers

Now let's look at the two Biblical accounts which do not say *specifically* that the believers spoke with other tongues when they received the Holy Spirit, but which do *infer* that speaking in tongues was the initial evidence.

In Acts chapter 8 we read the account of the Samaritans receiving the Holy Spirit.

ACTS 8:14-18
14 Now when the apostles which were at Jerusalem heard that Samaria had received the word of God, they sent unto them Peter and John:
15 Who, when they were come down, prayed for them, that they might receive the Holy Ghost:
16 (For as yet he was fallen upon none of them: only they were baptized in the name of the Lord Jesus.)
17 Then laid they their hands on them, and THEY RECEIVED THE HOLY GHOST.
18 And WHEN SIMON SAW that through laying on of the apostles' hands THE HOLY GHOST WAS GIVEN, he offered them money.

Notice the Bible says, *". . . when Simon SAW . . ."* (Acts 8:18). That phrase indicates there had to be some kind of a sign or evidence that registered on Simon's physical senses for him to know that the Samaritans had received the Holy Ghost.

Some people say that what Simon saw was the great joy of the new Samaritan believers. But Simon must have seen more than just the joy of the believers. For in reading Acts chapter 8:5-8, we find there was *already* "great joy in that city" because of the message of salvation or the new birth (Acts 8:8).

Likewise, the sign or evidence Simon saw couldn't have been devils being cast out or healings taking place, because these things had also occurred previously, as mentioned in this same chapter in Acts (Acts 8:7,8).

We cannot see the Holy Ghost with our physical eyes for He is a Spirit. But there had to be some physical evidence that registered on Simon's physical senses for him to know that the Samaritans had received the Holy Spirit. And it is only logical to assume that it is the same evidence of believers receiving the Holy Spirit that is recorded elsewhere in the Scriptures, that is, speaking in tongues.

And, in fact, Bible students know the Samaritans *did* speak with tongues, for every one of the Early Church fathers say they did. One does not need to be a student of church history, however, to realize this because the Bible itself gives conclusive proof that tongues are the evidence of receiving the infilling of the Holy Spirit, as we have seen in the three accounts in Acts 2,10, and 19.

Fifth Witness: Saul

The other account in Acts that *infers* that speaking in tongues was the evidence of receiving the Holy Spirit is found in Acts 9. In the case of Saul (who was later named Paul), the account in Acts 9 says Ananias was sent by Jesus to lay his hands upon Saul that Saul might be filled with the Holy Spirit.

ACTS 9:17
17 And Ananias went his way, and entered into the house; and putting his hands on him said, Brother Saul, the Lord, even Jesus, that appeared unto thee in the way as thou camest, hath sent me, that thou mightest receive thy sight, and BE FILLED with the Holy Ghost.

"But it doesn't say Saul, or Paul, spoke with tongues," someone might object.

While it is true the Bible doesn't specifically say in Acts 9:17 that Paul spoke with tongues, we do know that Paul spoke with tongues because he said in another passage, *"I thank my God, I speak with tongues more than ye all"* (1 Cor. 14:18).

We know that Paul didn't begin speaking with tongues *before* he received the Holy Ghost, so it is logical to assume that when Ananias laid hands on him, Saul received the Holy Ghost just as everyone else did — *with the evidence of speaking in other tongues.* Paul received the Holy Ghost and spoke in tongues just like the rest of us do when we receive the Holy Ghost, because tongues go along with this biblical experience.

The Baptism of the Holy Spirit and Speaking in Tongues Go Hand in Hand

I know in my own case as a denominational pastor more than fifty years ago, that as I read the New Testament and the Spirit of God helped me understand these verses, I was convinced that if I received the same Holy Ghost the Christians in the Book of Acts received, I would have the same initial sign or evidence they had — I would speak with tongues too. I wasn't satisfied with anything else.

We need to understand that speaking in tongues is not the Holy Ghost and the Holy Ghost is not speaking in tongues, but the two do go hand in hand. For example, it is just like the tongue of a shoe. The tongue isn't the shoe and the shoe isn't the tongue, but the tongue is a part of the shoe, and it's an integral part of the shoe; a shoe is not a shoe without it.

To further illustrate this point, when you buy an automobile in the United States, you receive a certificate of title. That certificate of title is evidence that the automobile is yours. Certainly the automobile is not the certificate of title, and the certificate of title is not the automobile. But you'll never get very far in the automobile without the certificate of title because the car would not be considered legally yours without it! Therefore, the automobile is not fully of benefit to you without the certificate of title.

It's the same way with receiving the Holy Spirit. If you have the infilling of the Holy Ghost, then you should have the biblical evidence that goes along with that experience, which is speaking in tongues.

To answer the question, *Is it necessary to speak in tongues?* let me put it this way: If you want a New Testament experience of the baptism in the Holy Ghost and you want the same Holy Spirit the apostles and the Early Church had, then you will want to speak with tongues. That is what the Christians in the Early Church did, and that is consistent with what the scriptures teach.

The Ephesian Disciples:
Speaking in Tongues *and* Prophesying

It is interesting to note that in the account of the Ephesian disciples in Acts 19, the Bible says that the believers spoke in tongues *and* prophesied when they received the Holy Spirit.

ACTS 19:6
6 And when Paul had laid his hands upon them, THE HOLY GHOST CAME ON THEM; and THEY SPAKE WITH TONGUES, and PROPHESIED.

Sometimes believers receive additional spiritual gifts as well as tongues when they are filled with the Spirit. However, tongues always comes first and is the evidence of having received the Holy Spirit. Acts 19:6 doesn't say that they prophesied and then spoke with tongues. It says they spoke with tongues and then prophesied.

I have seen folks receive the Holy Ghost and speak with tongues and then prophesy. I have also seen folks receive the Holy Ghost and speak with tongues and interpret the tongues (1 Cor. 12:10). But don't expect any more at the moment you are filled with the Spirit than what the Word of God teaches, which is that the believer will speak in tongues as the initial evidence of being filled with the Holy Spirit (Acts 2:4).

If another spiritual gift is added, well and good. However, we must also remember that spiritual gifts are given to the believer as the Holy Spirit wills, not as we will (1 Cor. 12:11). But, again, every believer should expect to speak with tongues as the initial evidence of having received the Holy Spirit.

When I received the Holy Ghost, I knew I had received Him because I spoke with tongues. But I also received an additional gift of the Spirit, too, although I didn't realize it at that time.

But I will be perfectly honest with you, when I received the Holy Spirit and spoke in tongues, I felt a little disappointed in a way. I think maybe I expected some kind of overwhelming spectacular experience. Having heard some Pentecostal folks testify about receiving the Holy Spirit, I thought I would have some sort of experience that was out of this world, so to speak. But I didn't.

I said to myself afterwards, *Well, all I did was talk in tongues. I've gotten a bigger blessing than this many times just praying in English with my understanding.*

But the baptism in the Holy Spirit is not just receiving a *blessing*. It is more than that. I knew the Bible and I knew about walking by faith, so I said, "I don't care what I feel or what I don't feel. I know I have received the Holy Spirit because I have spoken with other tongues. I have the Bible evidence for the baptism in the Holy Spirit."

I kept speaking in tongues and praising God almost continuously for about three days. Later I realized that at the same time I had received the Holy Spirit and had spoken with tongues, I had also received another gift of the Spirit, the word of knowledge.

The Fruit of the Spirit Is Not the Evidence
Of Receiving the Holy Spirit

So many times people have listened to others and not to what the Bible teaches. Or sometimes people draw their own conclusions about Bible experiences, such as salvation or receiving the Holy Spirit instead of relying on what the Word says. They want to accept their own conclusions instead of accepting what the Bible says.

For example, some people argue against the baptism of the Holy Spirit by saying, "But a lot of these Full Gospel folks who speak with tongues don't have the fruit of the Spirit as they ought to have; therefore, they could not be filled with the Holy Spirit." However, the fruit that Paul talks about in Galatians 5:22 and 23 is not the fruit of the baptism of the Holy Spirit at all. It is the fruit of the recreated human spirit.

GALATIANS 5:22,23
22 But the fruit of the Spirit is love, joy, peace, longsuffering, gentleness, goodness, faith,
23 Meekness, temperance: against such there is no law.

Most Bible translators and scholars agree that the word "Spirit" is erroneously capitalized in verse 22, and that it should be "spirit" indicating that it is the fruit of the born-again, recreated *human* spirit.

Therefore, Galatians 5:22 and 23 is talking about the fruit that should be in the life of *every* believer, not just in the life of Spirit-filled believers. Jesus said, *"I am the vine, ye are the branches . . ."* (John 15:5).

Fruit grows on *branches,* and Jesus said believers are the *branches.* Therefore, the fruit of the spirit grows in the life of the born-again, recreated believer because of the life of Christ resident and developed within believers — the branches.

The first fruit of the spirit listed in Galatians chapter 5 is love. Believers who are filled with the Holy Spirit don't necessarily have any more love than Christians who are not filled with the Spirit, for the simple reason that Jesus said all believers are to have love: *"By THIS shall all men know that ye are my DISCIPLES, if ye have LOVE one to another"* (John 13:35).

Every *believer* is to have the fruit of love. The Bible further states that *"We [every believer] know that we have passed from death unto life, because we LOVE the brethren . . ."* (1 John 3:14). Love is the fruit of the born-again human spirit, not the fruit of the baptism of the Holy Spirit; therefore, *every* Christian should have the fruit of the spirit regardless of whether or not he is filled with the Holy Spirit.

Another fruit of the spirit listed in Galatians chapter 5 is peace. I didn't have any more peace *after* I received the baptism of the Holy Ghost than I had *before.* The Word of God says in Romans 5:1, *"Therefore being justified by faith* [in Jesus Christ], *we have peace. . . ."* Therefore, peace is a fruit that should be resident in the life of every Christian because of the life of Christ within through the new birth.

However, one thing we must understand about the fruit of the spirit is that, just as with natural fruit, the fruit of the spirit can grow and be developed in the believer's life. Baby Christians, for example, don't produce and grow fruit all at once. After all, you don't expect a baby tree to produce fruit all at once. It takes time for a tree to mature and for the fruit on its branches to grow and develop. It's the same way with a baby Christian.

A baby Christian *can* be filled with the Holy Ghost, however, and have power, and can even have the gifts of the Spirit operating in his life. For example, the Corinthians were babes. Paul called them babes in Christ: *"And I, brethren, could not speak unto you as unto spiritual, but as unto carnal, even as unto babes in Christ"* (1 Cor. 3:1). Yet he also said, *". . . ye come behind in no gift . . ."* (1 Cor. 1:7).

Therefore, even though the Corinthians were babes in Christ and didn't have a lot of fruit of the spirit evident yet in their lives, they did have gifts of the Spirit operating in their lives.

The fruit of the spirit are for *holiness,* but the gifts of the Holy Ghost are for *power.* You can be holy without having much power, and you can have power without being so holy. Yet the combination of holiness and power in a Christian's life is best, and that is what God desires.

I have seen plenty of people who are wonderful Christians and who have marvelously developed the fruit of the spirit in their lives, but they have no power in their lives whatsoever. Then I know of other Christians who are certainly powerhouses for God, but it is obvious they need to grow a little more fruit of the spirit in their lives.

The Ministry of the Laying On of Hands

In a meeting I preached in Texas many years ago, we held day services for a number of months, as well as the night services. People came daily, some from more than one hundred miles away. After I taught on the baptism in the Holy Ghost for about seven weeks, no one came to the meetings without receiving the Holy Spirit. Folks received the Holy Ghost in every service.

We spent a week talking about the laying on of hands as a fundamental doctrine of the Bible (Heb. 6:2). As I've said, in the days of the Early Church the laying on of hands was widely practiced in receiving the Holy Ghost.

ACTS 8:18-20
18 . . . when Simon saw that THROUGH LAYING ON OF THE APOSTLES' HANDS the Holy Ghost was given, he offered them money,
19 Saying, Give me also this power, that on whomsoever I lay hands, he may receive the Holy Ghost.
20 But Peter said unto him, Thy money perish with thee, because thou hast thought that the gift of God may be purchased with money.

Some have thought Simon was trying to buy the gift of the Holy Ghost, but he wasn't. He was trying to buy the gift or *the ability* to impart the Holy Spirit to people through the laying on of hands.

The Lord Jesus appeared to me in a vision years ago in which He told me to lay hands on believers to receive the Holy Ghost. When I hesitated because that was not widely practiced in that day, the Lord led me to Acts chapter 8. He called my attention to the fact that the apostles who abode in Jerusalem sent Peter and John to Samaria *to lay hands on people* to receive the Holy Ghost.

Philip had a wonderful ministry in Samaria. He got people saved by the hundreds and healed by the scores. But he didn't get anyone filled with the Holy Ghost.

The Early Church believed in special ministries just as the Bible teaches. Therefore, the disciples sent Peter and John to Samaria because they had a special ministry of getting folks filled with the Holy Ghost. They had a ministry of laying on of hands. In fact, Peter called being able to lay hands on people to receive the Holy Ghost a "gift of God" (Acts 8:20).

When I lay hands on folks who have already received the Holy Spirit, I often know immediately by the Holy Spirit that they are Spirit filled without their telling me. But, remember, any revelation would have to be a manifestation of one of the revelation gifts in operation.

Helping Others Believe They Have Received

In this meeting in Texas that I mentioned, we were praying and laying hands on people to receive the infilling of the Holy Ghost. I had laid hands on several people and they all received.

Then I laid hands on a certain man and the minute I did, I knew by the manifestation of the Holy Spirit that this man had received the Holy Spirit some time in the past.

I stopped praying and said, "You have received the Holy Spirit sometime in your life. You have already been filled."

He said, "No, no, I haven't."

"Perhaps I am wrong then," I said. "After all, I am human."

But if I do miss it, it wouldn't be because God has missed it. It would be because I somehow failed to listen or respond to Him as I ought.

No human is ever going to get to the place of perfection. Even the great Apostle Paul said, *"Not as though I had already attained, either were already perfect . . ."* (Phil. 3:12).

Ministers can miss it, but that doesn't mean God misses it or that the ministers don't have the right gift operating in their lives. Sometimes we may just fail to receive accurately what God is saying to us.

For example, when talking on the telephone we sometimes fail to pick up everything that someone on the other end of the line has said. In the same way, I don't always get everything God is saying to me. But that doesn't mean that these gifts of the Spirit are not genuine.

I laid hands on this brother again and began to pray. I had the same manifestation again and knew that he had already been filled with the Holy Ghost.

I stopped praying, took my hands off of his head, and with more assurance this time, said, "Now, Brother, you *have* received the Holy Ghost at some time or another."

Again he stated very emphatically that he had not, so I began to pray for the third time.

When I had that manifestation again, I could no longer question it. I said, "Brother, I am not wrong. Open your eyes and look at me. I didn't miss it. You *have* been filled with the Holy Ghost at some time in your life. Has anyone ever told you that you have received the Spirit?"

"Well," he replied, "about eighteen months ago at a Full Gospel church, the pastor and two or three of the men praying with me at the altar told me I received the Holy Ghost."

"Then what makes you so sure you didn't receive Him?" I asked.

"Because my wife said. . . ," and about that time his wife who was standing nearby spoke up and began to tell me what she had said.

"Wait a minute, Sister," I said. "It is not you who is wanting the Holy Ghost. It's your husband. Let him explain."

This man then explained that his wife had said that receiving the Holy Spirit was a far greater experience than being born again. He said, "I doubted I had received the Holy Spirit because to me being born again was the greater experience of the two. Therefore, I was sure I had not received the Holy Spirit."

I said, "Then according to your wife, *I* am not filled with the Holy Spirit either, for becoming a child of God is the greatest thing that has ever happened to me too.

"You see," I explained, "you can go to heaven without being filled with the Holy Spirit, but you can't go to heaven without being born again. God did not promise to give you the Holy Spirit according to your wife. He promised to give you the Holy Spirit according to the Word."

I continued, "You have no right to expect to be filled with the Holy Spirit according to your wife's experiences or ideas or according to anyone else's. But you do have a right to expect to be filled with the Holy Spirit according to the Word of God."

"I guess I did receive the Holy Spirit back then," he answered, "because I did speak something that wasn't English. But I have never talked in tongues since then."

I said, "You didn't because you were doubting what you had received from God. Doubt will paralyze the power of God in your life. You don't need to receive the Holy Spirit again now. You just need to claim what you received eighteen months ago. You just need to reactivate the Holy Ghost within you."

I once heard a minister on the radio say, "You will not need anyone to tell you when you receive the Holy Ghost. If you are in doubt, then you've not received Him."

I can't agree with that statement entirely, however. We just discussed the example of a man who actually received the Holy Spirit with the accompanying evidence of speaking in tongues, but allowed another person's opinion to cause him to doubt.

That is why I cannot agree that people don't occasionally need someone to tell them whether or not they have received the Holy Spirit. This man was in doubt about it and needed someone's encouragement, even though he had actually received. He had listened to his wife instead of listening to the Word of God.

The devil, of course, will try to get believers to doubt any biblical experience they may have. But just because a believer is tempted to doubt doesn't mean that he didn't receive whatever it was he asked for according to God's Word.

People are often taught to believe that their receiving certain petitions from God depends upon experiencing some evidence the Bible does not teach us to expect. But we receive God's promises by *faith* in His Word. Yet in regard to the baptism of the Holy Spirit, God does give us physical evidence — speaking in tongues — to confirm to us that we have received the infilling of the Holy Spirit.

Expect the Biblical Evidence Of Receiving the Holy Spirit

Many people have different opinions about receiving the Holy Spirit that do not line up with God's Word. They form their own opinion about what the evidence should be of receiving the Holy Spirit. But we should expect to see the evidence that the *Word of God* teaches us to expect.

Misconceptions About Receiving the Holy Spirit

In the Early Church, they had no trial-and-error method of seeking and not finding, or of coming to receive the Holy Spirit and going away empty. We should be scriptural and tell people what the Word of God says. Too many times, people tell folks what *they* think. They give their theory or tell their experience. But did you know that you have no right to preach or to teach your *experience*?

Paul told Timothy, "*Preach THE WORD . . .*" (2 Tim. 4:2). He didn't say, "Timothy, tell folks what you think about the subject." He didn't say, "Now, Timothy, give people your theory on this subject." The preaching of opinion and theory just produces doubt and unbelief and holds people in bondage.

The truth of God's Word will liberate people: "*And ye shall know the truth, and the truth shall make you free*" (John 8:32). God's Word will also instill faith in people: "*So then faith cometh by hearing, and hearing by the word of God*" (Rom. 10:17).

Magnify the Word, Not Your Experience

Some people have unusual experiences beyond what most of us have when they are born again or receive the Holy Spirit. It is all right to refer to experiences one may have had, if those experiences are in line with the Word of God. But magnify the Word above experiences. Then let everyone have his or her own scriptural experience, for experiences will vary in many ways.

An example of an unusual born-again experience occurred when Paul was converted on the road to Damascus. A light brighter than the noonday sun shone round about him and he heard a voice speaking to him, saying, "*. . . Saul, Saul, why persecutest thou me?*" (Acts 9:3,4).

However, when I was born again, I didn't see any light or hear any voice speaking to me, but I am just as born again as Paul was.

Paul never told folks that they had to be converted in the same manner that he was. He never told folks that in order to be saved they had to see a light or hear a voice as he had. He referred to his experience occasionally, but he taught the scriptural way to be saved.

ROMANS 10:9,10
9 That if thou shalt confess with thy mouth the Lord Jesus, and shalt believe in thine heart that God hath raised him from the dead, thou shalt be saved.
10 For with the heart man believeth unto righteousness; and with the mouth confession is made unto salvation.

We thank God for Paul's born-again experience, but we should not hold one's experience up as the standard or criteria for being saved. No, we should magnify the Word, and let every person have his own experience as God wills.

Don't Seek Experiences To Receive the Holy Spirit

In the same way, some people have unusual experiences when they receive the Holy Spirit.

When I was a young boy preacher, I knew a fine denominational woman in whom I had great confidence. She related to me once how she received the baptism in the Holy Ghost.

She said she was seeking God, and she had her eyes closed, praising God. She saw in the spirit a beam of light about as big as a pencil. That beam of light seemed to come down through the roof and the ceiling and hit her right between the eyes. When it did, she started speaking with tongues.

Many people have told me, "I heard of people who were seeking the Holy Ghost, and they saw a ball of fire about as big as a basketball. It came and burst over their heads, and they started speaking in tongues."

My experience was different; I have never seen any beam of light or ball of fire, but I am just as much filled with the Holy Ghost as anyone. I had the Bible evidence of being filled with the Holy Spirit — I spoke with tongues.

I don't doubt that some of those other experiences happened, but God's Word really only promises the evidence of speaking with tongues as the initial sign that a person has been filled with the Spirit.

If other scriptural experiences occur, that's fine — as long as those experiences are in line with God's Word. But don't seek experiences. You do have a right, however, to seek to be filled with the Spirit and to speak with tongues.

All believers will speak with tongues when they receive the Holy Spirit, but some may also initially be given an additional gift of the Spirit. However, that doesn't mean they have any more of the Holy Ghost than you or I do.

The Need for Biblical Instruction For Receiving the Holy Spirit

Too many times folks have no instructions on how to receive the Holy Spirit. Or even worse, they receive wrong instruction, and therefore fail to receive the Holy Spirit.

I've also seen people come to receive the Holy Spirit, and they spoke a few words in tongues quietly.

Then I've seen someone slap them on the back and say, "Well, too bad you didn't receive this time! Better luck next time."

However, we don't receive from God by luck; the Bible says we receive the promises of God by faith (Heb. 11:6). The gift of the Holy Spirit is one of God's promises that we receive by faith in God's Word. And if a person spoke only two words in tongues, he has received the Holy Spirit just as much as anyone else who might speak fluently in other tongues.

Of course, I don't encourage people who only speak a few words in tongues to stop there. But just because people only speak a few words in tongues doesn't mean they haven't received. Acts 2:4 says, ". . . [they] *BEGAN to speak. . . .*"

Many people have gone away discouraged when they actually did receive the Holy Spirit. Many who should have received the Holy Spirit haven't because of wrong instruction and a lack of knowledge of God's Word.

An Example of Wrong Instruction For Receiving the Holy Spirit

Through the years, it has been my privilege to help many lawyers, doctors, college professors, school teachers, and others to be filled with the Holy Ghost. Many of these have related to me incidents of getting wrong instruction to receive the Holy Spirit, such as the story one man told me.

He said, "Brother Hagin, I saw this truth in the Bible about receiving the Holy Spirit years ago. I visited a Full Gospel church and came to the altar to receive the Holy Ghost. The people there said to me, 'Lift your hands.' I didn't mind lifting my hands, because I had read something about that in the Bible, so I lifted my hands.

"Then they told me to say, 'Praise God.' I didn't mind praising God. I knew that's in the Bible too. But then someone said, 'Say "Glory."'

"So I said, 'Glory.' Someone said, 'Say it faster.' So I said it faster. Then someone said, 'Say it like this: Glub, glub, glub . . .' So I said, 'Glub, glub, glub . . .'

"Then I got to thinking that I'd never read anything about that in the Bible, so I got up and left the church building, and I hadn't been back to a Charismatic service since."

Many honest, sincere, intelligent people have been driven away by unscriptural practices and wrong instruction. We must be simple in our teaching and just teach folks what the Word of God has to say. We must instruct them according to the Word.

After all, the Bible declares, *"The entrance of thy words giveth light . . ."* (Ps. 119:130). Proper instruction in the Word of God will save people hours of needless seeking.

Falling Into a Trance Is Not Biblical Evidence For Receiving the Holy Spirit

One minister said, "I know I received the Holy Ghost because I fell under the power of God and lay in a trance for three hours."

That is well and good, but that is not the Bible evidence that one has been filled with the Spirit. You could fall under the power of God and fall into a trance when you are filled, or you could do that after you were filled.

But the Bible doesn't say, "They were all filled with the Holy Ghost and fell into a trance." It says, *". . . they were all filled with the Holy Ghost, and BEGAN TO SPEAK WITH OTHER TONGUES . . ."* (Acts 2:4).

Experiencing Joy Is Not Biblical Evidence For Receiving the Holy Spirit

Others who have received the Holy Ghost have said, "I don't have the joy I think I should have. I expected to receive great joy."

But reading in Acts chapter 8, we find, *"And there was great joy in that city"* (Acts 8:8).

That's verse 8. We don't read that they were filled with the Holy Ghost, however, until verse 17. In other words, great joy is not the evidence of being filled with the Holy Ghost.

You should be joyous just because you are a Christian. For example, in Acts chapter 8, when Philip preached the Word in Samaria, there was great joy in the city because many folks were born again. Also, there was great joy in the city because many healings and miracles took place, and because devils were being cast out and people were being set free.

You see, *joy is a natural human reaction to faith.* If you will just believe God, the joy of the Lord will take care of itself.

One man was complaining to me that he didn't have the joy he thought he should have, although he was filled with the Spirit. I told him, "When you go home tonight, get on your knees and say, 'Thank you, Lord, for filling me with the Holy Ghost. I know I was filled because I spoke with other tongues just as they did in the Acts of the Apostles.'"

I told him, "Then when you get into bed, just praise yourself to sleep, thanking God because you received the Holy Ghost. The first thing when you wake up in the morning, give praise to the Lord for filling you with the Holy Ghost. Then throughout the day as you work, praise the Lord because you have received the Holy Spirit. If you are working where no one is around, just praise Him out loud while you work. Otherwise, just praise Him quietly to yourself while you work."

The next night as I stood on the platform in church, I saw this fellow in the congregation, beaming as if someone had turned on a neon sign in the dark. I knew without asking him that he had the joy of the Lord. He came to me immediately after the service and said, "Brother Hagin, it worked just as you said."

Joy is a natural reaction to faith. If you will believe God, you won't have to worry about having joy. If you don't have joy, it is simply because your faith isn't grounded securely in God and in His Word.

Not What You Feel, But What You Do

Then someone said, "But I don't feel like I think I ought to."

But Acts 2:4 doesn't say, "They were all filled with the Holy Ghost, and *felt* like they thought they ought to." And Acts 9:17 doesn't say, "And Ananias went his way, and entered into the house; and putting his hands on him said, Brother Saul, the Lord, even Jesus . . . has sent me, that you might receive your sight, and be filled with the Holy Ghost, and *feel* like you think you ought to."

Acts 19:6 doesn't say, "And when Paul had laid his hands upon them, the Holy Ghost came on them; and they spoke with tongues, and prophesied, and *felt* like they thought they ought to."

Acts 10:45 and 46 don't say that Cornelius and his household spoke with tongues and magnified God, and *felt* like they thought they ought to.

Acts 8:15 doesn't say that Peter and John laid hands on the Samaritans, and they received the Holy Ghost, and *felt* like they thought they ought to.

In fact, there is nothing in any of these scriptures about how the believers *felt*. If it were important how you felt, the Bible would have said so.

The important thing is not what you did or didn't feel when you received the Holy Spirit. The important thing is what you *did*; you believed you received and you yielded to the Holy Spirit and spoke in other tongues. In each of these instances I just mentioned, believers "spoke with tongues." And if *you* spoke with tongues, then you received the Holy Spirit too.

It doesn't matter how good you felt, if you didn't speak with tongues, you didn't receive the Holy

Spirit because speaking in tongues is the Bible evidence of the baptism of the Holy Spirit. In other words, when you are *filled* with the Spirit, you will speak in tongues.

I was preaching in Oregon once, and in the meeting a number of folks came forward to receive the Holy Ghost, so I laid hands on them. I went down the line laying hands on folks, and every one of them received the Holy Spirit and spoke with tongues until I came to the last woman.

I laid hands on this woman and the Holy Spirit came on her, but she didn't begin speaking with tongues. Therefore, she hadn't received the infilling of the Holy Spirit; she didn't speak with tongues that night, but she jumped up and began to shout and dance a little jig for joy. A woman sitting nearby said, "That's the way I like to see them get it."

I said, "But she hasn't received the baptism of the Holy Spirit. These other folks have, but she hasn't." You see, this woman who was sitting nearby assumed that because the woman was shouting and dancing, she had received the infilling of the Holy Spirit.

In another one of my meetings, a man in the church came forward to receive the baptism of the Holy Spirit. I laid hands on him and he began to speak in tongues. He spoke in tongues for fifteen minutes while I laid hands on others to receive.

Then I went back to him and said, "Brother, the Lord reveals to me that there is a thought in your mind that is hindering you from accepting the fact that you have received the Holy Spirit. The Holy Spirit told me that you have always thought that when you got the Holy Spirit, you would jump or dance or run and just have a 'high time.'"

He said, "Yes, that is exactly what I have always thought."

I said, "Well, if you want to run, go ahead. It's all right with me. Or if you want to jump, go ahead. But whether you run or jump or not, you have received the Holy Spirit."

"But if you ever see me shout," this man said, "it will have to be God."

"What do you mean it will have to be God?" I asked. "It wouldn't be God shouting or dancing or running."

"Well, I mean if I ever did that, it would be because God made me do it," he replied.

"You'll never do it then, because God will never *make* you do anything," I said.

He left the church, and as he told us later: "I went home disappointed, mumbling to myself, 'I don't feel like I thought I would, so I must not have received the Holy Spirit. If I had received, I would have felt differently than this. I am not happy, I am not exuberant, and I am not in a state of ecstasy. I have felt better than this and have gotten a bigger blessing than this many times. I just know I didn't receive the Holy Spirit.'

"In the night," he continued, "I couldn't sleep, and I began to think, *How am I going to know that I've received the Holy Spirit? Just what does the Bible say?* The scripture in Acts 2:4 came to me: '. . . and [they] began to speak with other tongues. . . .'

"Then it dawned on me and I said, 'Dear Lord, forgive me for being a doubter. I did receive the Holy Spirit. Acts 2:4 doesn't say they felt better. It doesn't say they were all filled with the Holy Spirit and were full of joy, and felt like they thought they ought to. It says they spoke with tongues. And *I* spoke with tongues.' Then I just lay there and spoke in tongues and praised the Lord for the rest of the night."

So we see that folks do need help and encouragement sometimes. Instruction will help people. It is a mistake to tell folks that they will be joyous after receiving the Holy Spirit. Immediately after the Holy Spirit came upon Christ, He was led into the wilderness to be tempted of the devil (Matt 4:1).

Sometimes the greatest temptations of life come immediately after we are filled with the Holy Spirit. We shouldn't ask for any more evidence than what the Bible teaches, but neither should we expect any less. We should expect to speak with tongues as the Word of God teaches.

Questions for Study

1. Name five recorded instances or witnesses in the Book of Acts of believers receiving the Holy Ghost.

   _____

   _____

2. On the Day of Pentecost, how many were gathered in the Upper Room and were all filled with the Holy Ghost?

   _____

   _____

3. How did the brethren of the circumcision know that the Gentiles had received the Holy Spirit?

   _____

   _____

4. What does the phrase, "*. . . when Simon SAW . . .*" in Acts 8:18 indicate?

   _____

   _____

5. What do some people say that Simon saw?

   _____

   _____

6. Why couldn't the sign or evidence that Simon saw have been devils being cast out or healings taking place?

   _____

   _____

7. What should you say to answer the question, "Is it necessary to speak in tongues?"

   _____

   _____

8. The fruit that Paul talks about in Galatians chapter 5 is not the fruit of the baptism in the Holy Spirit at all. What is it the fruit of?

   _____

   _____

9. In Acts 8:18-20, what was Simon trying to buy?

   _____

   _____

10. We don't receive the promises of God by luck. What does the Bible say is the way to receive them (Heb. 11:6)?

    _____

    _____

Ten Reasons Why Every Believer Should Speak in Tongues

I thank my God, I speak with tongues more than ye all.

— 1 Corinthians 14:18

The apostle Paul wrote and spoke much about the subject of speaking in other tongues, and he apparently practiced what he preached for he said, *"I thank my God, I speak with tongues more than ye all"* (1 Cor. 14:18). I, too, thank God that I speak in tongues regularly, and I wish every believer would make this his habit and enjoy this same blessing and source of power in his everyday life.

The purpose of this particular lesson is to set forth ten reasons why every Christian should speak in tongues, and to help believers see the blessings that can be theirs through daily appropriating the power of the Holy Spirit in their lives.

Reason Number 1

The Word of God teaches that when we are filled with the Holy Ghost, we speak with other tongues as the Spirit of God gives utterance. As we have seen, speaking in tongues is an initial evidence or sign of the baptism of the Holy Spirit: *"And they were all FILLED WITH THE HOLY GHOST, and began to SPEAK WITH OTHER TONGUES, as the Spirit gave them utterance"* (Acts 2:4).

In Acts 10, the brethren of the circumcision who had come with Peter to Cornelius' household were astonished when they saw that the gift of the Holy Ghost was poured out on the Gentiles too. They thought salvation and the baptism in the Holy Ghost were just for the Jews.

How did these Jews know that Cornelius' household had received the gift of the Holy Ghost? *"For they HEARD THEM SPEAK WITH TONGUES, and magnify God . . ."* (Acts 10:46). Speaking in tongues was the supernatural sign and initial evidence that convinced them that the Gentiles had the same gift they had.

Reason Number 2

Paul, in writing to the Church at Corinth, encouraged the Corinthian Christians to continue the practice of speaking with other tongues in their worship of God. He also encouraged them to speak in tongues in their individual prayer lives as a means of spiritual edification or building up. The Bible says, *"He that speaketh in an unknown tongue edifieth himself . . ."* (1 Cor. 14:4).

Jude 20 also links praying in tongues with building yourself up spiritually.

JUDE 20
20 But ye, beloved, BUILDING UP YOURSELVES on your most holy faith, PRAYING IN THE HOLY GHOST.

Howard Carter, who was one of the Pentecostal world's most renowned teachers on the subject of spiritual gifts, said we must not forget that speaking with other tongues is not only the initial evidence of the Holy Spirit's infilling, but is also a continual experience for the rest of one's life.

For what purpose? *To assist us in the worship of God.* "Speaking in tongues," Rev Carter said, "is a flowing stream that should never dry up, and that will enrich one's life spiritually." [1]

The Apostle Paul said that speaking with tongues will edify or build us up spiritually. *"For he that speaketh in an unknown tongue speaketh not unto men, but unto God: for no man understandeth him; howbeit in the spirit he speaketh mysteries"* (1 Cor. 14:2).

Moffatt's translation of this verse says, ". . . he is talking of divine secrets in the Spirit." Paul was saying here that God has given to the church a divine, supernatural means of communication with Him.

Paul also stated in First Corinthians 14:14, *"For if I pray in an unknown tongue, MY SPIRIT PRAYETH, but my understanding is unfruitful."* Notice he said, ". . . *my spirit prayeth.* . . ."

The Amplified Bible reads, ". . . my spirit [by the Holy Spirit within me] prays. . . ." God is a spirit. When you pray in tongues, your spirit is in direct contact with God, who is a Spirit. When you speak in tongues, you are talking to Him by divine, supernatural means.

Reason Number 3

The third reason people should speak with other tongues is that tongues keeps us continually aware of the Holy Spirit's indwelling Presence. Not only is speaking with tongues the initial sign or evidence of the Holy Spirit's infilling, but *continuing* to pray and to worship God in tongues helps us to be ever conscious of His indwelling Presence. And if you are conscious of the indwelling Presence of the Holy Ghost every day, that is bound to affect the way you think and live.

I once heard an evangelist tell of an experience he had in a pastor's home. As he walked into a room unexpectedly, he heard the pastor's twelve-year-old daughter just throwing a fit. She had lost her temper and was bawling her mother out.

Suddenly she looked up and saw the evangelist. She stopped and put her head in her hands and began to cry. She said, "I am so sorry you saw me act this way and heard what I said."

He said to her, "Honey, there is One who is greater than I am who heard you and saw you act that way. You are a Christian, aren't you?"

"Yes," was her tearful reply.

"Filled with the Spirit?" he asked.

"Yes," she answered.

"Well, the Holy Ghost is in you, and He knows what you said and how you acted," he told her. "Just repent and the Lord will forgive you." They prayed together and she repented. Then in a little while she began to worship God in tongues.

This evangelist then said to her, "There is one secret that will help you curb your temper. If you will just pray and worship God every day in tongues, it will help you to be conscious of the indwelling Presence of the Holy Ghost.

Then he said, "If you will remember that the Holy Spirit is in you, you won't act that way. You were ashamed because *I* saw you lose your temper. You were embarrassed because *I* heard you talk the way you did to your mother. But the Holy Ghost is greater than I am, and *He* saw and heard you too."

Some years later when this same evangelist returned to preach at that church, the pastor's daughter told him, "I have never forgotten what you said. Every day for the past few years I have prayed and worshipped God in tongues, and I have never lost my temper again."

Unfortunately, we all know people who have been filled with the Holy Ghost, yet still lose their temper and say and do things they shouldn't. It is because they have been walking in the flesh instead of in the Spirit, and they haven't been fellowshipping with God as they should have been.

It is so easy, when you are not conscious of God's Presence, to become aggravated and easily exasperated, and to allow yourself to lose your temper. But if you will take time to fellowship with God by speaking in tongues, you can continually be conscious of God's indwelling Presence.

Reason Number 4

Speaking in tongues eliminates the possibility of selfishness entering our prayer life. For instance, if I pray a prayer out of my own mind and out of my own thinking, it may be unscriptural. It may be selfish. Too many times our prayers are like the old farmer who always prayed, "God bless me, my wife, my son John, his wife — us four and no more."

Paul wrote to the Church at Rome, ". . . *we know not what we should pray for as we ought . . .*" (Rom. 8:26). He didn't say we didn't know how to pray, because we do know *how* we are to pray. We are to pray to the Father in the Name of the Lord Jesus Christ (John 16:23,24).

That is the correct way to pray. But just because I know *how* to pray doesn't mean that I know *what* to pray for as I ought. So Paul said, ". . . *we know not what we should pray for as we ought: but the Spirit itself* [Himself] *maketh intercession for us with groanings which cannot be uttered*" (Rom. 8:26).

P. C. Nelson, a Greek scholar and the founder of Southwestern Bible Institute, said that the Greek in Romans 8:26 literally reads, ". . . the Holy Ghost maketh intercession for us in groanings that cannot be uttered in *articulate speech.*"

Articulate speech means your regular kind of speech. He went on to point out that the Greek stresses that this not only includes groanings escaping your lips in prayer, but also praying in other tongues. That agrees with what Paul said in First Corinthians 14:14, *"For if I pray in an unknown tongue, my spirit prayeth. . . ." The Amplified Bible* says, ". . . my spirit [by the Holy Spirit within me] prays. . . ."

People should be careful making fun of tongues, because when people make fun of tongues, they are making fun of the Holy Ghost. When you pray in tongues, it is your spirit praying by the Holy Spirit within you. It is the Holy Spirit within giving you the utterance, and you are speaking from out of your spirit. You do the talking; the Holy Spirit gives the utterance.

By praying with groanings and with other tongues, the Holy Spirit is helping you to pray according to the will of God — to pray as things should be prayed for. This isn't something the Holy Ghost does apart from you. He doesn't groan or speak in tongues apart from you. Those groanings that cannot be uttered in articulate speech come from inside of you — from your spirit — and escape your own lips.

The Holy Ghost is not going to do your praying for you. He is sent to dwell in us as a Counselor, Helper,

Intercessor, Advocate, Strengthener, and Standby (John 14:16 *Amp.*). The Holy Spirit is not responsible for our prayer life. He is sent *to help* us pray. Speaking with other tongues is praying as the Spirit gives utterance. It is Spirit-directed praying. It eliminates the possibility of selfishness in our prayers.

Many times when people have prayed out of their own minds, they have prayed for circumstances to change that were actually not the will of God and were not best. If God's people want things a certain way, even if it isn't best for them or is not God's will, He will often permit it.

For example, God did not want Israel to have a king, but they wanted one, so He permitted them to have one (1 Sam. 8:4-7). But a king was not His perfect will for them.

Therefore, speaking in tongues eliminates selfishness and praying outside of the will of God because when we pray in tongues, we are praying the perfect will of God.

Reason Number 5

The fifth reason believers should speak with tongues is that it helps them learn to trust God more fully. It builds one's faith to speak in tongues. The Bible says, ". . . *building up yourselves on your most holy faith, praying in the Holy Ghost*" (Jude 20).

Speaking in tongues stimulates faith and helps us learn how to trust God more fully. For example, faith must be exercised to speak with tongues because the Holy Spirit supernaturally directs the words we speak. You see, we don't know what the next word will be — we have to trust God for that. *And trusting God in one area helps us learn to trust Him in another area.*

As a young denominational minister I was pastor of a community church, and there was a fine Christian woman in our church who dearly loved the Lord. But she was afflicted in her body with sickness. She had an ulcerated stomach, and the doctors feared that it would lead to cancer of the stomach. Her husband made good money, but he had spent everything he had on doctor bills until finally they didn't even own an automobile. He had spent thousands of dollars.

This woman received the baptism of the Holy Spirit and shortly after that I visited in their home again. I noticed that she could eat almost anything, whereas before she could eat only a little baby food and milk, and had even had difficulty keeping that in her stomach.

She told me, "I not only received the baptism of the Holy Ghost and spoke with other tongues, but I received my healing as well. I am perfectly healed."

I have seen this happen many times. What is the connection? We know that receiving the baptism of the Holy Ghost doesn't heal you. However, speaking with tongues helps you to learn how to trust God more fully in other areas of life — including in the area of healing.

Reason Number 6

The sixth reason every Christian ought to regularly speak in tongues is that speaking in tongues is a means of keeping us free from the contamination of the ungodly and profane elements of the world. For example, there is much vulgar talk that goes on around us on the job or out in public. But we can speak in tongues to ourselves (1 Cor. 14:28).

In other words, if you can speak in tongues to yourself and to God in church, then you can speak in tongues on the job, too, in a way that won't disturb anyone. In the barber shops, for instance, if the men are telling jokes that are not edifying, I just sit there quietly and speak to myself and to God in tongues.

Riding the train, bus, or airplane, you can speak to yourself and to God. On the job you can speak to yourself and to God. Speaking in tongues to yourself and to God is a means of keeping yourself free from the contamination of the world.

Reason Number 7

The seventh reason every believer should speak in tongues is that it provides a way for things to be prayed for about which no one thinks to pray, or is even aware of. We already know that the Holy Spirit helps us pray for things we do not know how to pray for as we ought. In addition, the Holy Spirit, who knows everything, can pray through us for things about which our natural mind knows nothing.

When a missionary to Africa was speaking at a missionary conference in England once, a woman asked him, "Do you keep a diary?"

When he replied that he did, she said, "Two years ago I was awakened in the night with a burden to pray. I got out of bed and I was speaking in tongues before I ever got down on my knees."

She continued, "I prayed for an hour in tongues. It just seemed as if I was wrestling in the spirit. I didn't know what I was praying for, but as I finished praying, I had a vision in which I saw you in a little old grass thatched hut. There weren't any other white people there. The natives were gathered around you, and you were extremely sick. Then you died. The natives pulled a sheet up over your head and went outside of the hut.

"Suddenly," she said, "I saw you come out of the hut and stand in their midst, and they all rejoiced! Did anything like that ever happen to you?"

In response, he asked her, "Do you keep a diary?"

"Yes," she answered.

"Bring your diary this afternoon and I will bring mine, and we can compare notes," he said. They had never had any connection with one another before this time; this woman only knew that this man was a missionary.

Comparing their diaries and making allowances for the differences in time between the countries of England and Africa, they learned that the time of the woman's prayer burden coincided exactly with the time when the missionary was sick with a deadly fever.

The missionary related that his partner had gone to a neighboring village and he had been left alone with the natives. Things happened just as she saw them. The missionary had died, the natives saw him die, and they pulled a sheet over his head. Then suddenly the missionary rose up well because of the power of God made available through this woman's praying in other tongues.

In 1956 when my wife and I were in California ministering, I was awakened suddenly in the night. It was as if someone had laid a hand on me. I sat bolt upright in bed, my heart beating fast as though I were afraid.

I lay back down and said, "Lord, what is the matter? I know something is wrong somewhere." It was as if the Spirit of God had awakened me.

I said, "Holy Spirit in me, You know everything. You are everywhere. You are everywhere present at once, as well as dwelling within me. Whatever is the matter, please give me utterance to pray about it."

Then I began to pray in tongues, and I lay there and prayed quietly to God for about an hour. Then I began to laugh and sing in tongues. When you pray this way, always continue praying until you have a note of praise or victory. Then that means whatever it is you were praying about has been prayed through.

When I got that note of victory in my praying, I knew that what I had been praying about had been prayed through. I had the answer, so I went back to sleep.

As I slept, I dreamed that I saw my youngest brother in a motel in Louisiana. I saw him awaken at midnight. I saw someone summon the doctor, and I saw an ambulance come. I saw them put my brother in an ambulance, and I saw the red light flashing as they took him to the hospital.

In the dream I stood in the corridor of the hospital just outside his door. When the doctor came out, he pulled the door closed behind him and then he saw me standing there. He shook his head and said to me, "He's dead."

In the dream I said, "No, doctor, he is not dead. The Lord told me he would live and not die."

The doctor became angry and said, "I know when people are dead. I have pronounced many hundreds of people dead." He grabbed me by the hand and said, "Come, I'll let you see for yourself."

He opened the door, led me to the bed, and jerked the sheet from my brother's face. When he did, he saw that my brother was breathing and his eyes were open.

The doctor said, "Why, you knew something I didn't know! He is alive, isn't he?" I saw my brother rise up well. Then that was the end of the dream. I knew that was what I had prayed about.

Three months later we came back to Texas. My brother stopped by to see me and said, "I nearly died while you were gone."

"Yes, I know," I said. "You were down in Louisiana, weren't you? It was in the nighttime and you had an attack and you were taken to the hospital in an ambulance."

"Yes. How did you know?" he asked.

When I told him about my burden for prayer followed by the dream, he said, "It happened just like that. They told me that for about forty minutes there at the hospital, the doctor thought I was dead."

Praying in the Spirit provides a way for things to be prayed for that people wouldn't know anything about in the natural. The Holy Ghost, however, knows everything. And He is our Helper in prayer.

Reason Number 8

Paul says in First Corinthians 14:21, "*. . . With men of other tongues and other lips will I speak unto this people. . . .*" Paul was saying this in reference to Isaiah 28:11 and 12. And this passage in Isaiah gives us the eighth reason that every Christian should speak in tongues.

ISAIAH 28:11,12
11 For with stammering lips and ANOTHER TONGUE will he speak to this people.
12 To whom he said, THIS IS THE REST wherewith ye may cause the weary to rest; and THIS IS THE REFRESH-ING: yet they would not hear.

What is the rest? What is the refreshing? Isaiah 28:11 and 12 says the rest and the refreshing is speaking with other tongues.

Sometimes the doctor recommends a rest cure for exhaustion or for some sicknesses. And often when you take a vacation, you have to come home and rest before you go back to work!

But I know the best rest in the world! Isn't it wonderful that we can just take this "rest cure" every day? The Bible says, ". . . *This is the rest . . . this is the refreshing . . .*" (Isa. 28:12). We need this rest in these days of turmoil, perplexity, and insecurity.

Reason Number 9

The ninth reason we are to pray in tongues is to give thanks to God.

1 CORINTHIANS 14:15-17
15 What is it then? I will pray with the spirit, and I will pray with the understanding also: I will sing with the spirit, and I will sing with the understanding also.
16 Else when thou shalt BLESS WITH THE SPIRIT, how shall he that occupieth the room of the unlearned say Amen at thy GIVING OF THANKS, seeing he understandeth not what thou sayest?
17 For thou VERILY GIVEST THANKS WELL, but the other is not edified.

When Paul said, ". . . *he that occupieth the room of the unlearned. . . ,*" he was referring to those who are unlearned in spiritual things.

Let me illustrate these verses of Scripture. For example, if you invited me to dinner and said, "Brother Hagin, please say the 'thanks' for the meal," if I prayed in tongues, you wouldn't know what I said. You wouldn't be edified.

Therefore, Paul said in a situation such as this, it would be better to pray with the understanding. If I did pray in tongues, I should interpret it so you would know what was said. Then you could be edified too, for Paul said, ". . . *thou verily givest thanks well, but the other is not edified*" (1 Cor. 14:17).

In other words, praying in tongues is the best way to give thanks. But in the presence of people who are unlearned, pray also with your understanding so they can be edified. Offering your thanks in your understanding allows people to be edified because then they will understand what you are saying.

Pay special attention to what Paul said in First Corinthians 14:17. He said praying in tongues provides the most perfect way to pray and to give thanks to God. Paul said when you offer thanks in other tongues, ". . . *thou verily givest thanks well . . .*" (1 Cor. 14:17).

Reason Number 10

The tenth reason why every believer should speak with tongues is found in James 3:8. *"But the tongue can no man tame; it is an unruly evil, full of deadly poison."* Yielding your tongue to the Holy Spirit to speak with other tongues is a big step toward being able to fully yield all of your members to God; for if you can yield your tongue, you can yield any member of your body to God.

Speaking in tongues is the initial evidence of the infilling of the Holy Spirit. God has given us this wonderful spiritual gift to bless us, edify us, and refresh us throughout our lives on this earth. Let's receive what God has provided, and enjoy the benefits of speaking in tongues!

------

[1] Howard Carter, *Questions and Answers on Spiritual Gifts* (Tulsa, Oklahoma: Harrison House, Inc., 1976), p. 120.

Questions for Study

1. This chapter lists ten reasons why every believer should speak in tongues.
   What are they?
   _____
   _____

2. How did the Jews know that Cornelius' household had received the gift of the Holy Ghost?
   _____
   _____

3. When you are not conscious of God's Presence, what can you easily become ?
   _____
   _____

4. What can happen if you will take time to fellowship with God by speaking in tongues?
   _____
   _____

5. According to John 16:23,24, to whom are we to pray?
   _____
   _____

6. According to P.C. Nelson, a noted Greek scholar, how does the Greek in Romans 8:26 literally read?
   _____
   _____

7. What does "articulate speech" mean?
   _____
   _____

8. Why should people be careful about making fun of tongues?
   _____
   _____

9. What have people prayed for many times when they have prayed out of their own minds?
   _____
   _____

10. Speaking in tongues stimulates _____ and helps us learn to _____ God more fully.

Chapter 10

Seven Steps To Receiving the Holy Ghost

And I will pray the Father, and he shall give you another Comforter, that he may abide with you for ever;

Even the Spirit of truth; whom the world cannot receive, because it seeth him not, neither knoweth him: but ye know him; for he dwelleth with you, and shall be in you.

— John 14:16,17

This Jesus hath God raised up, whereof we all are witnesses.

Therefore being by the right hand of God exalted, and having received of the Father the promise of the Holy Ghost, he hath shed forth this, which ye now see and hear.

— Acts 2:32,33

This lesson has a twofold purpose: Number one is to help those who have not yet received the infilling of the Holy Ghost. Number two is to help Spirit-filled believers pray with those who are seeking to receive the baptism of the Holy Ghost. Any layperson can take the following seven steps and help any Christian get filled with the Holy Ghost without any tarrying or waiting.

I was preaching in a certain meeting once where about sixty-five people had been filled with the Holy Ghost. In one of the daytime services, someone asked, "What are we going to do when you leave, Brother Hagin?"

You see, all that the people had known in the past was to struggle and struggle in order to get believers filled with the Holy Ghost. One of the women who was an outstanding altar worker said, "In every meeting, I always pray with people to receive the Holy Spirit until my throat almost gives out. And after the meetings sometimes I've had laryngitis for a month."

I told them about these seven steps to receiving the infilling of the Holy Ghost. That night seven believers came forward to receive the Holy Ghost, but I didn't pray for them. Instead, I prayed for the sick who came forward for healing and sent these seven people into a prayer room, telling the altar workers, "All right, go back there and get them filled, following the instructions I gave you earlier today."

They went to the room and came out in ten minutes' time with six of the seven having been filled

with the Holy Ghost! They apologized for not getting the seventh one filled, but it turned out that he wasn't even a Christian, and he didn't want to get saved. You see, you can't get the Holy Ghost without getting saved first.

One of these workers was so thrilled to learn how to help people receive the Holy Ghost that she could hardly wait to go visit her mother who lived some distance away and help her be filled with the Holy Spirit. "Mama has been seeking the baptism for nineteen years," she told me, "but now I know she will receive."

Several months later I was back in the same church to hold meetings again, and this woman told me, "I drove about one hundred and fifty miles to my mother's home, and Mama was outside waiting for me. I said, 'Mama, just come on into the house. I can't stay long. I'm going to have to get back home. I only have time to attend to the business I came for — to get you filled with the Holy Ghost.'"

"But, you know, I have been seeking a mighty long time," her Mama answered.

The woman related, "I told her, 'I know it, Mama, but now you are going to receive.' We went into the house and I said, 'Just sit down and open your Bible to Acts chapter 2.' I sat down on the seat next to her and spent ten minutes with her just sharing the Word. Then I laid hands on her and she received the Holy Spirit and started speaking in tongues!"

The Seven Steps To Receiving the Holy Spirit

I list here the same seven steps which I have used in my revival meetings across the country to help believers receive the Holy Spirit.

Step Number 1

Help the believer see that God has already given the Holy Spirit and that it is now up to that person to receive God's free Gift.

Above everything else, help the believer see that he is not to beg God to fill him with the Holy Spirit. The promise that the Holy Spirit was to be *given* was fulfilled in Acts chapter 2. The Holy Spirit came on the Day of Pentecost, and He has been here ever since. After that time God hasn't *given* the Holy Spirit to anyone. Now people simply have *to receive* the Holy Spirit.

For instance, let's look at what the Apostle Paul said some years after the incidents recorded in Acts chapter 2.

ACTS 19:1-6
1 . . . Paul having passed through the upper coasts came to Ephesus: and finding certain disciples,
2 He said unto them, Have ye RECEIVED the Holy Ghost since ye believed? [He didn't say, "Has God given you the Holy Ghost?" He said, "Have ye received the Holy Ghost?"] And they said unto him, We have not so much as heard whether there be any Holy Ghost.
3 And he said unto them, Unto what then were ye baptized? And they said, Unto John's baptism.
4 Then said Paul, John verily baptized with the baptism of repentance, saying unto the people, that they should believe on him which should come after him, that is, on Christ Jesus.
5 When they heard this, they were baptized in the name of the Lord Jesus.
6 And when Paul had laid his hands upon them, the Holy Ghost came on them; and they spake with tongues, and prophesied.

Paul didn't tell these disciples to pray that God would give them the Holy Ghost. The Bible says, "*. . . the Holy Ghost came on them; and they spake with tongues, and prophesied*" (Acts 19:6).

Notice also Acts chapter 8 which occurred some years after the Day of Pentecost.

ACTS 8:14,15
14 Now when the apostles which were at Jerusalem heard that Samaria had RECEIVED THE WORD OF GOD [concerning salvation], they sent unto them Peter and John:
15 Who, when they were come down, prayed for them, that they might RECEIVE the Holy Ghost.

The apostles didn't pray that God would *give* the Samaritans the Holy Ghost. They prayed that they might *receive* the Holy Ghost: "*Then laid they their hands on them, and they RECEIVED the Holy Ghost*" (Acts 8:17).

God hasn't given the Holy Ghost to anyone since the Day of Pentecost, but people have received Him. The Holy Ghost is already here for believers to receive.

Step Number 2

Show the person who has come to receive the Holy Ghost that anyone who is saved is ready to *immediately* receive the Holy Spirit.

ACTS 2:37,38
37 Now when they [the unsaved multitude who gathered as a result of the outpouring of the Holy Spirit and to whom Peter had preached quoting Joel's prophecy] heard this, they were pricked in their heart, and said unto Peter and to the rest of the apostles, Men and brethren, what shall we do?

38 Then Peter said unto them, Repent, and be baptized every one of you in the name of Jesus Christ for the remission of sins, and ye shall receive the gift of the Holy Ghost.

Verse 38 shows us that anyone who is saved is *immediately* ready to receive the gift of the Holy Ghost.

Some people think there are certain things they have to do to qualify to receive the baptism of the Holy Spirit. For example, some think they have to make restitution for past sins. One fellow in east Texas once said, "I had to return a pig that I had stolen before I could get the Holy Ghost."

It is true that sin which has not been confessed can hinder people from receiving the blessings of God. However, if folks are saved and walking in fellowship with God, they couldn't possibly be any cleaner than they are right then. Once we confess our sins, the blood of Jesus Christ cleanses us from all unrighteousness (1 John 1:9). I believe that saved people go to heaven when they die. And if they are good enough to go to heaven, they are good enough to have a little bit of heaven in them here on earth!

Some people think they have to follow certain standards of dress in order to receive the Holy Spirit. For example, we were preaching at a certain place and in the meeting a woman came forward to receive the Holy Spirit. She did receive and spoke with tongues for fifteen or twenty minutes.

Afterwards, she was sitting down and praising God in English. One fellow walked over to her and thought she hadn't received because he hadn't heard her speaking in tongues. He also noticed that she was wearing a wedding ring and he said to her, "Sister, if you will take that wedding band off, God will fill you with the Holy Ghost."

I whispered to him, "Brother, you are too late. He has already filled her, wedding band and all."

You see, some people have the mistaken idea that they have to court God's favor in order to get Him to do something for them. All we have to do is to be saved and walk in the light of salvation. A person who is out of fellowship, of course, would have to come back into fellowship with Him.

As I said, some people have imagined that one has to be perfect before he can get the Holy Ghost. However, even the great Apostle Paul said he wasn't perfect. Yet we know he had the Holy Spirit.

PHILIPPIANS 3:12,13
12 Not as though I had already attained, either were already perfect. . . .
13 . . . I count not myself to have apprehended: but this one thing I do, forgetting those things which are behind, and reaching forth unto those things which are before.

If you could do everything you ought to do and be everything you ought to be without the Holy Ghost, what would you need Him for? If you can do everything for yourself, why do you need the Holy Ghost?

Carnal Christians (or Christians who are sense-ruled or dominated by the flesh) can be filled with the Holy Ghost. How do we know that? Because the Bible says the Corinthian Christians were carnal, and yet Paul prayed for them that they would come behind in no gift (1 Cor. 1:7). He was not endorsing carnality, to be sure. He was trying to get them to grow up in God and outgrow carnality. But as believers yield to Him, the Holy Ghost will help them grow out of carnality.

Baby Christians can be filled with the Holy Spirit. Carnal Christians and baby Christians — indeed, *all* believers — greatly need to be filled with the Holy Spirit because then they will receive power that will help them (Acts 1:8). Also, if they will walk in the light of God's Word and be led by the Holy Spirit, He will lead them into all truth and help them to outgrow some things in their lives which have perhaps hindered their Christian walk (John 16:13).

Therefore, if a person is saved, he is ready to receive the Holy Ghost now. Always lead the believer who is seeking the Holy Ghost to see that truth.

Step Number 3

Tell people that when you lay hands on them, they are to receive the Holy Ghost.

Anyone can lay hands on another in faith, for God honors faith. However, there is also a ministry of laying on of hands, and some are used along these lines more than others. But anyone can lay their hands on a person in faith as a point of contact, and tell them, "This is the time — right now — that you are to receive the Holy Ghost." The Holy Ghost is received *by faith*, and faith is always "now" or present tense (Heb. 11:1).

Step Number 4

Tell the candidate what to expect as he receives the Holy Spirit; otherwise, he won't know what is happening when the Holy Spirit begins to move on him.

Tell the candidate that he is to expect the Holy Spirit to move upon his vocal organs and put supernatural words on his lips which he will have to speak out himself in cooperation with the Holy Spirit.

Remember, the person is the one who does the actual speaking, not the Holy Spirit. *The Holy Spirit gives the utterance*, but man does the actual speaking.

Some people have taught things that are unscriptural for so long that it is hard for them to break the habit of teaching them. For example, I have seen someone about to speak with tongues; the Spirit of God would be moving on his lips and vocal cords. Then I would hear someone say to him, "Let the Holy Ghost talk." But it is not the Holy Ghost who is to do the talking. It is the person receiving the Holy Ghost who is to do the talking.

Now it is all right to tell the person *to yield* to the Holy Ghost. But notice again Acts 2:4: "*. . . they were all filled with the Holy Ghost, and* [they] *began to speak with other tongues, as the Spirit gave them utterance.*" Notice, *they* were all filled and *they* began to speak. In other words, the Holy Spirit gives the utterance; the person who is receiving the Holy Spirit does the speaking.

Many people have thought, *If I do the speaking, that would just be me.* Well of course, it will be you talking. It sure won't be me! And it sure won't be the person praying with you who will be doing the talking. Anytime you ever speak with tongues, it will surely be *you* doing the talking. But the Holy Ghost gives you the *utterance*, and it is a supernatural utterance.

The point is this: the Holy Ghost doesn't take you over, so to speak, and force you to do anything. But you can respond to Him and follow His promptings. He will give you the utterance, but *you* do the talking. Nowhere in the Bible do we find that the Holy Ghost spoke in tongues. Every scripture reference tells us that the person receiving the Holy Ghost does the talking and speaks the supernatural utterance — tongues — the Holy Spirit gives him.

Let's look at what the Scriptures say about the believer's role in speaking in tongues and the Holy Spirit's role in giving the utterance.

ACTS 2:4
4 . . . [They] **began to SPEAK with other tongues, as THE SPIRIT gave them UTTERANCE.**

ACTS 10:46
46 **For they heard THEM SPEAK with tongues, and magnify God.** . . .

ACTS 19:6
6 **And when Paul had laid his hands upon them, THE HOLY GHOST CAME ON THEM; and THEY SPAKE with tongues, and prophesied.**

1 CORINTHIANS 14:2,4,5
2 **For HE THAT SPEAKETH in an unknown tongue speaketh not unto men, but unto God: for no man understandeth him; howbeit in the spirit HE SPEAKETH mysteries.** . . .
4 **HE THAT SPEAKETH in an unknown tongue edifieth himself.** . . .
5 **I would that YE ALL SPAKE with tongues.** . . .

1 CORINTHIANS 14:14,15,18
14 For if I PRAY in AN UNKNOWN TONGUE, my spirit prayeth, but my understanding is unfruitful.
15 What is it then? I WILL PRAY with the spirit, and I will pray with the understanding. . . .
18 I thank my God, I SPEAK with tongues more than ye all.

1 CORINTHIANS 14:27,28
27 IF ANY MAN SPEAK in an unknown tongue, let it be by two, or at the most by three, and that by course; and let one interpret.
28 But if there be no interpreter, let him keep silence in the church. . . .

Notice that every one of these scriptures shows that in receiving the Holy Ghost and in praying in tongues and in ministering tongues in public assembly, it is always *the person* himself that does the actual speaking. But *the Holy Spirit* gives the supernatural utterance.

When I tell this to people who have been seeking the Holy Ghost for thirty or forty years, they often look at me in amazement and say, "If I had known that, I could have been speaking in tongues for the last thirty years. I had the urge — I had the prompting all the time. In fact at times, it was all I could do to keep from speaking in tongues, but I was waiting for the Holy Ghost to come and take my tongue over."

Some people think that the baptism in the Holy Ghost is as if someone swallowed a small radio. And then when God gets ready, He just turns on "the radio" and it starts playing or speaking automatically. However, the *Holy Ghost* gives you *the utterance*, but *you* do *the talking*.

When the Spirit of God is moving on your tongue and lips, what you must do is lift your voice and put sound to it. If you will obey those promptings of the Holy Spirit, you will find yourself speaking with tongues. You see, you must cooperate with the Holy Ghost. Speaking with tongues isn't entirely you, and it isn't entirely the Holy Ghost. Speaking with tongues is *a cooperation* between you and the Holy Ghost.

Step Number 5

It may be necessary to help some folks get over their fears first before they can receive the baptism in the Holy Spirit.

Many seekers have been told by well-meaning people that they might get something that is false or counterfeit when receiving the baptism in the Holy Spirit. I have heard people say, "You know, there is a wrong spirit as well as a right one. I want to be certain and be sure I get the right thing."

When I hear people talk like that, I point out Luke 11:11-13 to them.

LUKE 11:11-13
11 If a son shall ask bread of any of you that is a father, will he give him a stone? or if he ask a fish, will he for a fish give him a serpent?
12 Or if he shall ask an egg, will he offer him a scorpion?
13 If ye then, being evil, know how to give good gifts unto your children: HOW MUCH MORE SHALL YOUR HEAVENLY FATHER GIVE THE HOLY SPIRIT TO THEM THAT ASK HIM?

Jesus was saying in this passage of Scripture, "If your child asked you as a parent for bread, would you give him a stone? If your child asked you for a fish, would you give him a serpent? If your child asked you for an egg, would you offer him a scorpion?"

No, of course you wouldn't. *"If ye then, being evil, know how to give good gifts unto your children: how much more shall your heavenly Father give the Holy Spirit to them that ask him?"* (Luke 11:13). We can be assured that God will not give His children a counterfeit when they ask Him for the Holy Spirit.

It is a different thing entirely, of course, when a sinner is seeking the Holy Spirit because the sinner cannot receive the Holy Spirit (John 14:17). But if a person who is a child of God is seeking the Holy Spirit, he is not going to receive an evil spirit.

Notice that the words "serpent" and "scorpion" are used here in Luke chapter 11. Turning to Luke 10:19, we read that Jesus said, *"Behold, I give unto you power to tread on serpents and scorpions, and over all the power of the enemy. . . ."*

Jesus used the terms "serpents" and "scorpions" to talk about evil spirits. So He said in Luke 11 you are not going to get a "serpent" or a "scorpion" when you ask for the Holy Spirit. If you are a child of God and you go to your Heavenly Father to receive the Holy Ghost, then that is what you are going to get — the Holy Ghost.

When I have given these scriptures to those who have been misled by false teaching, I have seen them immediately begin to speak with tongues. They later told me, "If I had known that, I could have been speaking with tongues and could have known the fullness of the Spirit for many years. But I was afraid I might get a wrong spirit." Thank God, we can be relieved of our fears through the Word of God.

Step Number 6

Tell the candidate to open his mouth and be ready to use his own mouth and vocal chords, for the Holy Spirit will give the utterance, but he must yield and give voice to that utterance. At the same time the believer should tell God in his heart, "I am receiving the Holy Spirit right now by faith."

I like to absolutely insist that people not speak one word in their natural language. And I will give Scripture further in this lesson why a person receiving the Holy Spirit shouldn't speak one word in his natural language.

Then when the Holy Spirit begins to move upon the believer, I tell him to lift his voice and speak out whatever utterance is given to him by the Holy Spirit, regardless of what it sounds like.

I tell the candidate to begin to speak the words and the language the Holy Spirit gives him, continuing to praise God and speak to God with those supernatural words until the language becomes more and more fluent.

When that person can hear himself speak in tongues in a distinct language, he will have assurance and confidence that he has received the Holy Ghost.

JOHN 7:37-39
37 In the last day, that great day of the feast, Jesus stood and cried, saying, If any man thirst, let him COME UNTO ME, AND DRINK.
38 He that believeth on me, as the scripture hath said, OUT OF HIS BELLY [spirit] SHALL FLOW RIVERS OF LIVING WATER.
39 (But this spake he of the Spirit, which they that believe on him should receive: for the Holy Ghost was not yet given; because that Jesus was not yet glorified.)

The Bible says the Holy Spirit will come to us as the rain. And Jesus said in John chapter 7 that we are to come and drink of the Holy Spirit.

In other words, Jesus said receiving the Holy Ghost is like drinking water. That is, the same principle is involved. The point is no one can drink with their mouth shut. And in the same way, in order to receive the Holy Spirit, a person must put action to his faith and give voice to the unction of the Holy Spirit; he can't do that with his mouth closed. Remember, the Holy Spirit gives the utterance; the person does the actual talking.

Secondly, no one can drink and talk at the same time. I have seen people come to receive the Holy Spirit and open their mouth in faith. I have never seen anyone who opened his mouth in faith to receive the Holy Spirit who didn't receive as quickly as you can snap your finger.

I have seen thousands upon thousands of folks filled with the Holy Ghost — preachers and pastors of every denomination, doctors, lawyers, school teachers, college professors, laborers, farmers, and people from every walk of life.

Once I saw five businessmen come down the aisle in one of my meetings to receive the Holy Spirit. They all opened their mouths in faith that they were going to receive the Holy Spirit, and they were all filled too!

That's scriptural because Jesus said, "Come and drink" (John 7:37). If you will act on God's Word, He will honor His Word, and you can receive the Holy Ghost or whatever it is that He has promised.

Step Number 7

Keep the candidate from being distracted.

For instance, don't permit a crowd to gather around the candidate, giving instructions all at once. This will confuse a person. I like to have only a few workers whom I have specially instructed to help folks receive the Holy Spirit.

Many times folks are a little slow about yielding to the Spirit, but if someone is there to help encourage them to yield to the Holy Spirit, people can more readily receive.

For example, when going swimming, sometimes it is hard to get some folks in the water, but if you will take the lead and get in the water and swim around and say, "The water sure feels good," they will be encouraged to get in the water too.

Similarly, sometimes you can simply speak in tongues yourself after praying with the candidate, and this will encourage the candidate to "follow you into the water," so to speak — into the baptism of the Holy Spirit.

I have been in Full Gospel circles more than fifty years, and I have seen nearly everything happen you can mention when people were seeking the Holy Ghost (and a lot I don't want to mention).

For example, I have seen dear folks at the altar seeking the Holy Spirit while someone on one side of them was yelling in one ear, "Hold on Brother, hold on."

Someone else might be hollering in the other ear, "Turn loose, Brother, turn loose."

Someone kneeling right behind them would be patting him on the back hollering, "Let go, Brother, let go." Then someone sitting right in front of them would be shouting something else at the top of his voice.

Many have still received the Holy Spirit this way, not because of this kind of behavior, but in spite of it! However, even though multitudes have received, many honest and sincere believers have been driven away. We will see more folks filled with the Holy Spirit if we will follow scriptural practices.

Therefore, don't allow several people to crowd around candidates who are seeking the Holy Spirit. And don't allow more than one person to give instructions at one time, because that would cause the candidate to become confused. Let one person instruct him how to yield to the Spirit.

If others are standing nearby, have them pray quietly in tongues, not in their own language. If people are praying in their own native language, that person receiving the Holy Spirit can hear what they are saying, and it will distract him. In other words, he might get his mind on the others and what they're saying. And many times people will not yield to God if they are listening to what people around them are saying.

You will find that by following these seven steps, you will help believers receive the Holy Spirit immediately without tarrying. As you assist believers in receiving the Holy Spirit, you will feel personally blessed and rewarded for your part in their receiving this wonderful gift of the Holy Ghost.

Questions for Study

1. What is the twofold purpose of this lesson?

   _____

   _____

2. This chapter lists seven steps to receiving the Holy Spirit. What are they?

   _____

   _____

3. The apostles didn't pray that God would _give_ the Samaritans the Holy Ghost. What did they pray?

   _____

   _____

4. According to Acts 2:38, who is ready to receive the gift of the Holy Ghost?

   _____

   _____

5. How do we know that carnal Christians (or Christians who are sense-ruled or dominated by the flesh) can be filled with the Holy Ghost?

   _____

   _____

6. What will happen if baby Christians will walk in the light of God's Word and be led by the Holy Spirit?

   _____

   _____

7. Why can anyone lay hands on another in faith?

   _____

   _____

8. How is the Holy Ghost received?

   _____

   _____

9. Anytime you ever speak with tongues, who will be doing the talking?

   _____

   _____

10. When the Spirit of God is moving on your tongue and lips, what must you do?

   _____

   _____

The Gift of the Word of Knowledge — Part 1

Now concerning spiritual gifts, brethren, I would not have you ignorant.

Ye know that ye were Gentiles, carried away unto these dumb idols, even as ye were led.

Wherefore I give you to understand, that no man speaking by the Spirit of God calleth Jesus accursed: and that no man can say that Jesus is the Lord, but by the Holy Ghost.

Now there are diversities of gifts, but the same Spirit.

And there are differences of administrations, but the same Lord.

And there are diversities of operations, but it is the same God which worketh all in all.

But the manifestation of the Spirit is given to every man to profit withal.

For to one is given by the Spirit the word of wisdom; to another THE WORD OF KNOWLEDGE by the same Spirit;

To another faith by the same Spirit; to another the gifts of healing by the same Spirit;

To another the working of miracles; to another prophecy; to another discerning of spirits; to another divers kinds of tongues; to another the interpretation of tongues:

But all these worketh that one and the selfsame Spirit, dividing to every man severally as he will.

For as the body is one, and hath many members, and all the members of that one body, being many, are one body: so also is Christ.

For by one Spirit are we all baptized into one body, whether we be Jews or Gentiles, whether we be bond or free; and have been all made to drink into one Spirit.

For the body is not one member, but many.
— 1 Corinthians 12:1-14

Don't Be Ignorant of Spiritual Gifts

Paul said by the Holy Spirit to the Church at Corinth, *"Now concerning spiritual gifts, brethren, I WOULD NOT HAVE YOU IGNORANT"* (1 Cor. 12:1). If the Spirit of God through Paul said that He didn't want the Church at Corinth to be ignorant concerning spiritual gifts, then I certainly do not believe He wants the Church today to be ignorant concerning spiritual gifts.

However, a gross ignorance does exist concerning these things. In some places people know nothing at all about the gifts of the Holy Spirit, or even that such gifts exist. They think these gifts have been done away with. In other places people know something about the gifts of the Spirit, but their knowledge is very limited.

Spiritual Gifts Will Exalt Jesus

Paul also said to the Church at Corinth, *"Ye know that ye were Gentiles, carried away unto these dumb idols, even as ye were led"* (1 Cor. 12:2). These folks had previously worshipped idols and in this idol worship, motivated by the wrong spirit, they would say a lot of things that were in error.

For instance, Church history tells us that some of these folks would come into the Christian assembly and when the Spirit of God began to manifest Himself, these people would yield to a wrong spirit and say things under the influence of the wrong spirit.

In fact, some of them would even rise up in the services when the gifts of utterance were in operation and they would say that Jesus was accursed. And the Bible says that no one speaking by the Spirit of God would call Jesus accursed.

1 CORINTHIANS 12:3
3 Wherefore I give you to understand, that NO MAN SPEAKING BY THE SPIRIT OF GOD CALLETH JESUS ACCURSED: and that no man can say that Jesus is the Lord, but by the Holy Ghost.

No, Paul said that when the Holy Spirit is in manifestation, He will make Jesus Lord. If an utterance gift, that is, a vocal gift — prophecy, divers kinds of tongues, or the interpretation of tongues — is in manifestation, then, of course, it will be clear by what is said that Jesus is Lord.

If the other gifts are in manifestation, they will always uplift the Lordship of Jesus, not the lordship of some man. They will not attract attention to some man, but rather to Christ.

You can be sure that if someone is operating in what appears to be one of the vocal gifts, and calls Jesus accursed or speaks against Him in any way, then he's not speaking by the Holy Spirit.

Then Paul said in First Corinthians 12:3 that no man can say that Jesus is Lord except by the Holy Spirit. In other words, Paul was saying that if someone is speaking by the right spirit — by the Holy Spirit — then what he *says* will exalt the Name of Jesus.

Once in a meeting while I was praying for folks for healing, I sensed that someone in the prayer line had a wrong spirit. I knew within my own spirit who this person was before she ever stood in front of me to be prayed for.

When she stepped up in front of me for prayer, I asked her, "Are you a Christian?" She replied that she belonged to a particular church.

I said, "Well, you can belong to any church and still not be a Christian. You have to be born again."

"Oh, I am saved and filled with the Holy Ghost," she said. "Do you want to hear me speak in tongues?" Then she started saying something that *sounded* like tongues.

I said, "Sister, say this prayer after me from your heart." I prayed a prayer to God the Father and she repeated the words after me. Then I said, "I acknowledge the Lord Jesus Christ as Your Son, and I acknowledge that He is come in the flesh."

But when I said that, she said, "Jesus Christ is *not* Your Son and He is *not* come in the flesh." It was immediately apparent that wasn't the right spirit speaking.

Those tongues she was rattling off — some kind of "gibberish" — weren't given by the Spirit of God. I tried two or three times to get her to repeat that prayer after me. Finally, she said, "Something on the inside of me won't let me say what you said."

"I know it," I said. "Do you want to be free from it?"

"I sure do!" she answered. I cast that spirit out of her in the Name of Jesus. Then I had her pray the sinner's prayer and she was born again. She was then filled with the Holy Spirit and went home speaking in tongues.

This woman was saying, "I am saved, I am born again, and I am filled with the Holy Ghost," but she wasn't at all. People can make a lot of statements, but that doesn't necessarily make them true. When the Spirit of God is in manifestation, He will make Jesus Lord. The wrong spirit won't acknowledge that Jesus is Lord and won't say that Jesus is Lord.

Gifts, Administrations, and Operations

1 CORINTHIANS 12:4-6
4   Now there are diversities of GIFTS, but the same Spirit.
5   And there are differences of ADMINISTRATIONS, but the same Lord.
6   And there are diversities of OPERATIONS, but it is the same God which worketh all in all.

There are two lines of thought on this particular passage of Scripture in First Corinthians chapter 12.

One line of thought says that the gifts of the Spirit are administered to different people in different ways. According to this line of thought, that is what First Corinthians 12:6 means by, *"And there are diversities of operations. . . ."*

In other words, there are those who think that diversities of operations in First Corinthians 12:6 means that the gifts of the Spirit will operate in different ways and not always in the same way through various people.

The other line of thought, however, says that diversities of operations is not referring to gifts at all. These people maintain that just as there are different *gifts* of the Spirit, there are also different *administrations* of the Spirit, as well as different *operations*.

In other words, they say that Paul was talking about three different things in First Corinthians 12:4-6, not just gifts. He was talking about *gifts*, *administrations*, and *operations*.

1 CORINTHIANS 12:7
7   But the MANIFESTATION of the Spirit is given to every man to profit withal.

Notice Paul was calling the gifts of the Spirit *manifestations*. And he said, *". . . the manifestation of the Spirit is given to every man to profit withal"* (1 Cor. 12:7). Paul was making the distinction here that "gifts" of the Spirit aren't gifts in the sense that the believer owns and operates the gift whenever *he* wants to. They are gifts of the Holy Ghost, *manifested* through individual believers as the Spirit of God wills. The gifts of the Spirit aren't just given for the individual, but they are given in order to profit the whole local assembly or local body of believers.

The Nine Gifts Categorized

1 CORINTHIANS 12:8
8   For to one is given by the Spirit the word of wisdom; to another THE WORD OF KNOWLEDGE by the same Spirit;

Paul goes on to list nine manifestations or gifts of the Spirit. The nine manifestations or gifts of the Holy Spirit are generally divided as follows:

Three revelation gifts
Spiritual gifts that *reveal* something:
    The word of wisdom
    The word of knowledge
    The discerning of spirits
Three power gifts
Spiritual gifts that *do* something:
    The gift of faith
    The working of miracles

The gifts of healings

Three utterance or inspirational gifts
Spiritual gifts that *say* something:
    Prophecy
    Divers kinds of tongues
    Interpretation of tongues

Very often these gifts work together, as tongues and interpretation work together. But we divide them as they are divided here in First Corinthians chapter 12 in order to distinguish them and to talk about them.

We can readily see that very often these gifts of the Spirit are in manifestation together.

For example, sometimes what we call prophecy is actually a word of wisdom that is being given forth. It is not really the simple gift of prophecy at all because the simple gift of prophecy has no revelation; that is, no foretelling or element of prediction with it. The simple gift of prophecy brings edification, exhortation and comfort (1 Cor. 14:3). (We'll discuss this in greater detail in Chapter 13.)

These gifts are listed in the order of their importance. Of the three gifts of revelation, the word of wisdom is the best gift because it brings supernatural revelation of the plan and purpose of God.

Of the three gifts of power, the gift of faith is the best gift because it is the supernatural ability to work a miracle.

Of the three gifts of utterance, the gift of prophecy is the best gift because it is complete in and of itself and it brings edification, encouragement, and comfort to the Body of Christ (1 Cor. 14:3).

The Bible does say to seek earnestly the best gifts (1 Cor. 12:31).

The word of wisdom is the best gift of all, because as I said, it brings revelation about the divine plan and purpose of God. Although the word of wisdom is mentioned first, we will study the word of knowledge first because after discussing the word of knowledge, I think we can better understand the gift of the word of wisdom.

The Gift of the Word of Knowledge

Notice that this gift is called "the word of knowledge." It is not "the *gift* of knowledge." There is no such thing as a spiritual gift of knowledge. There is, however, a spiritual gift, called the *word* of knowledge. The word of knowledge is *the supernatural revelation by the Holy Ghost of certain facts in the mind of God.*

God is all-knowing. He knows everything. But He doesn't reveal everything He knows to man. He just gives him a *word* or a *part* of what He knows. A word is a fragmentary part of a sentence, so a word of knowledge would simply be a fragmentary part of the entire knowledge or counsel of God. God is all-knowing. He has all knowledge. But He doesn't impart all of His knowledge to us; He imparts a *word* of knowledge to us — just what He wants us to know at a given time.

The Word of Knowledge Is Not Natural Knowledge

This word of knowledge is a supernatural manifestation as are all of these gifts of the Spirit. None of them are natural gifts; they are all supernatural gifts. Since one of them is supernatural, they all are supernatural. If one of them were natural, then *all* of them would be natural.

There are those who say that this gift of the Spirit — the word of knowledge — refers to natural knowledge. If that were true, then all the gifts of the Spirit would be *natural*, not supernatural. If that were true, for example, then the gifts of healings would not be supernatural healing, but simply healing through what people have learned and achieved through medical science.

We certainly believe in medical science and thank God for all it can do. But this passage of Scripture is talking about gifts of the Holy Spirit — *supernatural* knowledge and *supernatural* healing and so forth.

If these gifts of the Spirit were only natural gifts, divers kinds of tongues would simply refer to speaking different languages that were learned naturally. Then folks who wouldn't even be saved would have that gift.

However, we know that divers kinds of tongues are supernatural. Divers kinds of tongues is the gift of the Spirit enabling one to speak in languages he has never learned, given by the Holy Spirit.

It stands to reason that if some of the nine gifts are supernatural, then all of the nine gifts of the Spirit are supernatural. Therefore, this gift of the word of knowledge is not natural knowledge, but is supernatural knowledge. It is supernatural revelation of certain facts in the mind of God.

Confusing this gift with natural knowledge, some have said, "We don't need some of these lesser gifts. We have the gift of knowledge." The knowledge that they were bragging about was intellectual knowledge; knowledge they had gained themselves apart from the Holy Ghost and apart from the Word of God. That is not what this scripture in First Corinthians 12:8 is talking about at all. The word of knowledge is a supernatural gift.

The Word of Knowledge Is Not a Profound Knowledge of the Bible

Also, this gift of the word of knowledge is sometimes confused with a profound knowledge of the Bible. A minister once tried to tell me that he had the word of knowledge because he had studied the Bible so much.

It is certainly true that God will help us understand His Word, but that is not a supernatural gift. The gift of the word of knowledge can work in connection with the Bible, however. For example, God does reveal things in connection with His Word that we didn't know. But if that were all there is to the word of knowledge, we wouldn't have to study because the word of knowledge is supernatural revelation by the Holy Ghost of certain facts in the mind of God. However, Paul told the young minister Timothy to study.

In his letter to Timothy, who was the pastor of a New Testament church, Paul said, *"STUDY to shew thyself approved . . ."* (2 Tim. 2:15). So that kind of knowledge — a profound knowledge of the Bible — comes by studying, but the word of knowledge comes by a *supernatural* revelation.

The Word of Knowledge Is Not Knowledge Of God Through Close Communion With Him

Another mistaken idea about the gift of the word of knowledge is that the word of knowledge is the knowledge that comes by walking closely with God. One does gain a real knowledge of God by walking with Him, but that is different from a supernatural impartation of knowledge of certain facts in the mind of God.

In the Old Testament, we read the story of how God spoke to the boy Samuel (1 Sam. 3:4-10). Samuel was in the temple helping the old prophet Eli.

One night Samuel heard a voice call his name. Thinking it was Eli calling him, he got up from his bed and went to him. Eli told him he hadn't called, so Samuel went back to bed. Just about the time Samuel had gotten settled, he heard a Voice saying, "Samuel, Samuel."

Again he ran to Eli, and again Eli sent him back to bed. When this was repeated for the third time, Eli realized that God must be talking to the boy, and Eli told him to answer the next time the Voice called. When God called to Samuel again, Samuel answered, *". . . Speak; for thy servant heareth"* (1 Sam. 3:10).

Eli had been walking with God, but he hadn't been as faithful to God in rearing his children as he ought to have been. He knew about the things of God, of course, but he didn't hear God's voice that night — Samuel did. So we see that this kind of knowledge doesn't necessarily come by a longtime experience of walking with God.

As I mentioned previously, there is a knowledge of God that is obtained by walking with Him, just as we walk with a friend or family member and become better acquainted with him or her. As we walk with God, certainly our knowledge of Him increases, but this is still not a spiritual manifestation of the gift of the word of knowledge.

Biblical Examples of the Word of Knowledge

Let's look at some biblical examples of the gift of the word of knowledge in operation in the New Testament.

The Word of Knowledge to John

For instance, on the Isle of Patmos, John was in the Spirit on the Lord's day and Jesus appeared to him in a vision (Rev. 1:10-20). Here we will learn something about how this word of knowledge will come.

As in this particular instance with John the apostle, the word of knowledge might come through a vision. Jesus revealed to John in a vision the condition of the seven churches in Asia Minor, as recorded in the Book of Revelation.

Although there is a prophetic message for us today in this revelation, these seven churches actually existed at that time in Asia Minor. John, exiled to the Isle of Patmos, couldn't possibly have known what was going on in these cities or churches, but Jesus revealed to him their spiritual condition. That was a word of knowledge.

Word of Knowledge to Ananias

Another example of this gift in operation is found in Acts chapter 9. *"And there was a certain disciple at Damascus, named Ananias; and to him said the Lord in a vision . . ."* (Acts 9:10). Here the word of knowledge came to a layman through a vision.

Ananias wasn't an apostle, as was John. He wasn't a pastor or evangelist or teacher. The Bible calls him a disciple. He was just a member of the church at Damascus. If the Lord wills, laymen as well as ministers can have a manifestation of the word of knowledge or any of the gifts of the Spirit.

ACTS 9:11,12
11 . . . ARISE, AND GO INTO THE STREET WHICH IS CALLED STRAIGHT, AND ENQUIRE IN THE HOUSE OF JUDAS FOR ONE CALLED SAUL OF TARSUS: FOR, BEHOLD, HE PRAYETH,
12 And hath seen in a vision [Saul also had a like vision] a man named Ananias coming in, and putting his hand on him, that he might receive his sight.

In a vision the Lord told Ananias what to do: "*. . . Arise, and go into the street which is called Straight, and enquire in the house of Judas for one called Saul of Tarsus: for, behold, he prayeth*" (v. 11).

Ananias couldn't have known in the natural that in a certain house on a certain street a man named Saul was praying at that minute. Ananias couldn't have known that Saul had had a vision in which he had seen a man called Ananias coming in and putting his hands on him that he might receive his sight. Ananias couldn't have known this any other way than by supernatural revelation. He knew it by the word of knowledge.

Of course, God knew about everyone who was praying everywhere at that time, but He didn't give Ananias knowledge of everyone who was praying; He just gave Ananias knowledge about one man who was praying — Saul of Tarsus. That was a supernatural revelation of a certain fact in the mind of God. It was the word of knowledge which came to Ananias in a vision.

The Word of Knowledge to Peter

Another example is found in Acts chapter 10. Peter was in the town of Joppa.

ACTS 10:9-19
9 . . . Peter went up upon the housetop to pray about the sixth hour [about noon]:
10 And he became very hungry, and would have eaten: but while they made ready, he fell into a trance,
11 And saw heaven opened, and a certain vessel descending unto him, as it had been a great sheet knit at the four corners, and let down to the earth:
12 Wherein were all manner of fourfooted beasts of the earth, and wild beasts, and creeping things, and fowls of the air.
13 And there came a voice to him, Rise, Peter; kill, and eat.
14 But Peter said, Not so, Lord; for I have never eaten any thing that is common or unclean.
15 And the voice spake unto him again the second time, What God hath cleansed, that call not thou common.
16 This was done thrice: and the vessel was received up again into heaven.
17 Now while Peter doubted in himself what this vision which he had seen should mean, behold, the men which were sent from Cornelius had made inquiry for Simon's house, and stood before the gate,
18 And called, and asked whether Simon, which was surnamed Peter, were lodged there.
19 While Peter thought on the vision, THE SPIRIT SAID UNTO HIM, BEHOLD, THREE MEN SEEK THEE.

Peter received a supernatural revelation — a word of knowledge: "*. . . Behold, three men seek thee*" (Acts 10:19). Peter did not know there were three men who were seeking him (v. 19). He had fallen into a trance and had seen the vision of the sheet descending out of heaven.

While Peter was thinking about what that vision meant, the Holy Spirit told him that three men were seeking him. The men were already standing at the gate. Peter hadn't seen these men. He had no way of knowing they were there except by the Spirit of God.

Modern Examples of the Word of Knowledge

This manifestation of the Spirit isn't just for the Early Church, but it is for us today. Many years ago, a Spirit-filled Baptist brother who was the president of his local chapter of the Full Gospel Businessmen's Fellowship and one of the executives for the company he worked for, told me of an experience he had along this line.

He related, "I passed by a large Roman Catholic Church in my automobile and something seemed to say to me to stop. I pulled into the church parking lot, stopped, and sat there praying for a little while. Then that something seemed to tell me that the priest would be praying in his office in the rectory and that I should go in, lay hands on him, and he would be filled with the Holy Ghost.

"I hesitated," the Baptist brother said. "I didn't want to make a fool of myself. I sat there and prayed a little while longer. Then I decided it wouldn't hurt just to go see if I could find him and see if God was really leading me."

Too many times folks get things messed up because they get ahead of God when He speaks to them instead of waiting and following Him softly and letting Him open the door.

The Baptist brother continued, "I finally found my way in and knocked on the door of the study. Someone invited me to come in. I opened the door to see a man sitting in a chair in front of a desk with some books opened in front of him. As I entered, the priest got up and greeted me and we introduced ourselves."

The Baptist brother said, "When the priest heard that I was the president of the local Full Gospel

Businessmen's chapter, he immediately said, 'Praise the Lord! I was just reading about what God is doing these days by the moving of His Spirit! I was reading about this baptism of the Holy Ghost and speaking in tongues, and the Lord just witnessed to my spirit that this is what I need.'"

The priest said to the Baptist man, "I am conscious of my own spiritual lack. Only ten minutes ago, I bowed my head on my desk and said, 'Dear Lord, I don't know any Full Gospel people. I don't know anyone in this town who has had this experience. Send somebody by to pray with me.' And here you are!"

That priest got down on his knees and I laid hands on him and he began speaking in tongues almost instantly, lifting both hands to heaven. Then the priest got up and hugged me because he was so grateful.

It was the word of knowledge in manifestation that revealed to this Baptist brother that there was a priest in that particular church who was praying to receive the Holy Spirit.

Word of Knowledge Used To Bless Others

I heard of a similar experience which happened to a group of women who would meet at a church to have a Bible lesson and then would go out and witness to people. They were more or less going in their own strength and were not accomplishing very much. They had been knocking on doors for a couple of weeks and talking to people, but they hadn't won anyone to the Lord.

One morning the pastor's wife suggested that they change their methods. Instead of reading something from the Bible, praying a little, and going out, she suggested they read the Bible and stay there to pray — maybe for an hour, maybe longer — until they definitely felt led to go out. "I believe we will get more done if we are simply led by the Spirit," she told them.

The next morning the women had been praying about an hour when the pastor's wife had a vision in which she saw a certain apartment house and felt impressed to go there. She took one of the women with her, and when they arrived at the apartment and knocked on the door, someone inside said, "Come in." They pushed open the door and saw a woman lying on a bed in the corner.

When the sick woman saw them, she started rejoicing and said, "I recognized you the minute you came in the door. I was praying at six o'clock this morning and in a vision I saw you come in and lay hands on me, and I was healed." The two women then laid hands on the sick woman and prayed for her in the Name of Jesus, and she was healed.

By natural knowledge the pastor's wife couldn't have known that woman was sick and that she was praying for healing; she didn't even know her. But while the pastor's wife was praying in the Spirit, the Holy Ghost gave her a word of knowledge. Now God knew where everyone was who was sick at that time, but He didn't tell the pastor's wife about every one of them; He just sent her to one. He gave her a word of knowledge in the form of a vision.

Sometimes the word of knowledge comes by *an inward revelation*. The word of knowledge can also come by an audible Voice, by the Spirit of God speaking to you. Also, the gifts of the Spirit often operate together. We just separate them in order to define them.

For example, as I said before, the word of knowledge may come through tongues and interpretation of tongues, or through the gift of prophecy. Or an angel might come to deliver a word of knowledge. A word of knowledge can also be accompanied by a word of wisdom. God has many means of doing things, including manifesting the word of knowledge in various ways.

These examples also show us that what God did in Bible times, He is still doing in our modern times. It is amazing what is happening in the earth today. God is visiting hungry hearts everywhere. He is

Questions for Study

1. Who will spiritual gifts exalt?

   _____

   _____

2. If someone is speaking by the right spirit — by the Holy Spirit — then what he *says* will exalt the _____.

3. What are the two lines of thought on the passage of Scripture in First Corinthians 12:4-6?

   _____

   _____

4. What are the three revelations gifts?

   _____

   _____

5. What are the three power gifts?

   _____

   _____

6. What are the three utterance or inspirational gifts?

   _____

   _____

7. What does the simple gift of prophecy bring (1 Cor. 14:3)?

   _____

   _____

8. Of the three gifts of revelation, which is the best gift? Why?

   _____

   _____

9. Of the three gifts of power, which is the best gift? Why?

   _____

   _____

10. Of the three gifts of utterance, which is the best gift? Why?

   _____

   _____

Chapter 12

The Gift of the Word of Knowledge — Part 2

But the manifestation of the Spirit is given to every man to profit withal.

For to one is given by the Spirit the word of wisdom; to another THE WORD OF KNOWLEDGE by the same Spirit;

To another faith by the same Spirit; to another the gifts of healing by the same Spirit;

To another the working of miracles; to another prophecy; to another discerning of spirits; to another divers kinds of tongues; to another the interpretation of tongues:

But all these worketh that one and the selfsame Spirit, dividing to every man severally AS HE WILL.
— 1 Corinthians 12:7-11

The Epistle of First Corinthians is not a letter written to just one person; it is a letter written to the entire Church at Corinth, as well as to the Church — the Body of Christ — in our day.

Some folks have thought these verses applied to an individual person, but Paul was telling the entire Church to covet or desire spiritual gifts, because as an entire body of believers covets them, the Holy Spirit will divide the gifts of the Spirit to every man severally as *He* wills (1 Cor. 12:11).

As the Spirit Wills

Paul infers here that not every man is going to have all these gifts operating through him because he said, *"For to ONE* [not to everyone] *is given by the Spirit the word of wisdom; to ANOTHER the word of knowledge . . ."* (1 Cor. 12:8). Some people have taken this verse out of its setting and have thought the Bible was just telling individual people to desire all of these gifts, when actually Paul was telling the church as a group or body to covet them.

Lacking understanding, many people try to operate a gift of the Spirit themselves — without the unction of the Spirit of God. Perhaps a gift of the Spirit has manifested in their lives on occasion and they think, *Now I possess that gift and I can operate it at will.*

However, if people try to do that, they will invariably get into trouble, because they will be opening themselves up to satanic deception and to a wrong spirit. The gifts of the Holy Spirit operate as *the Holy Spirit* wills, not as *we* will (1 Cor. 12:11).

When you get away from the Word, then Satan can accommodate you, even with supernatural manifestations. Remember, the Holy Spirit operates in line with the Word of God, and the Word says His gifts operate as *He* wills.

If an entire local body of believers will covet the gifts of the Spirit, the Holy Spirit will divide to every man severally as He wills — not as I will, not as you will, but as *the Spirit* wills.

The Word of Knowledge Manifested in Different Ways

The gifts of the Spirit aren't just manifested in a public assembly, however. As I mentioned previously, the word of knowledge will sometimes manifest through a vision, through a dream, through a message from an angel, or through the gift of prophecy.

The word of knowledge can also be manifested through interpretation of tongues. However, interpretation of tongues is usually not the vehicle through which the word of knowledge manifests in public assemblies, except perhaps through the *ministry gift* of diversities of tongues (1 Cor. 12:28).

The reason for that is the ministry gift of diversities of tongues is more closely related to the office of the prophet. The prophet's ministry will more consistently manifest the revelation gifts. Interpretation of tongues in the local body is usually the equivalent of simple prophecy (for edification, exhortation, and comfort) and contains no revelation in it.

The Word of Knowledge in the Old Testament

There were supernatural manifestations of the word of knowledge in the Old Testament as well as in the New Testament. In fact, all the gifts of the Spirit were in operation in the Old Testament except tongues and the interpretation of tongues. We will cover the reasons why these two gifts were not included when we study them in a later chapter.

We do find all the other gifts of the Spirit — the word of wisdom, the word of knowledge, special faith, gifts of healings, working of miracles, prophecy, and discerning of spirits — manifested in the Old Testament. These gifts of the Spirit were manifested in the New Testament first in the ministry of Jesus. Then after the Day of Pentecost, the gifts of the Spirit, with tongues and interpretation of tongues as well, began to be manifested through Spirit-filled believers.

Let's look at the gift of the word of knowledge and how it was manifested in the Old Testament.

The Word of Knowledge to
Samuel Regarding Saul's Donkeys

We find in the Old Testament how the gift of the word of knowledge was used to help recover lost property.

When Saul was out looking for his father's donkeys that had either strayed or were stolen, someone said to him, "Why don't you go ask Samuel? He would know where they are."

1 SAMUEL 9:3,5,6,15,16,19,20
3 And the asses of Kish Saul's father were lost. And Kish said to Saul his son, Take now one of the servants with thee, and arise, go seek the asses....
5 And when they were come to the land of Zuph, Saul said to his servant that was with him, Come, and let us return; lest my father leave caring for the asses, and take thought for us.
6 And he said unto him, Behold now, there is in this city a man of God, and he is an honourable man; all that he saith cometh surely to pass: now let us go thither; peradventure he can shew us our way that we should go....
15 Now the Lord had told Samuel in his ear a day before Saul came, saying,
16 To morrow about this time I will send thee a man out of the land of Benjamin, and thou shalt anoint him to be captain over my people Israel, that he may save my people out of the hand of the Philistines: for I have looked upon my people, because their cry is come unto me....
19 And Samuel answered Saul, and said, I am the seer: go up before me unto the high place; for ye shall eat with me today, and tomorrow I will let thee go, and will tell thee all that is in thine heart.
20 AND AS FOR THINE ASSES THAT WERE LOST THREE DAYS AGO, SET NOT THY MIND ON THEM; FOR THEY ARE FOUND. And on whom is all the desire of Israel? Is it not on thee, and on all thy father's house?

Of course, Samuel only knew what God revealed to him, because if Samuel knew everything, that would make him omniscient or all-knowing. Samuel had a word of knowledge for Saul. He said to Saul, "...The asses which thou wentest to seek are found: and, lo, thy father hath left the care of the asses, and sorroweth for you, saying, What shall I do for my son?" (1 Sam. 10:2).

The Word of Knowledge to Samuel Regarding Saul

The word of knowledge also operated in the Old Testament to discover a man in hiding.

Although Samuel had already anointed Saul to be king over Israel, when it came time to reveal him as the king, Saul hid "...among the stuff..."

(1 Sam. 10:22). When the people couldn't find him, they inquired of the Lord instead of sending everyone to look for him. (Many times that is the quickest way to find an answer.)

The people knew that the Lord knew where Saul was. And the Lord told them exactly where Saul was. When they looked where God told them to look, they found Saul. That was the word of knowledge in operation. Remember, the word of knowledge reveals certain facts in the mind of God.

The Word of Knowledge
Manifested To Locate a Lost Daughter

Before we discuss other Old Testament examples of the word of knowledge in operation, let me give you a modern-day example of how God uses the word of knowledge to locate someone who is lost. That is scriptural, as we have seen in the examples of Samuel locating both Saul's donkeys and Saul himself when Saul was hiding.

I was teaching on the subject of the gifts of the Spirit in a church in 1943, when a couple asked me if the Lord could show them how to find their lost daughter.

This daughter had been involved with a gang when she was sixteen years old, and when she disappeared, the police thought the gang had killed her. Twenty-two years had gone by and in the meantime her mother and daddy, brothers, and sisters had all gotten saved and filled with the Holy Ghost.

The family, with the exception of her mother, had all given the girl up for dead. The mother kept saying that something on the inside of her told her the girl was still alive.

After I taught on the gift of the word of knowledge, the couple asked me, "Doesn't God know where our daughter is or whether or not she is alive? Would it be all right for us to pray about it?"

I said, "Surely," and while they were praying about it one day in the church, one of the women present had a vision. She saw a woman, now thirty-eight years of age, in a garage apartment with two children, a boy and a girl. She saw the woman chained and held captive in that apartment. Then in the vision she saw a letter come and she saw the girl's father going to the post office to get the letter. Later, the woman told the couple about her vision and said that within thirty days they would receive a letter saying their daughter was alive.

At the end of thirty days, the father went to the post office and got a letter from his daughter who had been missing and presumed dead for twenty-two years. She was in Houston, Texas. The letter began, "Dear Mom and Dad, I don't know whether you are alive or not, but if you are and answer this, I will come and see you. I am alive and well, and will explain everything to you when I see you."

The daughter was reunited with her parents and her entire family. One Sunday morning soon after that, the daughter came to our service, together with her two children and her parents. That morning she and her son were saved, and her daughter was saved later.

The woman had told her parents, "Twenty-two years have come and gone since I was taken away. The law was cracking down on the gang I was in and because I was just sixteen, the gang was afraid I would squeal on them."

This woman continued, "One of the boys knew this so he took me and ran away with me. We eventually got married, but I knew enough about him to send him to the electric chair, so he just kept me prisoner for a number of years. He would chain me before going to work every morning. I could get around the apartment, but I couldn't get out."

For twenty-two years these parents didn't know that God could really tell them about their daughter who was missing. They hadn't even thought to pray about it. But after hearing teaching along this line, they, along with others, were inspired to pray about it, and as they prayed God gave them a word of knowledge revealing that the woman was alive. God also gave them a word of wisdom (which we will discuss in the next chapter) indicating that they would hear from her in a short time.

The Word of Knowledge to Elijah

Then we see that the word of knowledge was manifested to enlighten and to encourage a discouraged servant.

Elijah had a great time up on the mountaintop when he prayed the fire down from heaven (1 Kings 18:37,38). But when someone told him, "Queen Jezebel said that about this time tomorrow she is going to take your head off your shoulders" (1 Kings 19:2), Elijah became worried and fearful.

He climbed under a Juniper tree and begged God to let him die. Later he said to God, ". . . *I have been very jealous for the Lord God of hosts: because the children of Israel have forsaken thy covenant, thrown down thine altars, and slain thy prophets with the* *sword; and I, even I only, am left; and they seek my life, to take it away*" (1 Kings 19:14). In other words, Elijah was saying, "Everyone is backslidden but me. Everyone has bowed their knee to Baal, and I am the only one left."

But God gave Elijah a word of knowledge that encouraged and enlightened him.

God said, "No, you aren't the only one left. I have seven thousand people reserved to Myself" (1 Kings 19:18).

Elijah couldn't have known that any other way. I am sure it encouraged him to know that he wasn't the only one left; that God had seven thousand who hadn't bowed their knees to Baal.

The Word of Knowledge To Elijah Regarding Gehazi

The word of knowledge was also used in the Old Testament to expose a hypocrite.

When Naaman was healed of leprosy and wanted to give the prophet Elisha changes of raiment and silver and gold, Elisha refused it. But his servant Gehazi ran after Naaman and lied to him.

2 KINGS 5:21-24
21 So Gehazi followed after Naaman. And when Naaman saw him running after him, he lighted down from the chariot to meet him, and said, Is all well?
22 And he said, All is well. My master hath sent me, saying, Behold, even now there be come to me from mount Ephraim two young men of the sons of the prophets: give them, I pray thee, a talent of silver, and two changes of garments.
23 And Naaman said, Be content, take two talents. And he urged him, and bound two talents of silver in two bags, with two changes of garments, and laid them upon two of his servants; and they bare them before him.
24 And when he came to the tower, he took them from their hand, and bestowed them in the house: and he let the men go, and they departed.

Naaman was so thrilled to be healed that he gave him twice the amount of money Gehazi asked for, and Gehazi hid it because he was a thief as well as a hypocrite and a liar.

When Elisha asked Gehazi where he had been, he said, ". . . *Thy servant went no whither*" (2 Kings 5:25).

Elisha said, ". . . *Went not mine heart* [or spirit] *with thee, when the man turned again from his chariot to meet thee? . . .*" (2 Kings 5:26).

How could Elisha be sitting in his own house and yet know what was going on several miles away? God revealed it to him through a word of knowledge. God gave Elisha a supernatural revelation of what had happened, and it exposed Gehazi, a hypocrite.

The Word of Knowledge to Elisha Regarding Syria

Also in the Old Testament, a word of knowledge was given to warn a king of the enemy's plan of destruction.

2 KINGS 6:8-12
8 Then the king of Syria warred against Israel, and took counsel with his servants, saying, In such and such a place shall be my camp.
9 And the man of God sent unto the king of Israel, saying, Beware that thou pass not such a place; for thither the Syrians are come down.
10 And the king of Israel sent to the place which the man of God told him and warned him of, and saved himself there, not once nor twice.
11 Therefore the heart of the king of Syria was sore troubled for this thing; and he called his servants, and said unto them, Will ye not shew me which of us is for the king of Israel?
12 And one of his servants said, None, my lord, O king: but Elisha, the prophet that is in Israel, telleth the king of Israel the words that thou speakest in thy bedchamber.

Every time an enemy would set up an ambushment against Israel, the prophet of God would tell Israel their plans. Finally this king got his servants together and said, "We must have a traitor among us who is giving us away" (2 Kings 6:11).

The servants replied, "No, it is not us. A prophet of God in Israel tells the king of Israel what you speak in your bedchamber." That was a supernatural revelation that God gave the prophet Elisha to warn him of the enemy's plan to harm Israel.

The prophet couldn't have known what the king had said in his bedchamber and what he was plotting because he wasn't there. No, the plans were revealed to him supernaturally by the word of knowledge, and it saved Israel from danger.

The Word of Knowledge in the New Testament

Now let's look at some other examples of the word of knowledge in operation in the New Testament. First of all, we see an example of the word of knowledge operating in Jesus' ministry when He ministered to the Samaritan woman in John chapter 4.

The Word of Knowledge to Jesus Regarding the Woman at the Well

In dealing with the woman at the well in Samaria recorded in John chapter 4, Jesus operated in the word of knowledge to convince a sinner of the need of a Savior.

JOHN 4:7,9,10,13-19,25,26
7 There cometh a woman of Samaria to draw water: Jesus saith unto her, Give me to drink. . . .
9 Then saith the woman of Samaria unto him, How is it that thou, being a Jew, askest drink of me, which am a woman of Samaria? for the Jews have no dealings with the Samaritans.
10 Jesus answered and said unto her, If thou knewest the gift of God, and who it is that saith to thee, Give me to drink; thou wouldest have asked of him, and he would have given thee living water. . . .
13 Jesus answered and said unto her, Whosoever drinketh of this water shall thirst again:
14 But whosoever drinketh of the water that I shall give him shall never thirst; but the water that I shall give him shall be in him a well of water springing up into everlasting life.
15 The woman saith unto him, Sir, give me this water, that I thirst not, neither come hither to draw.
16 Jesus saith unto her, Go, call thy husband, and come hither.
17 The woman answered and said, I have no husband. Jesus said unto her, Thou hast well said, I have no husband:
18 FOR THOU HAST HAD FIVE HUSBANDS; AND HE WHOM THOU NOW HAST IS NOT THY HUSBAND: in that saidst thou truly.
19 The woman saith unto him, Sir, I perceive that thou art a prophet. . . .
25 The woman saith unto him, I know that Messias cometh, which is called Christ: when he is come, he will tell us all things.
26 Jesus saith unto her, I that speak unto thee am he.

Jesus asked this woman for water. She asked Jesus who He was and He replied, *". . . If thou knewest the gift of God, and who it is that saith to thee, Give me to drink; thou wouldest have asked of him, and he would have given thee living water"* (John 4:10).

Jesus said, *". . . the water that I shall give . . . shall be . . . a well of water springing up into everlasting life"* (John 4:14). This Samaritan woman wanted that water. "Give me this water, so I won't have to come here and draw," she said, thinking about the water in the well.

Then Jesus told her to go get her husband. When she said she didn't have a husband, He said, in effect, "You are right about that. You have had five husbands, and the man you are living with right now isn't your husband" (John 4:17,18). Jesus knew that by an inward revelation — a word of knowledge — and used this gift to bring this woman to salvation.

The Word of Knowledge to Peter Regarding Ananias and Sapphira

In the New Testament, the word of knowledge was also used to reveal corruption in the local church.

In Acts chapter 5, we read that Ananias and Sapphira had lied to the church and to the Holy Ghost.

ACTS 5:1-4
1   But a certain man named Ananias, with Sapphira his wife, sold a possession.
2   And kept back part of the price, his wife also being privy to it, and brought a certain part, and laid it at the apostles' feet.
3   But Peter said, Ananias, why hath Satan filled thine heart to lie to the Holy Ghost, AND TO KEEP BACK PART OF THE PRICE OF THE LAND?
4   Whiles it remained, was it not thine own? and after it was sold, was it not in thine own power? why hast thou conceived this thing in thine heart? thou hast not lied unto men, but unto God.

It would have been all right if Ananias and Sapphira had sold their property and given only half of the money to the church, but they lied about it. They kept back part of the money for themselves and said they were giving the entire profit from the sale of the land to the church.

As Ananias laid the money at the apostles' feet, Peter must have asked Ananias something such as, "Is this the price of the land?" When Ananias said that it was, Peter asked, "*. . . why hath Satan filled thine heart to lie to the Holy Ghost . . .*" (Acts 5:3).

The entire transaction was revealed to Peter through a word of knowledge. Ananias' wife Sapphira came in and the same thing happened. And both of them fell dead the same day.

My Experiences With the Word of Knowledge

I have had many experiences in my own ministry in which the Lord used me in the word of knowledge. A couple of weeks after I was baptized in the Holy Ghost, the gift of the word of knowledge began to operate through me.

The first manifestation occurred when I was dismissing a service one night. I closed my eyes to offer the benediction. As I did, a quick vision appeared before me.

I saw a person in that congregation who I knew by the Holy Spirit was a new convert. In the vision, I saw the people she had been with the night before and what she had done. She was less than a month old in the Lord and had been forced by two other people to do something that was wrong.

I knew by revelation — by the word of knowledge — that this woman felt that God didn't love her anymore because she had sinned. She had decided that once she left this service, she would never go to church again because she had failed.

This was a spiritual vision that came to me in a second of time. I spoke to the congregation in such a way that no one else would know what had happened, but that this woman would know that God loved her and was dealing with her.

Before I finished speaking, this woman ran to the altar crying. I knew she was saved, but she hadn't been filled with the Spirit. By the time her knees hit the floor, she received the Holy Ghost. She found out how much the Lord *did* love her!

Another instance in which the Holy Spirit spoke to me by the word of knowledge concerning a new convert, occurred in the last church I pastored. While I was shaving one morning, the Holy Spirit said to me, "I want you to go pray for So-and-so. He has sinned."

This new convert was a forty-three-year-old man, but he had just gotten saved two weeks before. He had lost his temper on the job and the Holy Spirit showed me that he had sinned and that now he was home in bed. He had gotten sick as a result of losing his temper. The Lord wanted me to go restore him.

Here was a man in need, and the Spirit of God knew all about it. No doubt there were other people in my congregation who were in need, but God didn't send me to minister to all of them. He sent me to minister to this man, and we did get him restored.

While I was ministering in a church in Lubbock, Texas, years ago, the Spirit of God moved upon me just as I finished my message. I suddenly found myself saying to quite a large fellow whom I had never seen before, "You — standing in the back next to the aisle. Step out into the aisle."

This man was quite tall and wore cowboy boots which made him even taller. He was as far back in the church as he could get. Without question or hesitation, he stepped into the aisle.

I heard myself say to him, "Before you came to church tonight you said to your wife. . . ," and I began to tell him exactly what he had said to her. He had not wanted to come to church. Before I finished speaking, he began to cry and sob. God revealed the secrets of his heart through the word of knowledge.

This man ran down the aisle and slid into the altar. He had never been saved in his life. His wife was saved, but he fought her about salvation and the things of God. However, as the secrets of his heart were manifested, he repented and was born again.

I would not have known what he had said to his wife just before they came to church any other way than by the Spirit of God. God used that supernatural manifestation of the Spirit to bring this man to Him.

I remember when we were pastoring our last church, my wife and I took our fifteen-year-old niece into our home to help her. My sister's home had been broken by divorce and she had to go to work to make a living. Her five children were left alone too much of the time, and as a result, this fifteen-year-old girl got into bad company. I had to get permission from the judge to get custody of her because she had gotten involved with a gang and was about to get into trouble with the law.

My niece wasn't a Christian, and she was stubborn and hardheaded. For example, when we would pray and read the Bible every morning with our children before they went to school, she would just stand by the door and watch.

I didn't try to force her to do anything; I just let her stand there if she wanted to. After a while she would sit down when we prayed, and later she even began to get on her knees and join with us as we prayed.

We laid down certain rules for her to follow. For example, she could date only on weekends, and she was always to tell us where she was going. I told her, "I am going to put confidence in you. But the minute you betray my confidence, these privileges are over."

She was taking a home economics class in school and once as an assignment, her class was to prepare a meal for the entire school board. One Tuesday evening she said, "We are supposed to meet at a friend's house tonight to discuss what we are going to do and how we are going to decorate the hall." I knew in my spirit that part of what she was saying was true and part of it wasn't true.

I said, "All right, but you must be home this evening at 10:00. Also, don't drive up in front of the parsonage with some boy and sit there with him in the car. The living room is open and you can come inside and sit with him, but don't sit outside in the car."

Ten o'clock came that night and she wasn't home. I went to bed and was lying there meditating with my eyes closed, when suddenly I had a vision. I saw my niece over at her girlfriend's house. I saw her dancing with other teenagers; in fact, she was teaching them some new dance steps. Then at about 11:00 in the evening, my niece and a boy drove up in a car and stopped the car in front of the house. My niece sat out in the car until 11:30 that night before she finally came in.

I didn't say anything to her that night. Neither did I mention it the next morning at the breakfast table. I didn't say a word about it until Friday when she said, "I'm going to run down to the drugstore with a young man to get something to drink."

"No," I said, "you aren't going anywhere. You are grounded for thirty days. You are not to go anywhere except to school and church."

"Well, I would like to know why," she retorted.

I said, "I told you if you didn't betray my confidence, I would put more trust in you. However, you did betray my confidence. I told you to be home at 10:00 last Tuesday night and you didn't come in until 11:30."

"Well, we were late getting our plans made," she said.

I said, "You sat out in front of the parsonage for thirty minutes. Besides that, you were over there teaching those young folks new dance steps."

"Who told on me?" she asked.

"The Holy Ghost told me. I was lying in bed with my eyes closed when suddenly in a vision, I was over at your girlfriend's house. I will tell you exactly how the furniture was arranged."

As I told her how it was arranged, her eyes got big and she began to stammer and stutter. I said, "The Lord didn't lie on you, did He?"

"No," she said, "He didn't lie. But they didn't know some of these new steps and I just thought I would show them."

I said, "But you have betrayed my confidence, so for thirty days you won't go anywhere except to school and to church." Before the thirty days were ended, she was saved and baptized with the Holy Ghost, and she hasn't been in trouble since then.

The Word of Knowledge as an Aid to Prayer

One of the greatest areas where the word of knowledge can be used is as a mighty aid in effectual prayer, either for God's servants in distress or for those in need of spiritual help.

I once read of a minister and his wife who took a teenage boy into their home after their own daughter was grown and had become a missionary. They wanted to help this boy because he had no parents. They got custody of the boy through the judge because he had been in some trouble and had become a ward of the court.

The boy got saved and was filled with the Holy Spirit, and he did all right in his Christian walk for a while. After he finished high school, however, he had a tendency to fall back into some of his old ways, and this caused great grief and concern to the minister and his wife.

One day the boy went to look for a job. The pastor's wife was at home washing dishes when suddenly she felt compelled to pray. She didn't know what it was all about, but she stopped right in the middle of her work and began to pray fervently.

While praying in the Spirit, this mother had a vision and saw the young man downtown and he was about to go into a pool hall. In those days pool halls were dark dives. She was concerned and prayed earnestly for him.

Then in the vision, she saw him as he got about three feet inside the door. Suddenly he stood up straight, turned around, walked back out the door, and continued walking down the street. Then the vision ended. She began to sing and rejoice in the Spirit because she knew she had won a victory. Then she got up from praying and went back to finish her dishes.

That afternoon the boy came in, kissed her on the cheek, and said, "Well, Mom, I won a great victory today, and besides that I got a job."

She said to him, "I'll tell you what victory it is that you won today." And she told him how he had started to go in the pool hall and how he stepped three feet inside, then turned around and went back out.

He said, "That is exactly what happened!" That was a supernatural revelation of the word of knowledge and it was a mighty aid in prayer. This mother wouldn't have known those details except by the Spirit of God.

We all need the gifts of the Spirit in operation in every area of our lives. Parents of teenagers especially need the Holy Spirit's guidance and the operation of the gifts of the Spirit in these troubled times.

The word of knowledge can also be used to reveal sickness and the presence of an evil spirit. For instance, in my own ministry I would sometimes know by a word of knowledge that an evil spirit was oppressing the body of someone who was sick. (Of course, if the person I was ministering to was a believer, the evil spirit would not be in the person's spirit; it would only be in his *body*.) I would speak to the spirit and command it to leave in Jesus' Name and the person would be healed.

A Mentally Ill Person Set Free By the Word of Knowledge

Many times an evil spirit is involved in cases of mental illness, although this is not always true. A person can be sick mentally just as he can be sick physically.

Now every time a person has a stomachache, for example, that doesn't mean an evil spirit is oppressing him or that a demon is present in his body. There could be any number of natural reasons why a particular physical ailment exists. But on the other hand, an evil spirit could also be present and could be enforcing the sickness or disease. The same is true with mental illness.

The first experience I ever had along this line occurred while my wife and I were pastoring a church in Texas. A woman brought her sister home on a furlough from a mental asylum. The doctor had told the woman that her sister would never be right in her mind and that she would always need institutional care.

This mentally ill woman had been violently insane. She had tried to kill herself and others, and for more than two years she had been locked away in a padded cell. As a result of having no exposure to sunshine and very little exercise, her general health had deteriorated.

The doctors said they didn't believe she would ever be violent again but that she would always need institutional care. They allowed her sister to take her home on a two-week furlough so she could walk in the sunshine and get some exercise.

However, if the sunshine, exercise, and change of environment didn't improve her health, the doctors said she wouldn't live much longer. She had wasted away to almost nothing.

Her sister brought her over to the parsonage, and as we were praying, the Spirit of God told me to go and stand in front of her and say, "Come out, thou unclean spirit in the Name of Jesus."

I hadn't done anything like that before in my life. For several years I had been acquainted with this area of the supernatural in praying for folks for healing. But operating in the gifts of the Spirit in this area was new to me, and I was reluctant. I wanted to be sure the Lord was talking to me, and yet I sensed He was.

After some persuasion I stood in front of the woman and said, "Come out, thou unclean spirit in the Name of Jesus." You see, it was revealed to me that her trouble was caused by an unclean spirit.

This revelation came by a word of knowledge, not the discerning of spirits, because I didn't *see* any spirit (we'll discuss the gift of discerning of spirits in Chapter 14).

But the Holy Spirit did give me *knowledge* of the presence of an evil spirit causing the insanity. No matter how the presence of an evil spirit is revealed in another person, it still takes faith to deal with it, and many times the gift of faith will be in operation.

For instance, when I said, "Come out, thou unclean spirit in the Name of Jesus," there was no visible manifestation. As far as I could see, there was no change in the way the woman looked or behaved. Her eyes didn't look any different; she was just as she had been. Yet I knew that the command of faith was spoken and that the woman was delivered.

Forty-eight hours later this woman's sister called, saying, "Brother Hagin, pray! My sister is having a terrible attack like she did when she first lost her mind."

That news didn't bother me a bit because on the inside of me there was a supernatural faith or knowing that sustained me which was beyond me from a natural standpoint. It was more than ordinary faith — it was the gift of faith in operation. We'll discuss the gift of faith in chapter 15.

Casually, I said to her, "Don't worry. I spoke the word of faith and it *has* to be. The devil knows he has to go. Have you ever read in the Bible where Jesus told an evil spirit to leave a person, and sometimes before the evil spirit would leave, he would throw the person down and tear him [Mark 1:26]? The devil knows he has to go. When that attack is over, that evil spirit will be gone and your sister will never have another attack. She will be all right."

Sure enough, when that attack was over, that woman's mind was clear. They had to take her back to the institution because she was still a ward of the asylum, but the psychiatrist examined her and dismissed her. He pronounced her well. That was many years ago, and we had contact with her after that and she was still well.

This was a manifestation of the word of knowledge and the gift of faith operating together to set this woman free.

Remember, the revelation that the word of knowledge brings is *never* future tense — it's present or past tense. The word of wisdom, on the other hand, reveals plans and purposes concerning the future.

By the manifestation of the gift of the word of knowledge, the Church can be purified, the distressed comforted, the saints gladdened, lost property recovered, the enemy's plans defeated, and the Lord Jesus Christ glorified.

Questions for Study

1. To whom was the Epistle of First Corinthians written?

   _____

   _____

2. Why was Paul telling the entire Church to covet or desire spiritual gifts?

   _____

   _____

3. What does the Holy Spirit operate in line with?

   _____

   _____

4. How will the word of knowledge sometimes be manifest?

   _____

   _____

5. List two Old Testament examples of how the gift of the word of knowledge was manifested.

   _____

   _____

6. List two examples of the word of knowledge in the New Testament.

   _____

   _____

7. What is one of the greatest areas where the word of knowledge can be used?

   _____

   _____

8. What can the word of knowledge also be used to reveal?

   _____

   _____

9. The revelation that the word of knowledge brings is _never_ future tense. What tense is it?

   _____

   _____

10. What are six things that can happen by the manifestation of the gift of the word of knowledge?

   _____

   _____

Chapter 13

The Gift of the Word of Wisdom

But the manifestation of the Spirit is given to every man to profit withal.

For to one is given by the Spirit THE WORD OF WISDOM; to another the word of knowledge by the same Spirit;

To another faith by the same Spirit; to another the gifts of healing by the same Spirit;

To another the working of miracles; to another prophecy; to another discerning of spirits; to another divers kinds of tongues; to another the interpretation of tongues:

But all these worketh that one and the selfsame Spirit, DIVIDING TO EVERY MAN SEVERALLY AS HE WILL.

— 1 Corinthians 12:7-11

In studying the nine gifts of the Spirit, we can see from the Scriptures that all of these gifts work according to *". . . that one and the selfsame Spirit, dividing to every man severally as he will"* (1 Cor. 12:11).

The Holy Spirit Distributes Spiritual Gifts as He Wills

Let me emphasize again that as a church — a local body of believers — we are to desire that these gifts be made manifest among us, and we are to leave it up to the Holy Spirit to use whomever He wills. He will not use everyone the same way.

The Bible plainly states that the Holy Spirit divides the manifestation of the gifts of the Spirit to every man severally as He wills. Someone may want to be used in a certain gift; however, this may not be what God wills for him. We must stay open to God and let His will be done, even in the area of spiritual gifts. We get into trouble many times by wanting to do something ourselves and to have what we want instead of what God wants.

For example, not everyone will have all of these manifestations of the gifts of the Spirit in his life for the simple reason that the Bible says, *"For to ONE is given by the Spirit the word of wisdom; to ANOTHER the word of knowledge by the same Spirit"* (1 Cor. 12:8). It is quite obvious, then, that all the gifts aren't given to everyone.

As the Body of Christ, let us desire these manifestations and then let the Holy Spirit manifest Himself in our midst as *He* wills. That way we will be scripturally based. Some of our wrong thinking keeps us from the best that God has for us, so let's stay with the Word.

The Gift of the Word of Wisdom

Regarding the scripture, *". . . to one is given by the Spirit the word of wisdom; to another the word of knowledge by the same Spirit"* (1 Cor. 12:8), people sometimes call these the *gift* of wisdom or the *gift* of knowledge. That is not correct, however. We must call spiritual gifts what the Bible calls them or we will become confused.

For example, if you called a dog a cat, people would say you were confused. The gift of the word of knowledge is not the gift of knowledge, and the gift of the word of wisdom is not the gift of wisdom any more than a dog is a cat.

First Corinthians 12:8 is not talking about natural wisdom and knowledge in the general sense. It is talking about just what it says — the *word* of wisdom and the *word* of knowledge. And these gifts of the *word* of wisdom and the *word* of knowledge are given supernaturally. They are not natural gifts.

God has all knowledge. He knows everything, but He never reveals to anyone *everything* He knows. He just gives various people *a word*, a part, or a fragment of what He knows. A word of knowledge, for example, is just a fragmentary part of God's knowledge.

And so it is with the gift of the word of wisdom; it is not the *gift* of wisdom, it is the *word* of wisdom. God has all wisdom and all knowledge. But He only reveals a part of it to man — that which He wants him to know at a given time.

The Word of Wisdom Is Not Wisdom in the Affairs of Life

The word of wisdom is confused many times with simple wisdom in the affairs of life, but simple wisdom in the affairs of life is not a spiritual gift. In the beginning of Joshua's ministry, God told him that the key to his success would lie in meditating on the Word of God, and that is how Joshua was to obtain wisdom in the affairs of life.

JOSHUA 1:8
8 This book of the law shall not depart out of thy mouth; but thou shalt meditate therein day and night, that thou mayest observe to do according to all that is written therein: for then thou shalt make thy way prosperous, and then thou shalt have good success.

Another translation says, "Thou shalt make thyself prosperous and thou shalt be able to deal wisely in the affairs of life." There is a wisdom that is gained through the knowledge of God's Word, but that is not the supernatural manifestation of the gift of the word of wisdom.

Some people think that Solomon's wisdom was a manifestation of this word of wisdom, but it wasn't. Solomon's wisdom was given to him by God, just as we read in James 1:5: *"If any of you lack wisdom, let him ask of God, that giveth to all men liberally, and upbraideth not; and it shall be given him."*

God has promised that this wisdom, which I simply call general wisdom to deal in the affairs of life, is available to everyone who will ask for it. God will impart wisdom, but that is not a supernatural manifestation of the *word* of wisdom.

In writing to the Church, James said that if *any* lack wisdom, let him ask God for it (James 1:5). So we see that this general wisdom to deal wisely in the affairs of life will be given to anyone who asks for it.

The wisdom that James is talking about is the wisdom to deal wisely in the affairs of life and the wisdom to know how to conduct yourself as a Christian.

However, when God sees fit to reveal His own mind and purpose and plan to man in a supernatural way, He does so by this supernatural manifestation of the word of wisdom.

The supernatural manifestation of the *gift* of the word of wisdom is *not* given to everyone. Paul said in First Corinthians 12:8, "To *one* is given the word of wisdom." This verse says the manifestation of the word of wisdom is given to *one*; not to all, stating that spiritual gifts are divided severally as the Spirit wills. This infers that not everyone is going to have these manifestations.

The Word of Knowledge vs. the Word of Wisdom

I said that the word of knowledge is a supernatural revelation by the Spirit of God concerning certain facts in the mind of God — facts about people, places, or things in the past or present.

The word of wisdom is a supernatural revelation by the Spirit of God concerning the divine *purpose* and *plan* in the mind and will of God. The word of wisdom is the best gift because it is a revelation concerning the plans and the purposes in the mind of God.

The difference between the two gifts — the word of knowledge and the word of wisdom — is that the revelation the word of knowledge brings is always present tense or concerning something that has happened in the past. On the other hand, the word of wisdom always speaks of the future.

The Word of Knowledge and the Word of Wisdom Can Operate Together

We divide the two gifts of the word of knowledge and the word of wisdom and deal with them singularly. However, as I mentioned, very often spiritual gifts operate together.

We see these two gifts of the Holy Spirit — the word of knowledge and the word of wisdom — in operation throughout the Old Testament as well as in the New Testament.

In particular, we can see how the word of wisdom and the word of knowledge flowed together as the prophets prophesied. The Old Testament prophets often operated in these gifts along with the gift of prophecy.

The Old Testament prophets not only prophesied about the present, which is the word of knowledge in operation, but they also prophesied about things in the future, which is the word of wisdom in operation. And their prophecies foretold of events in the near future as well as events in the distant future, including the New Covenant and the coming Messiah.

Prophecy Can Be a Vehicle Through Which Other Gifts Can Flow

The prophet of the Old Testament had to have the word of wisdom in manifestation in his ministry to be able to stand in the office of the prophet because he made predictions concerning the future, and the simple gift of prophecy does not include with it the element of predicting or foreseeing into the future. The prediction the Old Testament prophet gave, even though it came by prophecy, was actually a word of wisdom in operation.

For example, you may *ride* in an automobile, but that doesn't make *you* an automobile. In other words, sometimes a word of wisdom is *conveyed* through the vehicle of prophecy, but it really isn't prophecy in and of itself. It is a word of wisdom. In other words, prophecy can just be the *vehicle* through which the word of wisdom comes.

The simple gift of prophecy as listed in First Corinthians 14:3 is given for ". . . *edification, and exhortation, and comfort."* There is no element of prediction or foretelling in the simple gift of prophecy whatsoever. Therefore, you can tell when an utterance is no longer just the simple gift of prophecy in operation because it will include some *revelation* in it.

When these elements of prediction and foretelling are in operation in one who is in the ministry (particularly in the office of the prophet), although the prediction may come by prophecy, it is really a word of wisdom in manifestation. This is particularly true if the prediction comes through a minister who stands in the office of the prophet. Prophecy, then, is just the vehicle through which the word of wisdom comes.

A word of wisdom may be manifested through the vehicle of prophecy in any Spirit-filled believer's life in his own *private* prayer life, as the Spirit wills, as the believer prays out the plan of God for his own life (John 16:13,14). We will discuss this in greater detail in Chapter 18. However, that is not to say that the word of wisdom will be manifested in the believer's life in *public* ministry through prophecy.

In public ministry, the word of wisdom or any of the revelation gifts coming through the vehicle of prophecy, especially on more of a continual basis, will normally come through the office of the prophet. Revelation gifts can also come through those who are called to the fivefold ministry, but will more frequently manifest in the office of the prophet.

If a person is just used in the simple gift of prophecy but does not have these revelation gifts in operation, then his prophesying is the simple gift of prophecy in demonstration. And it is used to bring edification, exhortation, and comfort — not revelation.

Therefore, the word of wisdom can come through the vocal gift of an utterance — through prophecy or through tongues and interpretation. The word of wisdom can also come through a vision or by a dream. For instance, in the Old Testament, Joseph received a word of wisdom through a dream which revealed to him God's plans and purposes for Joseph's future.

Moses received the revelation of the Law by an audible Voice as God gave him the Law. The Law concerned God's purpose for Israel; therefore, this was the word of wisdom in demonstration.

Also, the prophets of the Old Testament who prophesied concerning Israel's future — even things that are yet to be fulfilled — did so by the word of wisdom. The Old Testament prophets prophesied it, but it was a word of wisdom that was actually manifested because it foretold future events.

The Word of Knowledge and the Word of Wisdom Operating Together in the New Testament

John on the Isle of Patmos

An example in the New Testament of the gifts of the word of knowledge and the word of wisdom operating together is found in the Book of Revelation.

As we pointed out in the previous lesson, when the Lord spoke to the Apostle John on the Isle of Patmos, it was in the form of a vision. Jesus appeared to him in this vision and told him about the present condition of the seven churches in Asia Minor. The condition of those seven churches was a manifestation of the word of knowledge.

The present condition of these churches was revealed to John through a word of knowledge in a vision. Then the Lord went on to give John a word of wisdom. The Lord told each one of the churches what to do in the future, according to His plans and purposes for them.

Ananias

We also studied about a man named Ananias, as recorded in Acts chapter 9.

ACTS 9:10-16
10 And there was a certain disciple at Damascus, named Ananias; and to him said the Lord in a vision, Ananias. And he said, Behold, I am here, Lord.
11 And the Lord said unto him, ARISE, AND GO INTO THE STREET WHICH IS CALLED STRAIGHT, and ENQUIRE IN THE HOUSE OF JUDAS FOR ONE CALLED SAUL OF TARSUS: for, behold, HE PRAYETH,
12 AND HATH SEEN IN A VISION A MAN NAMED ANANIAS COMING IN, AND PUTTING HIS HAND ON HIM, THAT HE MIGHT RECEIVE HIS SIGHT.
13 Then Ananias answered, Lord, I have heard by many of this man, how much evil he hath done to thy saints at Jerusalem:
14 And here he hath authority from the chief priests to bind all that call on thy name.
15 But the Lord said unto him, Go thy way: FOR HE IS A CHOSEN VESSEL UNTO ME, TO BEAR MY NAME BEFORE THE GENTILES, AND KINGS, AND THE CHILDREN OF ISRAEL:
16 FOR I WILL SHEW HIM HOW GREAT THINGS HE MUST SUFFER FOR MY NAME'S SAKE.

Here we see the word of wisdom and the word of knowledge working together. The word of wisdom revealed to Ananias the plan and purpose of God, and the word of knowledge revealed specific facts to Ananias. It was God's plan for Ananias to go inquire for Saul. But the word of knowledge revealed exact facts as to where to go, even to the name of the street to go to, the very house to go to, and the person in the house to whom he was to speak (v. 11). The Lord even told Ananias that Saul was praying: ". . . for, behold, he [Saul] prayeth . . ." (v. 11). This was all knowledge of present-tense facts.

It was also revealed to Ananias that Saul *". . . hath seen in a vision a man named Ananias coming in, and putting his hand on him, that he might receive his sight"* (Acts 9:12). That was a revelation, given by a vision, to Ananias concerning *facts* about Saul; therefore, it was a word of knowledge.

Then Ananias said to Jesus in this vision, *". . . Lord, I have heard by many of this man, how much evil he hath done to thy saints at Jerusalem: And here he hath authority from the chief priests to bind all that call on thy name"* (Acts 9:13,14).

In response to that, the Lord spoke to Ananias again in the vision and gave him further revelation. This second revelation was a word of wisdom because it revealed God's plan and purpose: *"But the Lord said unto him, Go thy way: FOR HE IS A CHOSEN VESSEL UNTO ME, TO BEAR MY NAME BEFORE THE GENTILES, AND KINGS, AND THE CHILDREN OF ISRAEL"* (Acts 9:15).

That was a revelation concerning the plan and the purpose of God. It was a revelation of what Paul was eventually going to do for the Lord. It was a word of wisdom because it looked toward the future and revealed the *plans* and the *purposes* of God.

You see, God planned to use Paul in the future "to bear His Name before the Gentiles, and kings, and the children of Israel" (Acts 9:15). God said, *". . . he is a chosen vessel unto me . . ."* (Acts 9:15). That is a revelation of the future. It revealed God's plan and purpose for Paul in the future. We call that a word of wisdom.

In giving Ananias further revelation, God also said, *"For I will shew him how great things he must suffer for my name's sake"* (Acts 9:16). Now that didn't mean Paul was going to be sick, but that he would suffer much persecution and hardship in his circumstances and surroundings. And he did (2 Cor. 11:23-33). That also was a word of wisdom.

Paul was stoned and left for dead (Acts 14:19). Almost everywhere he went, there were people who became stirred up by Satan to oppose him. So we see that Paul did suffer many things for God. This aspect of Paul's future was a revelation given to Ananias, and it was a manifestation of this supernatural gift called the word of wisdom.

Philip

In Acts chapter 8 we see an example of the gifts of the word of knowledge and the word of wisdom operating together through a layman, Philip. At this time, Philip was still a deacon; he had been appointed to serve tables (Acts 6:2,3). God later moved him into the office of the evangelist (Acts 21:8).

A great persecution arose against the Early Church, and the Christians were scattered abroad. And as they were scattered, they went everywhere preaching the gospel. The preaching of the gospel wasn't limited to just the preachers of the day, however. The laity of the Early Church — believers — were also scattered abroad and preached the gospel.

The apostles were the only ministers the Early Church had at that time, and they remained in Jerusalem. But everywhere these laymen went, they told about Jesus: *"Then Philip went down to the city of Samaria, and preached Christ unto them"* (Acts 8:5).

After Philip's ministry to the Samaritans recorded in Acts 8:26, the Bible tells us an angel appeared to Philip to give him a message from the Lord.

Remember, we discussed how the word of knowledge and the word of wisdom can be manifested through various means, such as: the audible Voice of the Holy Spirit, a dream, a vision, a message from an angel, tongues and interpretation, or prophecy. God has various vehicles through which He manifests the gifts of the Spirit.

In Philip's case in Acts 8:26-29, the word of wisdom came through a message by an angel.

ACTS 8:26-29
26 And the angel of the Lord spake unto Philip, saying, ARISE, AND GO TOWARD THE SOUTH UNTO THE WAY THAT GOETH DOWN FROM JERUSALEM UNTO GAZA, WHICH IS DESERT.
27 And he arose and went: and, behold, a man of Ethiopia, an eunuch of great authority under Candace queen of the Ethiopians, who had the charge of all her treasure, and had come to Jerusalem for to worship,
28 Was returning, and sitting in his chariot read Esaias the prophet.
29 THEN THE SPIRIT SAID UNTO PHILIP, GO NEAR, AND JOIN THYSELF TO THIS CHARIOT.

The angel gave instructions regarding God's plan for Philip's immediate future. The angel said, "Go down to the desert" (v. 26). This was just a fragment or a "word" of the plan of God for Philip's life — a word of wisdom about something that was to transpire in the near future.

Philip obeyed and went to the desert, where he saw an Ethiopian eunuch. Then a word of knowledge was given to Philip by the Voice of the Holy Spirit: *". . . Go near, and join thyself to this chariot"* (v. 29).

God was giving Philip a present-tense fact — in this case, a present-tense instruction, to join the eunuch's chariot. This instruction was only a fragment or a "word" of knowledge from the mind of God to Philip at that time.

In this passage Philip was given both a word of wisdom through a message from an angel and a word of knowledge by the Voice of the Holy Spirit. Through the manifestation of two of the revelation gifts, God gave Philip instructions about what to do.

God gives instruction to each of us as believers, as He guides and leads us by the inward witness. But here Philip received instructions by spiritual gifts in operation through the manifestation of the word of wisdom and the word of knowledge.

However, it is important to note that even though the instructions were more spectacular than the inward witness or inward voice of the Holy Spirit that every believer has, Philip still had to obey God's instructions given through the word of knowledge *by faith*.

As I mentioned previously, these revelation gifts given supernaturally by God are only a *word* of knowledge and a *word* of wisdom. They are only a fragment of the knowledge and wisdom of God.

By way of illustration, if you needed legal advice concerning a particular situation in the present or in the future, you'd call your lawyer. But your lawyer wouldn't give you *all* the legal wisdom he has because you wouldn't need all of it. He would only give you a *word* or a fragment or a part of the legal wisdom he has that applies to your particular case. That would really be all you needed at the time.

Similarly, Philip only needed a part of God's wisdom and instruction, so God used an angel to give Philip a *word* of wisdom — a revelation concerning a part of God's plan and purpose for Philip's life — to go to the desert. And as a result, this Ethiopian received Jesus Christ as his Savior and Lord!

Old Testament Examples of the Word of Wisdom

Now let's look at some examples of how the gift of the word of wisdom was manifested in the Old Testament.

The Word of Wisdom to Noah

This gift of the word of wisdom was also used to warn people concerning future judgment or peril. Noah received a word of wisdom, for example, concerning peril and future judgment on the world through a flood, and he built the ark to save his household (Gen. 6:13-18).

If Noah could have gotten any of the other people to believe him, they could have been saved too. The

same was true concerning Lot and his family who were saved when God destroyed Sodom and Gomorrah (Gen. 19:29). And the word of wisdom was used to warn and to save a number of others in the Old Testament too.

The Word of Wisdom to Joseph

The manifestation of the word of wisdom was given in the Old Testament to reveal God's plan to those He was going to use in the ministry. For example, God spoke to Joseph through dreams concerning Joseph's own future.

Joseph's jealous brothers tried to dispose of Joseph, but God rescued him and fulfilled His plan for Joseph's life. Although Joseph was put in jail for a number of years and suffered numerous other hardships, he was finally made prime minister of the land of Egypt. And the time came when all of his brothers did bow down before him, as predicted in his dream (*see* Genesis chapters 37 through 50).

When I think about the story of Joseph, I think about the magnanimity of his soul. Under similar circumstances, how many others would have said to their brothers, "Well, what do you think about your baby brother now?" or "I told you so." But Joseph was not arrogant or overbearing.

Even as the second in authority under Pharoah, Joseph was a humble man with a noble and forgiving spirit; he didn't seek revenge. Nor did he even blame his brothers or scold them at all. He simply told them, "God just sent me before you to preserve the posterity of our people" (Gen. 45:5-8). Joseph knew about his calling and God's plan and purpose for his life through the word of wisdom.

The Word of Wisdom in the New Testament

We can also see examples of the word of wisdom in operation in the New Testament.

Agabus the Prophet

In the Book of Acts, we read that Agabus had prophesied and foretold that a drought and famine was coming (Acts 11:28). The people believed him because he was a man of integrity and had a proven ministry.

When Agabus prophesied about the drought, the people began immediately to make preparations in order to help the saints who lived where the drought was coming.

In Acts chapter 21 we read again about the prophet Agabus. Paul and his company (among whom was Luke, the writer of the Book of Acts) were at Philip's house.

ACTS 21:10,11
10 And as we tarried there many days, there came down from Judaea a certain prophet, named Agabus.
11 And when he was come unto us, he took Paul's girdle, and bound his own hands and feet, and said, THUS SAITH THE HOLY GHOST, So shall the Jews at Jerusalem bind the man that owneth this girdle, and shall deliver him into the hands of the Gentiles.

Notice that the Holy Spirit revealed something through Agabus. When any revelation is given by the unction of the Holy Spirit, it is always a word of wisdom, a word of knowledge, or discerning of spirits because these are the only three gifts of revelation. No others are listed in the Bible.

Note also that the spiritual gift demonstrated in Acts 21:11 was not a word of knowledge because it told of something that would take place in the future. The word of wisdom tells about something that is *going to happen*.

A *word* of knowledge has to do with the present and the past, but God in His divine wisdom knows all about the future, and He imparts certain facts about the future to man through the word of wisdom.

ACTS 21:12,13
12 And when we heard these things, both we, and they of that place, besought him not to go up to Jerusalem.
13 Then Paul answered, What mean ye to weep and to break mine heart? for I am ready not to be bound only, but also to die at Jerusalem for the name of the Lord Jesus.

After Paul made this statement, Luke recorded: *"And when he [Paul] would not be persuaded, we ceased, saying, The will of the Lord be done"* (Acts 21:14). What Agabus revealed by the Spirit of God was a revelation of the will of God that was to happen in the future; therefore, it was a word of wisdom. And it came to pass.

As I've said elsewhere, the word of wisdom may have been delivered through the vehicle of prophecy. Or when Agabus said, "Thus saith the Holy Ghost," he may just have been reporting what he had already received from the Lord. But whether it came through the vehicle of prophecy or not — it was a word of wisdom being delivered.

The Word of Wisdom to Paul

The word of wisdom is also given to assure of coming deliverance in the time of calamity.

Paul went aboard a ship when he was on his way to Rome to appeal his case to Caesar and a violent storm arose. He had a word of wisdom for those on the ship before they ever set sail. He said, ". . . *I perceive that this voyage will be with hurt and much damage . . ."* (Acts 27:10). But the south wind was blowing softly at the time, so they went ahead and set sail.

If those on the ship had listened to Paul, they would not have lost their ship and all their merchandise. Failing to heed his warning, however, they eventually had to throw everything overboard. Finally, all hope that they should be saved was gone. But in the midst of such calamity, Paul stood his ground because he had heard from heaven.

ACTS 27:23,24
23 . . . there stood by me this night the ANGEL OF GOD, whose I am, and whom I serve,
24 Saying, Fear not, Paul . . . GOD HATH GIVEN THEE ALL THEM THAT SAIL WITH THEE.

Paul said, "The ship will be lost, but if you listen to what I say and remain with the ship, you will not die."

You see, they were about to leave the ship, but because of the revelation Paul brought forth from the angel of God, everyone stayed with the ship, and not one of them perished. This wisdom concerning the future Paul had was by supernatural revelation. God revealed it to Paul, and Paul in turn revealed to those who were on the ship with him what was going to happen. Even though an angel delivered the message or revelation, it was a supernatural revelation from God.

Conditional Words of Wisdom

There were some incidents in the Old Testament when a prophet received a word from God which did not come to pass. Some manifestations of the word of wisdom are conditional, depending upon the person's obedience.

For example, in the case of Hezekiah the king, God told Isaiah to go and give him a word of wisdom concerning the future — the plan and purpose of God for Hezekiah's life under the present conditions. Isaiah was to tell Hezekiah, ". . . *Set thine house in order; for thou shalt die, and not live"* (2 Kings 20:1).

Isaiah delivered the message and then went his way. Hezekiah turned his face to the wall, repented of his wrongdoings, cried and prayed to God, and reminded God that he had walked before God wholeheartedly in times past. He told God that he had kept His commandments even though he had missed it in certain areas. And Hezekiah repented.

Then before Isaiah even got out of the courtyard, the word of the Lord came to Isaiah again, telling him to go back and give Hezekiah another word of wisdom. It was a word of wisdom because it still concerned the future. God said to Isaiah, "Tell Hezekiah I am going to give him fifteen more years" (2 Kings 20:5,6).

This first prophecy or word of wisdom, and even the second prophecy or word of wisdom which were given to Hezekiah, were conditional.

According to the first word of wisdom, under the existing conditions, Hezekiah was going to die. This promise was conditional, however. In other words, if Hezekiah had not repented, he would have died.

According to the second word of wisdom, Hezekiah would be spared and fifteen years would be added to his life. And it may have been that Hezekiah could have changed the latter part of this word of wisdom regarding the fifteen years that were to be added to him, just as he had changed the first part (Isa. 43:26).

Jonah

God spoke to the prophet Jonah and gave him a word of wisdom that Nineveh was going to be destroyed if the people of that great city did not repent and turn to God. This was a word of wisdom that Jonah received concerning the plans and purposes of God, and it was concerning a future event — the destruction of Nineveh.

Jonah didn't care whether Nineveh was destroyed or not, and as a result, he didn't want to go and warn the people. God dealt with him in the belly of a great fish, however, and he went and preached to the people of Nineveh, warning them of impending judgment if they didn't turn to God (Jonah 3:4).

The word Jonah gave to the Ninevites was conditional: if they repented, they would be spared. If they failed to repent, Nineveh would be destroyed. The people of Nineveh repented and judgment didn't fall on Nineveh in that generation, although it eventually did come (see the Book of Nahum).

The Word of Knowledge and the Word of Wisdom To Help a Fellow Minister

An example of a conditional word of wisdom was manifested through me years ago. The Lord through an audible Voice gave me both a word of knowledge and a word of wisdom. I had just been talking with a minister, and he had shown me his new building which would seat about four thousand people.

As I got in my car to leave, the Spirit of God said to me, "Go tell him that he is going to die unless he judges himself on three things: number one, his diet." This minister was greatly overweight and would practically eat anything he could get his hands on. You know, a person can actually "dig his own grave with his teeth."

"Number two," the Lord said, "he must judge himself on money." You see, preachers can become so money-minded that money can be first with them rather than God.

"Number three, he must judge himself on love." This minister needed to walk in love toward fellow ministers.

Here was an example of both the word of knowledge and the word of wisdom operating together. This word from the Lord spoke plainly about a present-tense condition that existed in this minister's life: the minister had not been judging himself. But it also included a word of wisdom: he would die unless he judged himself.

First Corinthians 11:30,31 says, *"For this cause many are weak and sickly among you, and many sleep. For if we would judge ourselves, we should not be judged."*

Paul inferred that those people who were physically weak and sickly and who died prematurely could have lived if they had judged themselves. Any of the things this minister was doing would *not* have kept him out of heaven, but they *would* rob him of his blessings down here.

This was a revelation concerning a present-tense fact: this minister should judge himself. It was also a revelation concerning the future. If he failed to judge himself, he was going to die. He didn't judge himself, and he died.

Thank God, we can and do hear from heaven through the manifestation of the gifts of the Spirit. But we need to take very seriously God's messages to us that come through these gifts.

How desperately we need supernatural manifestations of the gifts of the Holy Spirit today, such as the gift of the word of wisdom. As we learn to yield to God, His plans and purposes will be revealed to us through the word of wisdom as His Spirit wills.

Questions for Study

1. The Bible plainly states that the _____ _____ divides the manifestation of the gifts of the Spirit to every man severally as _____ wills.

2. God has all wisdom and all knowledge. How much of it does He reveal to man?

   _____

   _____

3. What is the word of wisdom many times confused with?

   _____

   _____

4. What kind of wisdom is James talking about in James 1:5?

   _____

   _____

5. What is the word of wisdom?

   _____

   _____

6. What can be a vehicle through which other gifts can flow?

   _____

   _____

7. Give two examples of the word of knowledge and the word of wisdom working together in the New Testament.

   _____

   _____

8. Give two Old Testament examples of the word of wisdom in operation.

   _____

   _____

9. Give two New Testament examples of the word of wisdom in operation.

   _____

   _____

10. Some manifestations of the word of wisdom are conditional. What do they depend upon?

    _____

    _____

Chapter 14

The Discerning of Spirits

But the manifestation of the Spirit is given to every man to profit withal.

For to one is given by the Spirit the word of wisdom; to another the word of knowledge by the same Spirit;

To another faith by the same Spirit; to another the gifts of healing by the same Spirit;

To another the working of miracles; to another prophecy; TO ANOTHER DISCERNING OF SPIRITS; to another divers kinds of tongues; to another the interpretation of tongues:

But all these worketh that one and the selfsame Spirit, dividing to every man severally as he will.

— 1 Corinthians 12:7-11

Our previous lessons have dealt with two of the three gifts that reveal something: the word of wisdom and the word of knowledge. In this lesson we will cover the third revelation gift: *the gift of discerning of spirits.*

The most important of the three revelation gifts, of course, is the word of wisdom. Listed in the order of their importance, the revelation gifts include: first, the word of wisdom. Second, the word of knowledge. And, third, the discerning of spirits.

Everything within the realm of knowledge, whether facts, events, purposes, motives, origins, or destinies — human, divine, or satanic; natural or supernatural; or past, present, or future — comes within the focal range of one or the other of these three revelation gifts.

The gifts can include in their comprehensive scope all that God knows. And there is nothing that God knows that may not be made known to man *as the Spirit wills* through the agency of one or more of these three revelation gifts.

The word of wisdom gives us the revelation of the plans and purposes in the mind of God. You could understand why that would be the greatest of all of these gifts. Naturally, it would be more important than anything else in all the world to have a revelation of the plans and purposes in the mind of God.

The word of knowledge gives us the revelation of facts that are now or that have been.

The discerning of spirits gives supernatural insight into the spirit world. "To discern" means *to perceive by seeing or hearing.* Therefore, discerning of spirits is the same as seeing or hearing in the realm of spirits.

The discerning of spirits actually has a more limited range of operation than the other two revelation gifts, the word of wisdom and the word of knowledge. That is because its revelation is limited to a single class of objects — spirits.

The revelation that the word of wisdom and the word of knowledge brings is broader and applies to people, places, and things. The discerning of spirits gives us supernatural insight only into the realm of *spirits.* Remember, the discerning of spirits is seeing or hearing into the spirit world. It also reveals the kind of spirit that is in operation behind a supernatural manifestation.

What the Discerning of Spirits Is *Not*

Someone has said that the best way to find out what something is, is to find out what it is *not.* So let's discuss what the discerning of spirits is not. It is not *discernment.* I've heard people say, "I believe I have the gift of discernment."

Actually, there is no such thing mentioned in the Bible as the gift of discernment. It is *the discerning of spirits.* Many times what people call the gift of discernment is really the gift of the word of knowledge in operation.

In other words, sometimes people know things by the Spirit of God and call it discernment. But that doesn't mean it is really discernment. It is actually the word of knowledge in operation.

Also, the discerning of spirits is not a kind of spiritual mind reading. And the discerning of spirits is not psychological insight, nor is it mental "penetration." It is *not* the power to discern the faults of others.

You will find that the power to discern faults in others is possessed not only by believers but by unbelievers as well. You don't even have to be a Christian to have that "gift"! As a matter of fact, the power to discover or discern the faults in others is absolutely forbidden in the Scriptures. *"Judge not, that ye be not judged"* (Matt. 7:1).

One purpose of the baptism in the Holy Ghost is *to destroy* this "gift" of discerning faults in others, which is nothing more than criticism, and then to replace it with the sweet gift of gentle forbearance. The gift of discerning of spirits is not faultfinding. If those who think they have the "gift" of faultfinding would just turn that "gift" on themselves for about fifteen seconds, they would never use it again.

Therefore, the discerning of spirits is not a spiritual gift to uncover human failures. Christians should walk in love, and the Bible says love covers a multitude of sins (1 Peter 4:8). Paul, writing to the Church at Ephesus, said, *"And be ye kind one to another, tenderhearted, forgiving one another, even as God for Christ's sake hath forgiven you"* (Eph. 4:32). Paul was talking here to Christians.

No, the discerning of spirits is not discerning of character or faults; it is not even the discerning of *people.* It is called the discerning of *spirits,* and it deals with spirits that exist in the spirit realm, whether they are divine, satanic, or human.

Discerning of Spirits Is Not Simply Discerning of Devils

Let me point out that this gift of discerning of spirits is *not* just the discerning of devils, nor is it the discerning of just evil spirits.

To say that the discerning of spirits has to do only with devils is misleading. This gift has to do with the entire class of spirits, including good spirits, bad spirits, and human spirits. It is supernatural insight into the realm of *spirits.* The discerning of evil spirits is included, of course, but too many times folks have thought that seeing demons and devils is all this gift encompasses and they have been misled.

Maintain Balance in Dealing With Demons

The way that some people teach about demons and casting out demons troubles me because it is not actually in line with the Word of God, and it binds people instead of delivering them.

For example, many things that people say are the devil, aren't the devil at all; they are works of the flesh. The works of the flesh are listed for us in Galatians 5:19-21.

GALATIANS 5:19-21
19 Now the works of the flesh are manifest, which are these; Adultery, fornication, uncleanness, lasciviousness,
20 Idolatry, witchcraft, hatred, variance, emulations, wrath, strife, seditions, heresies,
21 Envyings, murders, drunkenness, revellings, and such like. . . .

Envy is mentioned in this passage of Scripture as a work of the flesh. Yet when someone has a problem with envy, many times someone wants to cast the devil out of him! Hatred is also mentioned as one of the works of the flesh, but we wouldn't necessarily cast a demon of hatred out of a person. No, we have the flesh to deal with. And we are told in the Word

how to deal with it. We are to *crucify* or *mortify* the deeds of the flesh (Rom. 8:13; Col. 3:5).

We need to be careful about these things. We need to be scriptural and believe the truth of God's Word and practice it! We need to be careful to follow what the Word says if we are to receive lasting results. It is just like any other Bible doctrine. If you overemphasize any one Bible doctrine to the exclusion of others, you can go to the extreme and get out of balance. I always pray, "God, help me to stay balanced in my ministry."

For example, we know that water baptism is a scriptural doctrine. Yet there are people who have even distorted the doctrine of water baptism and have gotten out of balance. They tell people that if they are not baptized in water, they are not saved. Some will even tell people that water baptism is what saves them! Then there are others who will tell people that unless they are water baptized according to a certain formula or ritual, they are not saved.

I even heard one man on the radio say, "I don't care how many of you have been baptized in the Name of Jesus only, you are not saved unless I did it. I am the only one authorized to do it, and none of you will go to heaven unless I baptize you in water in the Name of Jesus."

That's ridiculous! But, you see, this man had gotten off into extremes. He wasn't following the Word and he got into error.

I believe in water baptism, but even if you take water baptism or any Bible doctrine for that matter to the extreme, you can certainly do more harm to people than good. I also believe in the reality of evil spirits, and I believe we need to know something about them and how to deal with them. But if you take it to the extreme, you can do more harm than good; you can begin to believe that everyone has a devil in them.

Some people become more devil conscious than they are God conscious. As a result, they give place to the devil and he defeats them in life. But Jesus said, *"And ye shall know the truth, and the truth shall make you free"* (John 8:32).

As I have already said, many things that happen which people are calling the devil are not the devil at all. Certainly, the devil may take advantage of a situation where the works of the flesh are being manifested. But if you will deal with the flesh, the devil won't have anything to work with.

If you will do what the Bible says, if you will *". . . present your bodies a living sacrifice, holy, acceptable unto God, which is your reasonable* [or spiritual] *service*" (Rom. 12:1) and "*Neither yield ye your members as instruments of unrighteousness unto sin . . .*" (Rom. 6:13), the devil won't be able to have any place in you.

It is certainly true that there are those who are bound by the enemy, and of course all bondage is of the devil, either directly or indirectly. That doesn't always mean there is a direct presence of an evil spirit, but an evil spirit could be enforcing the problem.

And at times when an evil spirit *is* the direct cause of a problem, a believer might see the evil spirit that is affecting the situation when the gift of discerning of spirits is in manifestation by the Holy Spirit. But as I said before, the discerning of spirits encompasses much more than just the discerning of evil spirits.

Discerning the Similitude of God

Also included within the scope of this gift is seeing the similitude of God. For example, Exodus 33 records an account of God allowing Moses to see into the realm of spirits to behold the similitude of God.

EXODUS 33:20-23
20 And he [the Lord] said, Thou canst not see my face: for there shall no man see me, and live.
21 And the Lord said, Behold, there is a place by me, and thou shalt stand upon a rock:
22 And it shall come to pass, while my glory passeth by, that I will put thee in a clift of the rock, and will cover thee with my hand while I pass by:
23 And I will take away mine hand, and thou shalt see my back parts: but my face shall not be seen.

Moses was seeing in the spirit realm. He was able to discern the similitude of God by the manifestation of this gift of the Spirit.

Another instance of a person seeing the similitude of God is found in Isaiah 6. The prophet Isaiah said, "*In the year that king Uzziah died I saw also the Lord sitting upon a throne, high and lifted up . . .*" (Isa. 6:1).

Throughout the Word of God we read about those who in vision form have been able to see the similitude of God through the gift of discerning of spirits. They didn't see God, but they saw *the similitude* of God. As He was revealed in vision form, they were seeing into the spirit world. That was a manifestation of discerning of spirits. So we see that the discerning of spirits isn't just seeing into the realm of evil spirits.

Discerning the Risen Christ

Through the discerning of spirits, or seeing into the spirit realm, one could also discern the risen Christ. No one has actually seen Jesus in His physical flesh and bone body (Luke 24:39) since His ascension and seating on High (Acts 1:9; Heb 1:3) because He is now seated on the right hand of the Father where He ever lives to make intercession for us (Heb. 7:25).

Therefore, since Jesus' ascension and seating on High, no one has ever seen Him except through the gift of discerning of spirits.

But through this supernatural gift of the discerning of spirits, some people have been able to see into the spirit realm and have seen the Risen Lord.

All such visions would be a manifestation of the gift of discerning of spirits. This gift of the discerning of spirits, however, might bring with it a word of wisdom or a word of knowledge. But the vision itself would be the discerning of spirits because the person would at that time be *seeing* into the spirit world.

Remember, the gift of the discerning of spirits is supernatural insight into the spirit world where there are divine spirits as well as evil spirits. Also, the discerning of spirits can be manifested to reveal the human spirit; that is, the good or evil tendencies of the human spirit. Discerning of spirits, then, deals with three kinds of classes of spirits: divine, satanic, and human.

So you see, discerning of spirits may be discerning the similitude of God, discerning the risen Christ, or even the discerning of the Holy Spirit.

Discerning the Holy Spirit

For instance, John, in his vision on the Isle of Patmos, saw the Holy Spirit as seven spirits before the throne of God (Rev. 4:5). That simply meant that in the spirit realm John was seeing these seven aspects of the Spirit of God.

The discerning of spirits can also reveal cherubim, seraphim, archangels, or a host of God's angels. It could reveal Satan and his legions. Discerning of spirits can reveal the power, whether good or evil, that may be enforcing a supernatural manifestation or influencing a type of behavior.

Discerning the Spirit Behind an Operation

Supernatural manifestations can come from different sources. In fact, many things that seem miraculous or supernatural to us actually do not come from God. We must remember that Satan is also a supernatural being. Too many times folks are ready to follow anything that is supernatural or spectacular, whether it is proven by the Scriptures to be of God or not.

It is good to have a genuine manifestation of the Spirit of God, but we must realize that all supernatural manifestations are not necessarily a demonstration of the Spirit of God. If the discerning of spirits is in operation, we can know the spirit behind a given manifestation or operation.

An example of this is found in Acts 16. Here Paul dealt with an evil spirit behind an operation. When the maiden who had the spirit of divination followed Paul and said, "*. . . These men are the servants of the most high God, which shew unto us the way of salvation*" (Acts 16:17), Paul finally turned to her and spoke directly to the spirit. He didn't deal with the woman at all.

It was probably the gift of discerning of spirits in operation because Paul spoke directly *to the spirit*; Paul was possibly talking to a spirit that he *saw*.

He spoke to the spirit and commanded it to come out of her. After that, the maiden couldn't tell fortunes any more. Paul dealt with the spirit involved, not the person.

The Inward Witness as Our Guide

On the other hand, without even having the discerning of spirits in manifestation, if we know the Word of God and if we are walking in the Spirit, we will have an inward witness if someone is operating by a wrong spirit. The Holy Spirit on the inside of us, in our spirits, will warn us if we are at all sensitive to Him.

I once knew a highly esteemed Bible teacher who was deceived by a preacher who was simply not right with God. Much of what the preacher was teaching was error and was not biblical. Unfortunately, this well-known Bible teacher also influenced others to believe in and follow this fellow's teaching.

Eventually, this Bible teacher began to see that some things about the preacher's doctrine weren't right. However, many times in such cases it is too late to rescue others because they've already been ensnared by the false teaching.

This Bible teacher finally went to the preacher and told him that some of the things he was preaching were not in the Bible. The preacher replied, "Brother, you won't get what I am teaching in that thing [referring to the Bible]. I am *beyond* that."

"Then you are too far out for me," said the Bible teacher and he broke his association with him. The Bible teacher was enlightened enough to get away from this false teacher, but unfortunately he had influenced others to believe this man and what this man was teaching.

One woman who had just been saved and who had recently converted from Buddhism said, "The first time I was in that preacher's meeting, the Spirit of God on the inside of me said, 'You get up and get out of here; that teaching is not right.'"

This new convert knew nothing about the Bible; she was just a few weeks old in the Lord. Yet, on the other hand, here was a well-known Bible teacher who had been in Full Gospel churches for thirty-five years and he was taken in by this preacher's false doctrine.

This is an example of how we can fail to follow that urging or witness on the inside of us which is the leading of the Holy Spirit. God communicates with our spirits, and our spirits know things our heads don't know. In the natural, this woman who was a new convert didn't know anything about this false teacher or whether or not what he was teaching was right because she was a baby Christian. She wasn't like some folks who think they know everything when they really don't. She was just depending on the Lord, and she had learned to depend on what she heard down on the inside of her spirit.

We don't need the discerning of spirits to know when something is out of order. We ought to know God's Word well enough for ourselves to know when something doesn't line up with the Word of God. And we ought to be led by the inward witness. "*For as many as are led by the Spirit of God, they are the sons of God*" (Rom. 8:14).

This verse implies that all the sons of God can be led by the Spirit of God. But the Scriptures certainly don't imply that all the children of God will have the gift of discerning of spirits operating in them because we read, "*For to ONE is given by the Spirit the word of wisdom; to another the word of knowledge* [or any gift of the Holy Spirit] *by the same spirit*" (1 Cor. 12:8).

That verse doesn't say or even imply that everyone would have these gifts in manifestation in their lives. But Romans 8:14 does imply that every believer can be led by the Holy Spirit. We need to distinguish the difference.

You see, we can have some facts regarding the spirit world revealed to us by the discerning of spirits. Other facts are revealed to our spirits by the inward witness of the Holy Spirit. He is our Guide. But the inward witness is not the same as seeing into the spirit world — the discerning of spirits.

The Word of Knowledge vs. the Discerning of Spirits

Another way that the Holy Spirit reveals facts to us about the realm of the spirit is through the gift of the word of knowledge. Howard Carter, who made a thirty-year study of the gifts of the Spirit, said that the word of knowledge gives one a revelation of anything that can be classified as existing or having existed. The fact of a spirit possessing a body could be revealed by the gift of the word of knowledge, but the person wouldn't have a *vision* of the spirit; he would not *discern* the evil spirit.

In other words, if you discerned a spirit, you would *see* the spirit, because the discerning of spirits is seeing into the spirit realm. If the word of knowledge is in operation, you may *know* that a spirit is present or is involved in a particular situation, but you wouldn't *see* the spirit. Remember, the word of knowledge is revelation by the Holy Spirit of certain facts in the mind of God.

The Spirit of God may impart a word of knowledge to us to let us know if someone is operating by another spirit and not by the Spirit of God. The Holy Spirit has done so with me.

Evil Spirit Revealed by the Word of Knowledge

In my own ministry, when praying for folks, I would sometimes know facts supernaturally before I had ever had any kind of a manifestation of discerning of spirits. I knew them by the gift of the word of knowledge. No one will know these things every time they are ministering to someone, because these manifestations are given as the Spirit wills.

One time a man was invited to the platform to speak for a few minutes in a church where I was conducting a meeting. I had heard that this man was not living right. Of course the Bible tells us that by their fruits we shall know them (Matt. 7:20).

As I sat on the platform while this man got up to say a few words to the congregation, I heard the Voice of the Holy Spirit say, "He has a familiar spirit." I looked behind me. I already knew that no one was sitting behind me; yet the Voice was so real I looked behind me. It was the Holy Spirit speaking to me.

Many folks thought this preacher operated in the word of knowledge because he could tell people many things about themselves. He could give them their names and addresses; he could tell them how much money they had in their purses or billfolds. He could even sometimes tell them what they had in their pockets.

But the Spirit of God said to me, "He has a familiar spirit." In the Old Testament God talks about familiar spirits and forbids the people of God to have anything to do with them. Familiar spirits are familiar with people and they can pass on information about one person to another.

Evil Spirit Revealed by Discerning of Spirits

The Lord appeared to me in a vision one time and said, "I am going to teach you about the devil, demons, and demon possession. From this night on what is known in My Word as the discerning of spirits will operate in your life when you are in the Spirit."

Of course, the vision itself — seeing Jesus — was a manifestation of the discerning of spirits because I *saw* Jesus. I was seeing into the realm of spirits. That's discerning of spirits.

After that visitation from the Lord, the first such manifestation occurred in a meeting in Tyler, Texas. The pastor told me about his niece who had cancer of the left lung. The doctors had wanted to operate on her, but she wouldn't submit to an operation. The malignancy had spread to her other lung as well, and then it was too late for an operation even if she had wanted one.

She was bedfast and had wasted away to nothing although she was being fed six times a day. They got her out of bed and brought her to church on Tuesday and Friday nights of the first week of meetings I was holding there. Tuesday and Friday were the healing meetings, and I prayed for her. They brought her again on Tuesday and Friday nights of the second week, and I prayed for her again.

On Tuesday night of the third week they brought her again, and she happened to be the first one in the prayer line. I laid hands on her and suddenly everyone and everything else in the room seemed to disappear. I was enveloped in a cloud and all I could see was myself and this young woman standing in a circle of light.

I was seeing into the realm of the spirit. I saw a demon or an evil spirit hanging on to her body over her left lung. I knew it was the cause of her physical condition and that it had to be dealt with. I commanded the demon to leave her in the Name of Jesus. In the realm of the spirit I saw this evil spirit and I heard him speak. No one else saw or heard anything.

This was a manifestation of the discerning of spirits, because I saw into the realm of spirits. When I commanded the demon to leave, he fell off of that woman's body and fell down on the floor. Then he just lay there and whimpered and whined like a whipped pup. He said, "I don't want to leave, but I know I have to if you tell me to."

I said, "Not only must you leave her body, but you must also leave these premises." He ran down the aisle and out the door of the church, and the woman was healed.

This woman went to the doctor the very next day and asked him to take X rays of her lungs. He said that wasn't necessary; they already had sufficient X rays of her lungs. "But something has happened to me, and I want you to take them again," she said.

They finally took the X rays, and they confirmed that something had indeed happened! "Your lungs have cleared up!" they said. "There's no more cancer!" The doctors wanted to run more tests, and after they did, they said her lungs were completely clear and all the other tests also proved negative.

The doctors asked her, "What happened to you?" When she told them how God had healed her, they said, "We don't know how it happened, but we know what has happened. The cancer was there, but now it is gone."

The doctors said they would give her a written affidavit that she had had cancer of the lungs, but that she no longer had it. These doctors were not against healing; doctors are in the healing business. And they are glad to see people delivered.

Three weeks later the pastor told me that his niece had gained sixteen pounds. That was many years ago, and in talking to this pastor years later, I found she was still well.

Howard Carter also said concerning this subject of a spirit being revealed through the word of knowledge versus the discerning of spirits:

> If one was informed about a spirit but had no vision of the spirit, he would not discern it. By the discerning of spirits we see beyond the sphere for which we have been created, since we are natural beings. It is only by the revelation of the Holy Spirit that we can perceive the beings that live in the spirit world. [1]

The realm of the spirit is very real, although we cannot perceive it with our natural senses. God has provided the gift of discerning of spirits to give the Church supernatural insight into this spiritual realm, as His Spirit wills.

------

[1] *Questions and Answers on Spiritual Gifts*, pp. 101,102.

Questions for Study

1. What does the discerning of spirits give supernatural insight into?

   _____

   _____

2. What does "to discern" mean?

   _____

   _____

3. Why does the discerning of spirits actually have a more limited range of operation than the other two revelation gifts?

   _____

   _____

4. Name five things that the discerning of spirits is _not_.

   _____

   _____

5. Many things that people say are the devil, aren't the devil at all. What are they?

   _____

   _____

6. How does the Word of God tell us to deal with the flesh?

   _____

   _____

7. Why has no one actually seen Jesus in His physical flesh and bone body since His ascension and seating on High?

   _____

   _____

8. Discerning of spirits deals with three classes of spirits: _____, _____, and _____.

9. What does Romans 8:14 imply?

   _____

   _____

10. Name another way that the Holy Spirit reveals facts to us about the realm of the spirit?

   _____

   _____

Chapter 15

The Gift of Faith

But the manifestation of the Spirit is given to every man to profit withal.

For to one is given by the Spirit the word of wisdom; to another the word of knowledge by the same Spirit;

TO ANOTHER FAITH by the same Spirit; to another the gifts of healing by the same Spirit;

To another the working of miracles; to another prophecy; to another discerning of spirits; to another divers kinds of tongues; to another the interpretation of tongues:

But all these worketh that one and the selfsame Spirit, dividing to every man severally as he will.
— 1 Corinthians 12:7-11

As I've mentioned in a previous lesson in this series, the nine manifestations or gifts of the Holy Spirit can be divided into three categories: Three spiritual gifts *reveal* something. Three spiritual gifts *do* something. And three spiritual gifts *say* something.

The three spiritual gifts that *reveal* something include: the word of wisdom, the word of knowledge, and the discerning of spirits.

The three spiritual gifts that *do* something, or the three power gifts as they are often called, include: the gift of faith, the gifts of healings, and the working of miracles.

The three inspirational gifts or vocal gifts — the spiritual gifts that *say* something include: the gift of prophecy, divers kinds of tongues, and the interpretation of tongues.

Gifts of the Spirit Are Supernatural

As I mentioned in previous lessons, all of the gifts of the Holy Spirit are supernatural; they are not natural. Every one of them is a supernatural manifestation of the Spirit of God.

There are Bible teachers who say that some of the gifts of the Spirit are natural and some of them are supernatural. But if one of them is supernatural, then all of them are supernatural. Every single one of the gifts of the Spirit listed in First Corinthians 12:8-10 is a supernatural manifestation of the Holy Spirit.

For example, speaking in tongues is supernatural, not natural. Speaking in your own language isn't supernatural because you were *taught* how to speak

that language. But you were never *taught* how to speak in tongues. Tongues — the supernatural utterance of the Holy Spirit — was divinely given when you received the baptism of the Holy Spirit.

It is true that in our own individual lives, the Spirit of God will lead and guide us in ways that are supernatural, because the Bible says we are led by the Spirit of God (Rom. 8:14). It is also true that everything God does is in a sense supernatural. But not everything God does would necessarily be a manifestation of the gifts of the Spirit in operation.

For example, in my own spirit I may have an inward witness to do or not to do something. And although that witness is supernatural, it is not a manifestation of one of these gifts. The inward witness is simply a matter of being led by the Holy Spirit, and every believer should be led by the Holy Spirit in their everyday Christian walk (Rom. 8:14).

I often receive guidance from God by an inward witness. Sometimes in praying for guidance, I am impressed in a certain direction. That doesn't mean I have a supernatural manifestation of a gift of the Spirit. I just have an inward impression or witness. That is the Holy Spirit leading and guiding me.

Sometimes when people have asked me to pray for them for direction, I have asked them, "What is your heart telling you?"

Very often they have laughed and said, "Well, I guess I really knew on the inside of me all the time what I ought to do."

This guidance by the inward witness is not a supernatural manifestation of a gift of the Spirit in operation; it is simply an example of being led by the Holy Spirit.

Wherever there is a supernatural manifestation that reveals something, that manifestation would be one of the revelation gifts in operation — the word of wisdom, the word of knowledge, or the discerning of spirits.

The Gift of Special Faith

In previous chapters, we covered the revelation gifts of the Holy Spirit: the word of wisdom, the word of knowledge, and the discerning of spirits.

Now let's study the three power gifts of the Holy Spirit: the gift of faith, the working of miracles, and the gifts of healings.

In this lesson, we will discuss the first of the power gifts: the gift of faith. *The Amplified Bible* reads, "To another (wonder-working), faith . . ." (1 Cor. 12:9). This gift of the Spirit is also called *special faith.*

The Gift of Special Faith Is Not the Same as Saving Faith

Every believer already has general faith or saving faith, which is also a gift. Ephesians 2:8 says, *"For by grace are ye saved through faith; and that not of yourselves: it is the gift of God."*

The faith that you are saved by is a gift of God, but it is not one of the nine gifts of the Spirit. Saving faith is given to you through hearing the Word, because the Bible says, *"So then faith* [saving faith] *cometh by hearing, and hearing by the word of God"* (Rom. 10:17).

The faith which we are talking about in this lesson — special faith — is something other than general faith or saving faith. It is a supernatural manifestation of the Holy Spirit whereby a believer is empowered with *special* faith, or wonder-working faith, and it is beyond simple saving faith.

The gift of faith is the greatest of the three power gifts. And this gift is miraculous just as the rest of the gifts of the Spirit are miraculous.

The gift of faith is a gift of the Spirit to the believer in order that he might *receive* miracles. The working of miracles, on the other hand, is a gift of the Spirit given to the believer that he might *work* miracles. One gift *receives*, the other *does* something.

Notice the Bible says, *"To another the WORKING of miracles . . ."* (1 Cor. 12:10). In other words, when you *receive* a miracle, you don't *work* the miracle. But when you *perform* a miracle by the unction of the Holy Ghost, you are *working* a miracle by this supernatural gift of the Spirit, the working of miracles.

These power gifts are very closely associated one with another and many times work together. The same is true of the revelation gifts; they also are closely related and work together as do the utterance gifts.

It is also important to note that all of the gifts of the Spirit operate by faith — by ordinary faith on the part of the believer through which the gift is being manifested. In other words, a person must step out in faith and yield to the promptings of the Holy Spirit. That's where simple *faith* is involved. This ordinary faith is the faith that comes by hearing God's Word. Therefore, the gifts of the Spirit do

not operate by the gift of faith, but they do operate by general or ordinary faith. Remember, the Bible says, *". . . If thou canst believe, all things are possible to him that believeth"* (Mark 9:23).

As we said, the gift of faith, one of the nine gifts of the Spirit, is separate and distinct from the simple gift of saving faith. The gift of faith — special faith — is also distinct from the faith that is a *fruit* of the Spirit (Gal. 5:22). We read about the fruit of the Spirit, one of which is faith, in Galatians chapter 5.

However, in the original Greek, the word "faith" in Galatians 5:22 could be translated *faithfulness.* The *fruit* of the Spirit are for *character*; the *gifts* of the Spirit are for *power*. Fruit is something that grows. Faith — or faithfulness — is a fruit that grows in the life of a Christian to establish him in godly spiritual character.

But the gift of faith is a special gift which is given supernaturally by the Spirit of God, as He wills. Those who operate in special faith, the gift of the Spirit, can believe God in such a way that *God* honors their word as His own, and miraculously brings to pass the desired result.

Thus, we learn that there are different kinds of faith. Saving faith brings one to salvation. Faith, or faithfulness, the fruit of the Spirit, comes after salvation. And the manifestation of the gift of special faith can come as a gift of the Spirit after one receives the baptism in the Holy Ghost. However, the gift of faith which is a gift of the Spirit, operates as *He* wills, not as we will.

Faith, like prayer, is something that is easily confused in the minds of some people. Many times we just put all kinds of faith in the same sack, so to speak, mix them up, and shake them all out together. But we must differentiate between saving faith, or the general faith that every believer has, and this special faith that God gives on certain occasions.

Referring to general or saving faith, I have heard people say, "Well, if God gives me faith I will have it, and if He doesn't I won't." They read the scripture, *"To another* [is given] *faith . . ."* (1 Cor. 12:9), and they think that is the way all faith works.

However, as we have already proven, this special faith, this gift of faith, is not the same saving faith or general faith which one needs in order to be saved. And special faith is not the faith needed for believing God to have your needs met according to His Word. The faith for believing God for your needs to be met comes by hearing the Word (Rom. 10:17), and *every* believer is given a measure of that kind of faith (Rom. 12:3).

Also, as I already pointed out, this gift of faith is not the fruit of faith that grows in a person's life to develop character in Christian living.

Special faith is not the general faith by which we ordinarily receive answers to prayer. We know that we are saved by general faith; we know that we receive the baptism in the Holy Ghost by faith — general faith. We know that we receive answers to prayer by this kind of ordinary or general faith because Jesus said, *". . . What things soever ye desire, when ye pray, believe that ye receive them, and ye shall have them"* (Mark 11:24).

Many of us have received many answers to prayer just through faith even before we ever received the baptism in the Holy Ghost. These answers came because we believed God and appropriated the promises in His Word by faith. But that is still not this *gift* of faith as described in First Corinthians 12:9.

If the gift of faith had to be in manifestation in order to get an answer to prayer, to receive the baptism of the Holy Ghost, to receive healing for your body, or to have a financial need met, then you could never get your prayers answered until after you got saved and received the baptism in the Holy Ghost. Yet many of us, including myself, did receive healing *before* we ever received the baptism of the Holy Ghost; we received healing by exercising simple faith in what God's Word says.

Also, if these general answers to prayer were the result of the gift of faith in operation, then not everyone — even if they had the baptism in the Holy Ghost — would be able to obtain answers to prayer, because not everyone will have this gift operating in them. Remember, the Bible says, *"For to ONE is given by the Spirit the word of wisdom. . . . To another faith by the same Spirit"* (1 Cor. 12:8,9).

Therefore, if we had to rely on this gift of faith to get our prayers answered, then not everyone could get their prayers answered, and we know that is untrue.

But there is a faith — I call it a general faith — that all believers have that can be increased by feeding on the Word of God and exercising it in the arena of life. We can all have an ever-increasing faith. The gift of faith, however, is a supernatural manifestation of the Holy Spirit given as the Spirit wills.

The Gift of Faith vs.
The Gift of the Working of Miracles

The gift of faith is also distinct from the working of miracles, although both gifts produce miracles. One of them is active and the other is passive.

The working of miracles is active; it actively *works* a miracle. The gift of faith doesn't work a miracle, but passively receives a miracle.

In other words, the difference between the working of miracles and the gift of faith is that the gift of working of miracles actively *does*, and the gift of special faith passively *receives*.

When Daniel was in the lions' den, he *received* a miracle. In those days as well as throughout history, there have been those who were thrown to the lions and the lions devoured them. Why didn't the lions devour Daniel? The Bible says that *". . . Daniel was taken up out of the den, and no manner of hurt was found upon him, because he believed in his God"* (Dan. 6:23).

There is no doubt that God gave Daniel special faith, a special manifestation of this gift of the Spirit, to receive deliverance. Daniel didn't *do* anything. He just lay down and went to sleep. His faith was *passive* rather than active, yet he *received* a miracle.

We see Jesus exercising this gift of faith as He slept in the back of the ship during a raging storm (Mark 4:38). Someone might argue, "Yes, but that was Jesus. He is the Son of God."

However, Jesus never did anything except by the power of the Holy Ghost. Jesus voluntarily stripped Himself of what power He had as the Son of God when He came to the earth (Phil. 2:7). Jesus was just as much the Son of God *before* the Holy Ghost came upon Him and anointed Him as He was *after* He was anointed. Yet because He stripped Himself of that power vested in Him as the Son of God when He came to the earth, Jesus never worked any miracles prior to the time He was baptized by John and the Holy Ghost came upon Him.

You see, when Jesus was on the earth, He ministered only as a man anointed by the Holy Ghost. If He had worked miracles by some power that was inherent in Him as the Son of God, He would not have told us we could do the works that He did. But Jesus plainly said, *"Verily, verily, I say unto you, He that believeth on me, the works that I do shall he do also . . ."* (John 14:12).

But if Jesus did the works as a man anointed by the Holy Ghost, then certainly under the inspiration and anointing of the Holy Ghost, believers could do the same thing.

While the raging storm swept the sea and threatened the safe journey of the disciples to the other side of the lake, Jesus was asleep in the hinder part of the boat (Mark 4:38). He wasn't bothered by the storm. And while the lions roamed about in the den,

Daniel lay down and slept in the face of danger in perfect peace and calm assurance. Why? Because Jesus and Daniel each possessed a faith beyond the simple general faith every believer can have through hearing the Word.

Throughout the Bible we see how the gift of faith worked primarily for people who were in danger. And through this gift of the Spirit, they possessed a calmness and quiet assurance that was supernatural.

The working of miracles employs faith that actively *works* a miracle. But the gift of faith employs faith that passively *expects* a miracle as a sustained or continuous action. That means when it is necessary, there is a duration to the gift of special faith — it is ongoing in its action.

When the gift of faith is in operation, it may be that nothing is seen at the time to confirm that the person has his answer. Therefore, special faith may carry over a long period of time and be sustained or continued in its action of passively receiving a miracle.

For example, it was by the gift of faith that the patriarchs of old would lay hands on their children and pronounce a blessing or curse on them which would sometimes come to pass many years later. We see this in the stories of Abraham, Isaac, and Jacob. This was the gift of faith in operation. By supernatural faith, special faith in operation, these patriarchs believed that what they said would come to pass, even if it took many years.

The gift of faith is a divine gift or enabling by the Spirit of God that causes what is spoken or desired by man, or spoken by God to ultimately come to pass. The human or divine miracle, utterance, certainty, cursing or benefit, creation or destruction, removal or change, will eventually come to pass when it has been spoken under the inspiration of this gift of special faith.

Wigglesworth and the Gift of Faith

Smith Wigglesworth said that if you will take a step of ordinary faith, when you come to the end of that faith, very often this supernatural gift of special faith will take over. One reason more folks don't see the manifestation of special faith operating in their lives is that they don't first use what faith they already have.

Under Wigglesworth's ministry, at least three different people were raised from the dead, and there were probably many more. One instance of a person who was raised from the dead was a man named Mr. Mitchell whom Wigglesworth personally knew.

One day when coming home from an open-air meeting, Wigglesworth learned that his wife, Polly, was at Mr. Mitchell's house. The day before when Wigglesworth had visited Mitchell, the sick man had been close to death.

As Wigglesworth hurried to Mitchell's house, he heard screaming coming from the house. On the way into Mr. Mitchell's room, he passed Mrs. Mitchell, who was crying, "He's gone! He's gone!"

Wigglesworth related his experience:

I just passed Mrs. Mitchell and went into the room, and immediately I saw that Mitchell had gone. I could not understand it, but I began to pray. My wife was always afraid that I would go too far, and she laid hold of me and said, "Don't, Dad! Don't you see that he is dead?"

But I continued praying. I got as far as I could with my own faith, and then God laid hold of me. Oh, it was such a laying hold that I could believe for anything. The faith of the Lord Jesus laid hold of me and a solid peace came into my heart. I shouted, "He lives! He lives! He lives!" And he is living today. [1]

Receiving the dead raised back to life again is beyond anyone's ordinary faith. In our ordinary faith, we could try what Wigglesworth did — we could pull someone off a deathbed and stand him up and tell him to walk, but that doesn't mean he would begin to walk. Why? Because it takes a *supernatural manifestation* of God's power to receive a miracle such as this.

The Power Gifts Often Work Together

As I have mentioned, the three power gifts — the gift of faith, the gifts of healings, and the working of miracles — will very often work together. In the case of raising the dead, all three of these power gifts — the gift of faith, the gifts of healings, and the working of miracles — operate together. This is one reason we don't see too many people raised from the dead; some of us may have one or more of these gifts operating in our lives, but not too many of us have *all* of them operating in our lives.

First of all, in raising the dead, it takes supernatural faith — the gift of special faith — to call a person's spirit back after it has left the body. Then it takes the working of miracles because the body would have started to deteriorate, as in the case of Lazarus (John 11:39).

Raising the dead also takes gifts of healings because if the person who was raised from the dead wasn't healed, whatever he died from would still affect his body and he would die again. So the person would have to be healed too. Therefore, all three of the power gifts are in manifestation when someone is raised from the dead.

Sometimes people have thought that it is the gift of faith in operation in the healing of the sick. But in the case of healing, it is the gifts of healings in operation. To cleanse a leper or to heal any incurable sickness, as well as cripples, the gifts of healings are in operation.

Casting Out Demons

Another area in which the gift of faith operates together with other gifts of the Spirit is the area of casting out evil spirits. In casting out demons, the gift of discerning of spirits and/or the gift of the word of knowledge, as well as the gift of faith, are in operation. If you don't discern or see the spirit, very often the presence of the evil spirit is revealed through the word of knowledge. But the gift of faith still has to be exercised in casting out the spirit.

We can't deal with the devil in our own strength. But God has given us His Word, His power, His authority, and all the spiritual equipment necessary to enforce Satan's defeat in our own lives. And a part of that spiritual equipment God has given us is this supernatural gift of faith.

So the gift of faith can operate, as I said, to cast out demons, to receive the dead raised back to life, and to supernaturally sustain a person beyond the ability of ordinary faith.

Purposes of the Gift of Faith

As I mentioned previously, the working of miracles is more of *an act*, whereas the gift of faith is more of *a process*. In other words, the working of miracles would *perform* a miracle, but the gift of faith would *receive* a miracle.

In summary, first, we've seen the gift of faith in operation in receiving blessings or the fulfillment of human utterances as in the cases of the patriarchs of old. As we said, many times when the patriarchs were ready to die, they would lay their hands on their sons and command blessings upon them, and whatever they said would come to pass. They did this by the supernatural manifestation of the gift of faith.

Second, we have seen how this gift of faith was manifested for personal protection in perilous circumstances, such as the case of Daniel in the lions' den.

Third, this gift of faith was manifested for supernatural sustenance in the time of famine. We can see this, for example, in the case of Elijah when he was fed by the ravens (1 Kings 17:3-6). Elijah's faith had to be given to him supernaturally because it was beyond ordinary faith to believe that ravens would feed him. But they brought food to him morning and night.

Remember, ordinary faith comes by hearing the Word of God (Rom. 10:17). But the gift of faith is manifested by the Holy Spirit to enable a person to receive a miracle beyond the capacity of ordinary faith to receive.

Fourth, this gift of faith is manifested to raise the dead, as I have already pointed out.

Fifth, the gift of faith is employed in casting out evil spirits. When you cast out devils, you are trusting God to honor your word as His own.

Sixth, in some instances this gift comes into operation in the laying on of hands for people to be filled with the Holy Ghost.

GALATIANS 3:5
5 He therefore that ministereth to you the Spirit, and worketh miracles among you, doeth he it by the works of the law, or by the hearing of faith?

When Paul said to the Galatians, ". . . [he that] *worketh miracles among you. . . ,*" he was referring to the working of miracles. But before that he said, *"He therefore that ministereth to you the Spirit . . ."* (Gal. 3:5).

Paul was talking about ministering the Spirit first and then he was talking about the gift of working of miracles. Then Paul adds, ". . . *doeth he it by the works of the law, or by the hearing of faith?*" (v. 5). Of course, it is by the hearing of faith, which belongs to every believer. But some in the Body of Christ have more of a ministry along this line, and the gift of faith accompanies their ministry.

In other words, this gift of faith is in operation many times when it comes to ministering the baptism of the Holy Spirit to believers. This gift comes into operation with the ministry of laying on of hands; as I said, there are those who are supernaturally equipped with a ministry more along this line.

Of course, any believer can lay hands on people in general faith and appropriate God's promises from His Word, even in receiving the Holy Spirit. But when it comes to a manifestation of the Spirit of God ministered through one person to another, that is a gift of the Spirit in operation.

If you lay hands on someone for healing or for any other blessing without a gift of the Spirit in operation, that person can simply receive by faith whatever the Word promises. The laying on of hands then is simply a point of contact for the one receiving to release his faith in the promises in God's Word. And, of course, if the person receives the blessing by faith, that is still a demonstration of God's power.

God works through sovereign demonstrations of power and through supernatural manifestations in the gifts of the Spirit, as well as through simple faith in His Word.

Therefore, this gift of faith can be in operation to minister the Holy Spirit to believers, imparting the fullness of God which is the promise of the Father, enriching the soul, and empowering one for spiritual service.

In summary, we can say that by the gift of faith the violence of fire has been controlled as in the case of Elijah (1 Kings 18:38). By the gift of faith, the miraculous has been supernaturally manifested and a man was supernaturally fed and sustained (1 Kings 19:4,6); another lived and labored for forty days without food or water and was sustained (Exod. 34:28).

Angels have stood guard over the servants of God, protecting them because this gift was in manifestation; men have been delivered from the ferocity of beasts, such as Daniel in the lions' den (Dan. 6:22). The gift of faith brings an inward calm within the spirit of those through whom this gift is manifested. For example, Peter, a man condemned to die, slept on the very eve of his execution, and he was delivered from death (Acts 12:6-11). And by this gift, a raging storm was stopped that threatened to wreck a ship at sea and destroy human life (Mark 4:39).

The gift of faith can expel unclean spirits from the bodies of men, which have been defiled by their presence. On the other hand, this gift can also be in operation in ministering the baptism of the Holy Spirit. Also by this gift of faith, we know that blessings can be pronounced which can miraculously and permanently change the entire course of one's life.

As we appropriate the Word of God concerning the gifts of the Spirit, there shall come more manifestations of the Spirit of God in greater frequency than in the past. And there shall be great manifestations of God's power through the gifts of the Spirit. In this day and hour in which we live, these gifts of the Holy Spirit are necessary to bring about that which God desires to do in the earth.

---

[1] Smith Wigglesworth, *Ever Increasing Faith* (1924; Springfield, Missouri: Gospel Publishing House, 1971), pp. 138,139.

Questions for Study

1. Name the three spiritual gifts that *reveal* something? That *do* something? That *say* something?

    _____

    _____

2. Guidance by the inward witness is a supernatural manifestation of which gift of the Spirit?

    _____

    _____

3. How is saving faith given to a person?

    _____

    _____

4. Special faith is something other than general faith or saving faith. What is it?

    _____

    _____

5. How do all of the gifts of the Spirit operate?

    _____

    _____

6. In the original Greek, how could the word "faith" in Galatians 5:22 be translated?

    _____

    _____

7. The *fruit* of the Spirit are for _____; the *gifts* of the Spirit are for _____.

8. What is the difference between the working of miracles and the gift of faith?

    _____

    _____

9. What two other gifts operate with the gift of faith to raise the dead?

    _____

    _____

10. Name the six purposes for the gift of faith listed in this chapter.

    _____

    _____

Chapter 16

The Gift of the Working of Miracles

But the manifestation of the Spirit is given to every man to profit withal.

For to one is given by the Spirit the word of wisdom; to another the word of knowledge by the same Spirit;

To another faith by the same Spirit; to another the gifts of healing by the same Spirit;

TO ANOTHER THE WORKING OF MIRACLES; to another prophecy; to another discerning of spirits; to another divers kinds of tongues; to another the interpretation of tongues:

But all these worketh that one and the selfsame Spirit, dividing to every man severally as he will.
— 1 Corinthians 12:7-11

After Paul listed the nine gifts of the Spirit as shown in the text above, he went on to say, *"But covet earnestly the best gifts . . ."* (1 Cor. 12:31).

The 'Best' Gift Is the Gift Needed at the Time

Sometimes people become confused about what the best spiritual gift is. They miss the fact that under some circumstances, even the very best gift of all the spiritual gifts, may not be the best gift in a given circumstance or the gift needed at that particular time.

For instance, the word of wisdom, which is a divine revelation of the plan and purpose of God, is the greatest of all the gifts of the Spirit. However, if you are sick, you don't need that manifestation; you need a manifestation of the gifts of healings.

In other words, under that particular circumstance, the "best" gift would be the gifts of healings, not the word of wisdom. So, you see, the best gift, the word of wisdom, is not always what's needed in every situation and circumstance. In that sense, the best gift would really be the one that is needed at the time.

Find Your Place of Ministry

We look at Paul's letter to the Corinthians in which he said, *". . . covet earnestly the best gifts . . ."* (1 Cor. 12:31). Paul also said, *". . . desire spiritual gifts . . ."* (1 Cor. 14:1). Paul was exhorting the Corinthians to desire spiritual gifts. Many times, we take this verse of Scripture personally and we think it means that each person is to desire spiritual gifts as his own *personal* possessions.

However, Paul was not writing this letter to an individual member of the Church of the Lord Jesus Christ. He was writing to the whole Church at Corinth. He was telling them as a church, as a *group*, to desire these gifts. And this also applies to the Church, the Body of Christ today.

Then if believers as a group would earnestly desire spiritual gifts to be manifested in their midst, the Holy Spirit would manifest Himself, "dividing to every man severally as He wills" (1 Cor. 12:11). The phrase, *". . . dividing to every man severally as he will"* in First Corinthians 12:11, infers that each of us will not all have the same spiritual gift manifested through us at the same time.

At some time or another, those who are called to the fivefold ministry would have to be equipped with certain gifts of the Spirit in order to stand in certain offices. Therefore, those people have more consistent manifestations of these spiritual gifts than others in the Body of Christ. But no one will have all the gifts operating through him.

Too many times, we try to be a "jack-of-all-trades and master of none," spiritually speaking, instead of just staying in our places and using whatever gift God has given us, or instead of functioning in the ministry to which we were called. For example, many times people try to do the other fellow's ministry or job, or try to be used in a gift that someone else is used in.

I have heard people say, "If they can do that, so can I." That causes confusion in the Body of Christ, and will eventually lead to error.

By way of illustration, you would really have confusion in your own physical body if your foot said, "If the eye can see, so can I." Of course, your foot can't see; it can't fulfill the role of the eye. It's not supposed to. And conversely, the eye cannot fulfill the role of the foot.

I once attended a meeting conducted by Howard Carter, and after the service, a woman came up to him and said, "Brother Carter, I want you to pray for my healing."

He said to her, "Sister, go see my wife. I seldom lay hands on the sick for healing. That's not my ministry. I know any of us can pray in faith for those who are sick if no one else is present.

"But God uses my wife in the gifts of healings," Rev. Carter explained. "That gift operates through her; it doesn't operate through me. God uses me in getting people filled with the Holy Ghost. I lay hands on people to be filled with the Spirit and seldom does one fail to receive. That's my ministry.

"The gift of faith operates through me, "Rev. Carter continued," and I impart the Holy Ghost to people through the laying on of hands. I seldom fail to get anyone filled with the Spirit, and she seldom fails to get anyone healed, so go see her."

Of course, God will honor the faith of people who will believe Him. But you can get things done more quickly by folks who are especially used along particular lines, because they are supernaturally endued with certain gifts of the Spirit. Naturally, then, they could get results quicker than others could.

The Working of Miracles Defined

In our studies on the gifts of the Spirit, we now come to the gift of the working of miracles. First of all, let us define the working of miracles. A miracle can be defined as *a supernatural intervention by God in the ordinary course of nature.*

As is the case with many words in the English language, when we use the word "miracle" generally speaking, it means one thing; but used specifically, it means something else. For example, sometimes the word "miracle" is used generally as a figure of speech. We talk, for instance, about miracle fabrics, miracle drugs, miracle detergents, and so forth.

In nature we might see a beautiful sunrise and say, "That's a miracle." We might look at a beautiful rose garden ablaze with glorious color, the perfume of the flowers ascending into the heavens, and say that it is a "miracle" of nature.

None of these things are a miracle specifically speaking, but generally speaking they are. In the magnificent sunrise, the sun is doing exactly what it ought to do according to the laws of nature. The rose is doing exactly what it was meant to do according to the laws of nature. Therefore, specifically, these are not miracles because a miracle is a supernatural intervention in the ordinary course of nature.

Another example of a natural miracle, or a miracle generally speaking, is the birth of a child. Sometimes the medical profession calls it the miracle of birth. Generally speaking, a natural birth is a miracle. But it is not a miracle in the specific sense, because it is an event occurring in the normal or ordinary course of nature.

The same is true in the spiritual realm regarding the "miracle" of salvation. Generally speaking, salvation is a miracle; but specifically speaking, salvation isn't any more a miracle than a natural birth is a miracle. In the supernatural realm, the new birth is a very natural or normal occurrence. It is a supernatural act, but it is not the gift of working of miracles in operation.

So, generally speaking, as a figure of speech, both the natural birth and the spiritual rebirth of one's spirit are miracles. But specifically speaking, neither is a miracle because they are not a supernatural intervention in the ordinary course of nature, neither in the natural realm nor in the spiritual realm.

The new birth is a supernatural act which takes place in the *spiritual* realm. We do not call that a miracle according to our definition of the word "miracle": *a supernatural intervention in the ordinary course of nature.* What we call a miracle in the specific sense, is a supernatural act on a *natural* plane.

Therefore, the new birth is not a supernatural act in the natural realm; it is a supernatural act in the spiritual realm. The natural birth is in the natural realm. One is spiritual and the other is natural, and neither are miracles in the specific sense.

Every one of the gifts of the Spirit is miraculous; they are all supernatural. In the *general* use of the word "miracle," all gifts of the Spirit are miracles, not just the gift of the working of miracles. But *specifically* speaking, all of them are not.

When the working of miracles is in manifestation, there is a divine intervention in the ordinary course of nature. For example, the dividing of a stream by the sweep of a mantle is an example of the working of miracles in operation (2 Kings 2:14). After Elijah ascended to heaven in a chariot in the whirlwind, Elisha received his mantle and smote the Jordan River. Dividing the waters by a sweep of his mantle was the working of miracles because that was a supernatural intervention in the ordinary course of nature.

In the area of healing, many times miracles are received, but this is not necessarily the *working* of miracles; they are simply called healing miracles. Everything that God does is miraculous in a sense, but receiving healing by supernatural means is not a miracle in the same sense that turning common dust into insects just by a gesture is a miracle (Exod. 8:16), or turning common water into wine just by speaking a word is a miracle (John 2:7-11). Those two occurrences are examples of the working of miracles.

Water turned into wine by the aging process, or the process of nature, is a natural phenomenon. But water turned into wine just by speaking a word, as

Jesus did (John 2:1-11), is a miracle according to our definition — a supernatural intervention in the ordinary course of nature.

A miracle, therefore, is a supernatural intervention in the ordinary course of nature, a temporary suspension of the accustomed order, or an interruption in the system of nature as we know it, operated by the power of the Holy Spirit.

Old Testament Examples of the Working of Miracles

We've defined the working of miracles. Now let's look at examples from the Bible of this gift in operation.

Moses and the Israelites

This working of miracles was used time and time again for miraculous deliverance of God's people. We see this gift used in Egypt when God convinced Pharaoh to let Israel go (*see* Exodus chapters 7 through 14). A number of miracles were wrought during this time.

When Aaron threw down his rod and it was turned into a serpent, for example, that was the working of miracles in operation (Exod. 7:9-12). When the dust was turned into insects (Exod. 8:16-18) and all the other plagues followed, this was the gift of the working of miracles in operation.

When the children of Israel came out of Egypt and approached the Red Sea, Pharaoh and his hosts were close behind, ready to recapture them and make them slaves again (Exod. 14:5-9). There the Israelites were with the wilderness on one side, mountains on the other, the sea in front of them, and the enemy behind them. It seemed hopeless.

But Moses looked to the Lord and the Lord told him to stretch forth his rod. Moses stretched it forth and the sea divided (Exod. 14:15-31). That was the working of a miracle. That was *a divine intervention in the ordinary course of nature.*

Actually, two gifts of the Spirit were in operation at the parting of the Red Sea. The working of miracles divided the sea, but what kept it divided? It took the gift of faith to do that. It took the gift of faith to sustain this miracle as an ongoing act.

God's people walked over dryshod to the other side. The enemy attempted to do the same, but the waters came together as they attempted to do so, and the Egyptians were drowned in the depths of the sea.

Elijah and the Widow

The working of miracles was also used in the Old Testament to provide for those in want. For example,

it was a working of miracles when the widow's cruse of oil didn't fail, but kept flowing out like a fountain of oil until it filled up every vessel she had, and still the cruse kept flowing with oil (1 Kings 17:8-16).

Working of Miracles in the New Testament

Now let's look at a few examples of the working of miracles in operation in the New Testament.

Jesus and the Feeding of the Five Thousand

We see the working of miracles in the New Testament when Jesus took the little boy's lunch and fed five thousand with it (John 6:5-14). I am sometimes amazed at the way some folks — even educated folks — try to explain away the Bible.

For example, I was reading after a fellow once who had all kinds of initials on the end of his name — X, Y, Z, Ph.D., and so on! Please understand that I am not against education. But sometimes people can educate their heads at the expense of educating their hearts.

This particular intellectual I was reading after was trying to explain away the miracles in the Bible. He explained the miracle of Jesus feeding the five thousand with the little boy's loaves of bread by saying, "The loaves of bread in those days were bigger than they are now"!

If he had really read this account in the Bible, he would have noticed that it was a *little boy's* lunch (John 6:9). In the first place, it is difficult to imagine that a little boy could have carried enough bread out there to have fed five thousand. In the second place, it is difficult to imagine that he had planned to eat all of that for lunch himself!

No, it was the working of a miracle that fed five thousand with just a little boy's lunch. The disciples even gathered up twelve remaining basketfuls when they were finished eating (John 6:13)!

Ananias and Sapphira

This working of miracles was also used to carry out divine judgment, as in the case of Ananias and Sapphira (Acts 5:1-10), because this was an example of divine intervention into the ordinary course of nature.

At one time, the Christians in the Early Church had sold all of their possessions and brought the money and laid it at the apostles' feet. They owned everything in common. God didn't tell them to do it. They evidently felt prompted by the Holy Spirit to do this, and it proved to be a wise move because within a few years the city was overrun, and they would have eventually lost everything they owned.

Ananias and Sapphira had sold their land, but kept part of the money they received. It would have been perfectly all right for them to have said to the disciples, "This is half of the money we received from the sale of our property."

God wasn't requiring them to give all their money to the disciples. There is nothing in the Scriptures that even infers that. It would have been fine if they had been honest and had said, "Here is half the money. We are going to keep the other half."

Ananias came in and laid his money at the apostles' feet, seemingly making the same consecration and dedication that the others had made. Peter asked, "Is that the price of the land?"

"Yes, that is the total price," Ananias answered in effect, but he was telling a lie because he had kept back part of it.

Peter knew through the operation of the gift of the word of knowledge that Ananias was keeping back some of the money. He said, "*. . . why hath Satan filled thine heart to lie to the Holy Ghost . . .*" (Acts 5:3).

Ananias fell down dead, as a result of divine judgment that came through the working of miracles in operation. The disciples didn't even dismiss for his funeral, and no one went to tell Ananias' wife that he had died.

Three hours later Ananias' wife, Sapphira, came in (Acts 5:7). I don't know how long the service had been going on when Ananias arrived, but three hours later it was still going on. Once while listening to a sermon on Ananias and Sapphira, I heard the preacher say, "Sapphira came in about *thirty minutes* later."

About that time I thought, *Wait a minute!* And I read that verse again. It was *three hours*, not thirty minutes later, that Sapphira came in (Acts 5:7).

Later I pointed this out to that minister. He read it again, shook his head, and said, "I guess I got it confused with our services. If it had been in one of our churches today, if she had come in more than thirty minutes after the service had begun, there wouldn't have been anyone there!"

I believe that most of the time, this is true. However, where the gifts of the Spirit are in operation, I have seen people stay in church all day. Where God's Spirit is moving, folks are not in any hurry to leave.

Divine judgment came to Sapphira and she, too, fell down dead. The working of miracles was again used to carry out divine judgment (Acts 5:8-10).

Paul and Elymas

The working of miracles is also used to confirm the preached Word. When Paul was preaching in Cyprus, Elymas the sorcerer withstood him. Elymas was struck blind for a season through the power of God in the operation of the gift of the working of miracles. That was a supernatural sign to others nearby (Acts 13:4-12).

The Gift of Faith vs. the Working of Miracles To Deliver From Danger

This working of miracles is used to deliver people from unavoidable danger or harm. The gift of faith would carry a person *through* the danger with great peace and calm without the person's being harmed at all. But the working of miracles is different.

For instance, when Paul was shipwrecked, the storm did not cease until it "blew itself out" (Acts 27:1-44). Paul didn't stand up and say, "Storm, you stop!" But because God had spoken to him through a message from an angel of God, Paul had extraordinary faith to believe for divine protection. Paul passively *received* a miracle. That was the *gift of faith* in operation, and he received divine protection and safety for everyone on board the ship, although the ship itself was greatly damaged.

In another incident, however, when Jesus stood on that ship and said, "*. . . Peace, be still . . .*" (Mark 4:39), and the storm ceased, *that* was the *working of miracles* and those on board were delivered from danger.

As I previously mentioned, the difference between the gift of faith and the working of miracles is that the gift of faith *receives* a miracle and the working of miracles *works* a miracle.

The working of miracles is used to display God's power and magnificence. In *Young's Analytical Concordance to the Bible,* the Greek word for "miracles" in First Corinthians 12:10 is "dunamis," and can also be translated *acts of powers.*

In other words, the working of miracles could also be called the working of *acts of powers.* According to the Greek concordance, the Greek word also means, *explosions of almightiness or impelling, staggering wonders or astonishments.*

In other words, the Greek could read, "To another the working of impelling, staggering wonders or astonishments, or the outworkings of explosions of almightiness and acts of powers."

Gifts of Healings More Prevalent in the New Testament

Although in the Old Testament people were healed and the gifts of healings were in operation, gifts of healings were more commonly in operation in the New Testament than they were in the Old Testament.

On the other hand, the working of miracles was more prominent or more commonly manifested in the Old Testament than in the New Testament, with the exception of the gift of working of miracles in Jesus' ministry.

However, the working of miracles could possibly be included where it says, *"And by the hands of the apostles were many SIGNS AND WONDERS wrought among the people . . ."* (Acts 5:12). According to the *Interlinear Greek-English New Testament*, verse 12 says, "And many *miracles* and *works* were worked among the people by the hands of the apostles."

Although the Bible doesn't specify what signs and wonders or miracles and works these were, it does go on to tell us about some healings which occurred through the ministry of the apostles (Acts 5:15,16). These healings were not actually the working of miracles in demonstration but gifts of healings in operation. Any spectacular manifestation that has to do with healing is the gifts of healings in operation.

But it could be that because Acts 5:12 does not specify whether these signs and wonders were specifically miracles of healing or not, that this verse could refer to the workings of miracles by the apostles, particularly when the Greek does say that *miracles* and *works* were worked by the apostles. But, again, the Bible does not specify what miracles and works these were.

Another example of the gift of working of miracles that is specifically mentioned in the New Testament is found in Acts 8.

ACTS 8:5,6
5   Then Philip went down to the city of Samaria, and preached Christ unto them.
6   And the people with one accord gave heed unto those things which Philip spake, hearing and seeing the MIRACLES which he did.

The passage goes on to tell about some of the miraculous healings which took place. However, again, that would not be the same as the gift of the working of miracles. It could be that verse 6 is talking about miraculous healings, or it could be that it is talking about some other miracles that were wrought.

The Bible does not specify what miracles were wrought, except to say, *". . . hearing and seeing the MIRACLES which he did"* (Acts 8:6). So it could also be that some miracles were wrought that weren't

healings. If so, that would be the gift of the working of miracles in operation.

We see other passages in the New Testament where the working of miracles is also directly mentioned.

ACTS 6:8
8   And Stephen, full of faith and power, did great wonders and MIRACLES among the people.

ACTS 15:12
12 Then all the multitude kept silence, and gave audience to Barnabas and Paul, declaring what MIRACLES and wonders God had wrought among the Gentiles by them.

ACTS 19:11
11 And God wrought special MIRACLES by the hands of Paul.

The word "miracles" in Acts 6:8 and Acts 19:11 is the same Greek word, "dunamis," meaning *acts of power* (*Young's*) or *mighty, wonderful works* (*Strong's*).

The word "miracles" in Acts 15:12 is the Greek word "semeion," which according to *Vine's Expository Dictionary*, translates as *a sign, mark, or token* and "is used of miracles and wonders as signs of divine authority." [1]

The Importance of the Working of Miracles

Howard Carter said in his book, *Questions and Answers on Spiritual Gifts*: "The working of miracles is a very important manifestation of the Spirit. It is the mighty power of God flowing through a person." [2]

We might say that when this gift is in manifestation through a believer, he participates in the same power of God that was in manifestation when God created the world.

God certainly worked a miracle when He spoke the earth and the world into existence. When the Lord permits a person through the power of the Holy Spirit to speak a word, and the miraculous occurs, then the same God who created the world is allowing some of His omnipotence to be manifested through that person. But, remember, these gifts of the Spirit, including the gift of the working of miracles, operate as the Spirit wills.

By the working of miracles, a nation was plagued to ensure the deliverance of God's people and to bring Him glory (Exod. 7:12). By the working of miracles, the shadow cast by the sun went back ten steps on a sun dial as a sign that King Hezekiah would live and not die (Isa. 38:1-8).

Through the working of miracles, suddenly and astonishingly a rod that was thrown to the ground miraculously became a serpent (Exod. 7:10). Through the working of miracles, fire flashed from the sky and consumed a sacrifice as well as the altar upon which it had been sacrificed (1 Kings 18:38). One time through the working of miracles, a prophet even made it thunder and hail (Exod. 9:23).

By the working of miracles through Samson, even lions were overcome and were slain. In the case of Daniel, however, the lions were not overcome and slain. Instead, an angel came down and shut the lions' mouths. Daniel received his miracle through the *gift of faith* in operation. He lay down and went to sleep among those hungry, ravenous lions and was kept in perfect safety.

The Bible says that when Daniel came out ". . . *no manner of hurt was found upon him, because he believed in his God*" (Dan. 6:23). That kind of faith *to receive* a miracle is beyond the ordinary faith that every Christian possesses (Rom. 12:3). It is the gift of faith in action.

Remember, the gift of special faith *receives* the miracle; the gift of the working of miracles *does* the miracle.

Through the working of miracles, loaves were multiplied (Matt 14:17-21; Mark 6:38-44; Luke 9:13-17; John 6:9-14).

Through the working of miracles, a solid iron axe head was made to float in water as if it were a piece of wood (2 Kings 6:5-7).

Through the working of miracles, the raging force of a storm was quieted (Mark 4:37-41; Luke 8:23-25).

Through the working of miracles, a multitude of fish filled the disciples' net when they let it down at Jesus' instruction (John 21:6-8,11).

Through the working of miracles, the widow's small pot of oil became a fountain of oil and provided sustenance for her and her son (2 Kings 4:1-7).

The Gift of Working of Miracles Is for Us Today

Someone said, "But the working of miracles is not for us today." Who said so? The Bible certainly does not say that (1 Cor. 14:1). Some answer, "Well, if the miraculous were for us today, then we would have it operating in our midst." But I say, if God says we can have the miraculous operation of spiritual gifts, then we ought to have them!

Full Gospel people often criticize denominational churches because many of these churches, while claiming to believe certain fundamental truths, in reality know little about them. For example, although church doctrine may state a belief in the new birth, the majority of their members and many of their pastors may have never experienced the new birth.

I once heard an example of this kind of problem. A woman left a certain church to join the church her husband attended. Shortly thereafter, she was born again. When she later saw her former pastor, she asked him, "Do you know the Lord Jesus Christ personally?"

"I know about Him, just as I know about George Washington," he replied. "I know Him as a historical person just like I know Abraham Lincoln as a historical person. I read about Lincoln in history books. And I read about Jesus in the Bible."

This woman began to talk to her former pastor about becoming personally acquainted with Jesus Christ and having the peace of God in his heart through the new birth.

He asked, "Can I really have that?" She assured him he could. Then she prayed with him to receive Jesus Christ as his Savior. The doctrines of his particular church stated a belief in a born-again experience, yet here was a pastor who had never experienced it!

I spoke to a prominent minister years ago who had retired from the ministry. He was about seventy-two years old at the time, but he was doing more for God than he had ever done in his life in the ministry. He told me that since he had retired, he had gotten saved. He had spent his whole life in the ministry and had never been saved!

Although Full Gospel people sometimes criticize other churches for their failure to put into practice what they have on paper as doctrinal tenets, Full Gospel churches can be guilty of the same fault. Many Full Gospel churches that claim to believe in the gifts of the Spirit don't have them in operation in their churches. We not only need to *believe* in the gifts of the Spirit, but we need to have them in *manifestation* in our churches too.

Desire Earnestly Spiritual Gifts

Why don't we have more manifestations of spiritual gifts then? Because we are not meeting God's conditions. God said, ". . . *covet earnestly the best gifts* . . ." (1 Cor. 12:31). If we as a local church, for example, don't have spiritual gifts in manifestation among us, it is because we are not coveting and desiring these things as we should.

I am thoroughly convinced that as we covet spiritual gifts and earnestly desire them, they will be more in manifestation than they have ever been. But it is not going to come just because we sit around and talk about it and just wish we could see them in demonstration.

God said *to desire* spiritual gifts. If someone really desires something, he is going to make some effort in that direction in order to see what he desires come to pass.

Paul said, *"But covet earnestly the best gifts . . ."* (1 Cor. 12:31). The dictionary defines "covet" as *to desire earnestly*. In other words, Paul said to desire earnestly spiritual gifts.

Many people have desires, but they are not very earnest about making sure those desires are fulfilled. But let's desire gifts of the Spirit to be made manifest among us.

Let's covet them as a body of believers — as a group — and let's pray for them to be manifested in our midst. It is all right to pray that the mighty Holy Ghost will manifest Himself among us dividing to every man severally as He wills according to the Scripture (1 Cor. 12:11). Let's pray that these gifts of special faith, the working of miracles, and gifts of healings, and all the gifts of the Spirit will be more in operation in our midst than they have been.

Let me encourage you as a believer to start praying for the fullness of the spiritual gifts to be in manifestation. That is not a prayer to pray once and then quit.

But daily say to the Lord: "Lord, these manifestations of your Holy Spirit are for us today. You haven't taken them out of the Church. You said these gifts are given to the Church; they belong to us and we ought to have them in manifestation. We pray, Lord, that they will be in manifestation in our midst." Then as a body of believers, let's covet them; let's desire spiritual gifts earnestly.

This working of miracles "is indeed a mighty gift, glorifying the God of all power," as Howard Carter said, and "stimulating the faith of His people and astonishing and confounding the unbelief of the wicked." [3]

I am convinced that in this hour, God wants this gift of the working of miracles to be more in prominence, for what "explosions of almightiness" that would be as a sign to the unbeliever and as a mighty demonstration of God's power to all. What it would do for the Body of Christ in this final hour of God's outpouring upon the earth!

---

[1] W. E. Vine, *Vine's Expository Dictionary of Biblical Words* (Nashville, Tennessee: Thomas Nelson Inc., 1985), p. 412.
[2] *Questions and Answers on Spiritual Gifts*, p. 63.
[3] *Ibid.*, p. 64.

Questions for Study

1. After Paul listed the nine gifts of the Spirit, he went on to say, *"But covet earnestly the best gifts . . ."* (1 Cor. 12:31). Generally speaking, which gift of the Spirit is the "best" gift?

   _____

   _____

2. At some time or another, those who are called to the fivefold ministry would have to be equipped with certain gifts of the Spirit for what purpose?

   _____

   _____

3. Define the term "miracle."

   _____

   _____

4. Why isn't the birth of a child considered a true miracle?

   _____

   _____

5. The new birth is a supernatural act that takes place in what realm?

   _____

   _____

6. Give two Old Testament examples of the working of miracles.

   _____

   _____

7. Give two examples of the working of miracles in the New Testament.

   _____

   _____

8. In *Young's Analytical Concordance* to the Bible, what is the Greek word for "miracles" in First Corinthians 12:10?

   _____

   _____

9. The working of miracles could also be called the working of _____ _____ _____?

10. How does the dictionary define "covet"?

    _____

    _____

Chapter 17

Gifts of Healings

But the manifestation of the Spirit is given to every man to profit withal.

For to one is given by the Spirit the word of wisdom; to another the word of knowledge by the same Spirit;

To another faith by the same Spirit; TO ANOTHER THE GIFTS OF HEALING BY THE SAME SPIRIT;

To another the working of miracles; to another prophecy; to another discerning of spirits; to another divers kinds of tongues; to another the interpretation of tongues:

But all these worketh that one and the selfsame Spirit, dividing to every man severally as he will.
— 1 Corinthians 12:7-11

The gifts of healings are manifested for the supernatural healing of sickness and disease without any natural source or means. As I've mentioned, every one of these nine gifts of the Spirit are supernatural.

Some gifts are more spectacular in demonstration than others, but they are all supernatural. We may have some difficulty, because of our limited knowledge, in defining some of the other gifts. But I think we should have little difficulty defining this gift, the gifts of healings.

Most of us basically understand the subject of healing. Healings were, of course, in prominence, in Jesus' ministry as He walked on the earth. Jesus had a healing ministry, and He also gave authority to His disciples to heal the sick (Matt. 10:8). Healing the sick is also included in the Great Commission (Mark 16:18).

Gifts of Healings: Not Medical Science

First, I want to emphasize the supernatural character of the gifts of healings. The gifts of healings have nothing to do with medical science or human learning.

Luke, who was a medical doctor, was with Paul on many of Paul's missionary journeys. Luke wrote the Acts of the Apostles as well as the Book of the Bible that bears his name. Luke was with Paul when he was shipwrecked and they were on the Island of Melita.

Nothing at all is said to the effect that Luke ministered to the folks on that island with his medical knowledge. But the father-in-law of the chief man of the island was sick, and Paul laid his hands on him and he was healed. He was healed by the supernatural power of God. This was the gifts of healings in manifestation.

Then the islanders brought the sick from all over the island, and Paul ministered to them, and they were healed.

Certainly I believe in medical science, and I thank God for what it can do. I am certainly not opposed to doctors, but some people confuse medical science with the gifts of healings.

I heard someone say on the radio one time that the gifts of healings were what God had given doctors and medical science. But the gifts of healings are not doctors and medical science. If that is God's method of healing, then doctors ought not to charge anything; medical treatment ought to be free because the Bible says, *". . . freely ye have received, freely give"* (Matt. 10:8).

However, as anyone who has had any experience with doctors knows, medical treatment is *not* free. Also, if doctors and medical science were God's method of healing, medical treatment would always be free from errors; doctors would make no mistakes. However, we know that this is not true either. Doctors and medical science are *natural* means of healing. The gifts of healings and other methods of divine healing are *supernatural*.

I would not speak disparagingly about doctors, hospitals, and medical science because they do much good for humanity. I thank God for the number of good Christian physicians who have the best interest of their patients at heart and who minister to them with their natural human ability as a trained physician.

But the healing that is supernatural doesn't come by diagnosis or by prescribing treatment. Divine healing comes by laying on of hands, anointing with oil, or sometimes just by speaking the Word, just to name a few examples from the Word of how healing is ministered.

I believe in natural healing and I thank God for it. I think one of the greatest areas in medical science, and one in which the greatest strides have been made, is in the field of preventive medicine. But not only do I believe in natural healing, I also believe in supernatural, or divine healing.

Gifts of Healings Prominent in the New Testament

It will help us to understand the operation and the purpose of these gifts of healings by looking at some of their uses in the Scriptures. We know, first of all, that the purpose of these gifts is to deliver the sick and to destroy the works of the devil in the human body. And the Bible is full of such examples.

We have discussed the working of miracles and the fact that the working of miracles is more prominent in the Old Testament than in the New Testament. It is just the opposite with the gifts of healings. The gifts of healings are more prominent in the New Testament than in the Old Testament.

In the New Testament, there aren't many records of the gift of the working of miracles in operation. There were a few instances in the ministry of Christ and less in the Acts of the Apostles. But in the New Testament, there are many examples of the gifts of healings in operation.

Jesus Ministered as a Man Anointed by the Holy Spirit

Jesus Himself ministered not as the Son of God but as a man anointed by the Holy Ghost. Jesus was just as much the Son of God when He was twenty-five as He was the Son of God when He was thirty years old. Yet at twenty-five years old, He had not healed a single person; not one miracle of healing had been wrought under His ministry prior to His receiving the anointing of the Holy Spirit at the age of thirty.

And Jesus was just as much the Son of God when He was *twenty-nine* years old as He was when He was thirty. Yet at the age of twenty-nine, not one single person was healed in His ministry, nor had He wrought one miracle of healing.

Even when Jesus was thirty years of age, on the day before Jesus was baptized by John in the River Jordan and the Holy Spirit descended upon Him to anoint Him to minister, Jesus was just as much the Son of God as He was after His baptism.

Yet until Jesus was anointed by the Holy Spirit, He never healed a single person. Before Jesus was anointed by the Holy Spirit, there was no manifestation of the power of God operating in His ministry. It was only *after* the Holy Spirit descended upon Him in the form of a dove in order to anoint Him to minister that the gifts of the Spirit began to be manifest in His ministry.

In fact, Jesus Himself said, *". . . the Father that dwelleth in me, HE doeth the works"* (John 14:10). He never did claim to do them Himself or on His own. He said, "My Father in Me, He does the works." How did He do them? Through the power of the Holy Spirit.

Jesus stood up and read in His hometown synagogue, *"The Spirit of the Lord is upon me, because he hath anointed me . . ."* (Luke 4:18). Then Peter, preaching to Cornelius and his household, said, *"How God anointed Jesus of Nazareth with the Holy Ghost and with power: who went about doing good, and healing all that were oppressed of the devil; for God was with him"* (Acts 10:38). Although Jesus had always been the Son of God, He never healed anyone until after He was anointed with the Holy Ghost and power.

This should prove conclusively that Jesus didn't heal the sick by some power that was inherent in Him as the Son of God, the second Person of the Trinity. Rather, He healed the sick just as anyone else called of God would minister to the sick today — by the anointing of the Holy Spirit, by the manifestation of these gifts of healings, and by the preaching of the Word of God.

The Word of God tells us in the Book of John that Christ had the Spirit without measure (John 3:34). Therefore, we would see a full manifestation of spiritual gifts operating in Jesus' ministry that we wouldn't see in anyone else's ministry because, as John 3:34 infers, Jesus had the Spirit without measure. No other person has the Spirit without measure.

However, it seems to me that John 3:34 infers that the entire Body of Christ has the same measure of the Spirit *collectively* as Jesus had *individually*. Therefore, just one person would not have the same measure of success in ministering even the gifts of healings that Jesus had in His earth walk because He had the Spirit without measure.

Having the Spirit without measure, Jesus would have the manifestation of all the gifts of the Spirit in His earth walk, except tongues and interpretation, which are exclusive to the dispensation of the church age which Jesus ushered in. Of course, *all* the gifts of healings would be included in the spiritual gifts which were manifested in Jesus' ministry.

The Gifts of Healings

I want to point out a few verses in First Corinthians chapter 12. In verses 9, 28, and 30 the gifts of healings are mentioned.

1 CORINTHIANS 12:9,28,30
9   To another faith by the same Spirit; to another the GIFTS OF HEALING by the same Spirit. . . .

28 And God hath set some in the church, first apostles, secondarily prophets, thirdly teachers, after that miracles, then GIFTS OF HEALINGS, helps, governments, diversities of tongues. . . .
30 Have all the GIFTS OF HEALING? do all speak with tongues? do all interpret?

Notice in verse 28, both the words "gifts" and "healings" are plural, and this is the way it should be listed in every one of the verses where this gift is mentioned.

In the Greek verse 28 is ". . . gifts of healings, helps, governments, diversities of tongues." And according to *Vine's Expository Dictionary of Biblical Words*, the word "healings" is plural in the Greek in verses 9, 28, and 30.

Notice that this is the only one of the spiritual gifts listed in First Corinthians 12 that is in the plural — gift*s* of healing*s*. All the other gifts of the Spirit are singular, except tongues, which will be covered in a later lesson.

Why are they "gifts of healing*s*" and not the "gifts of healing"? The Bible doesn't specifically say, but I have an opinion which I believe is well-founded as to why this is so. I don't think any of us could know for sure scripturally because the Scriptures don't specifically tell us. However, it may be that there are gift*s* of healing*s* because there are different kinds of diseases and one gift wouldn't heal every kind of disease.

For example, I have noticed in my own ministry, as well as in the ministry of others who have these gifts of healings in operation in their lives and ministries, that when it comes to healings, in some areas I have more success than in other areas. Other ministers have concurred that this is also true in their ministries.

For instance, other ministers have told me that there are certain kinds of diseases they seldom get people healed of in their ministry, and yet, when it comes to other diseases, nearly every person they pray for is healed.

Of course, this is not to negate the fact that believers can be healed on their own faith in God's Word. And yet we must also recognize that there are those in the Body of Christ who are endued with particular spiritual gifts, such as gifts of healings.

For instance, in my own ministry, ruptures, growths, hernias, or lumps of any kind are almost always healed when I pray for people. I once kept a record in every meeting I had over a period of several years. And in ninety-nine cases out of one hundred, these types of afflictions were eventually all healed.

Some of the growths disappear within a month. Others sometimes take several months before they completely disappear. But in most cases these growths disappear and the people are healed. That is a manifestation of the gifts of healings.

One fellow who was greatly used of God in praying for people who were deaf, said by his own admission that he very seldom got any other type of malady except deaf folks. I watched him several times in various meetings, and I never saw a deaf person fail to receive healing under this man's ministry.

In the ministry of Jesus, *every* manner of sickness and *every* manner of disease was healed (Matt. 9:35). That's because Jesus had the Spirit without measure and all the gifts of healings were in manifestation in His life and ministry.

Gifts of Healings vs. Receiving by Faith

There is a difference between receiving healing through the manifestation of gifts of healings and just simply receiving healing by our own faith in God's Word. God has taught me through the years the difference between the two. Both are scriptural ways to receive healing.

When I received healing for my own body, for example, no one laid hands on me. In fact, I didn't really know there was any church group that believed in divine healing. I didn't know there was such a thing as a Full Gospel movement.

But as a Baptist boy on the bed of sickness, I read Grandma's Methodist Bible and I was healed, not just because I believed in divine healing necessarily, but because I acted on and stood on Mark 11:24: ". . . *What things soever ye desire, when ye pray, believe that ye receive them, and ye shall have them.*"

So I prayed and began to say, "I believe I receive healing for my deformed heart. I believe I receive healing for my paralyzed body. I believe I receive healing from the top of my head to the soles of my feet." And God's healing power was manifested in my body.

My healing came because I acted in faith on God's Word. You can do the same thing. God's Word will work for you if you believe and act on it. Gifts of healings are manifested through another person to you. All healings are done by God, of course, but the difference is in the channel through which healing is manifested.

Someone has said that any time you receive healing, it is done by the gifts of healings in operation. In one sense of the word "gift," healing by any method is a gift because anything you get from God is a gift generally speaking.

However, all healing is not necessarily the gifts of healings in manifestation. My own healing, for example, was manifested as I believed God's Word and acted on it in faith.

Ministering by the Gifts of Healings

Look again at First Corinthians 12:28: *"And God hath set some in the church. . . ."* Paul was not talking here about spiritual gifts, or the gifts of the Spirit when he said, *"And God hath set SOME in the Church. . . ."* He was talking about *men and women* who were equipped with spiritual gifts and ministries.

The "some" that were set in the church includes *". . . first apostles . . ."* (1 Cor. 12:28). "Apostles" isn't an individual gift that someone might receive; it is a ministry gift to the Church. "Some" also includes *". . . secondarily prophets . . ."* (1 Cor. 12:28). That is a ministry, not to bless an individual, but it is a ministry that is given to bless the whole Church, the Body of Christ.

First Corinthians 12:28 says, *". . . thirdly teachers. . . ."* The teaching gift is not something that is given to bless the one who ministers in that anointing. It is a gift that is given to enable a person to bless others. It is a ministry gift *to* the Body of Christ.

Paul went on in this passage to talk about the working of miracles: *". . . after that miracles . . ."* (1 Cor. 12:28). He was saying that there are some people in the ministry who are equipped with the working of miracles in their ministry. That verse continues: *". . . then gifts of healings . . ."* (1 Cor. 12:28).

Then Paul asks the question, *"Are all apostles? . . ."* (1 Cor. 12:29). In other words, Paul was saying, "Does everyone have the ministry of an apostle?" The answer is no. *". . . are all prophets? . . ."* [No.] *". . . are all teachers? . . ."* The answer is no.

Not everyone has the ministry of a teacher to the Body of Christ. Certainly, we could all teach to the extent of our knowledge, but that's not the ministry gift of the teacher. There are those whom God has put in the Church who are equipped by the Holy Spirit with a teaching gift.

I wasn't always a teacher. In fact, for the first nine years of my ministry, I was strictly a preacher. I liked to preach. I was a sermonizer and I had received a great heritage and background along this line from the

Southern Baptists. I could read Spurgeon's sermons and preach them just as he did. I loved to preach, but I did not like to teach.

In my pastoral work, it was customary many times for me as the pastor to teach the Sunday School class in the main auditorium, which was attended by folks thirty-five years old and older. I didn't like that.

Sometimes I would wait until Sunday morning to prepare for it, because I knew I could read the lesson and get up and recite it without a lot of study. I took time to prepare my sermons and get ready to preach for my church services, but I just didn't do much about preparing when it came to teaching. I never was so glad about anything in my life when that Sunday morning ordeal was over.

But in May 1943 in the parsonage of the church that my wife and I pastored in Farmersville, Texas, God gave me a teaching gift. I knew what it was when it came. I didn't have it before, but I knew when I got it. It was just as real to me in the Spirit, as it would have been in the natural realm if someone had handed me a $500 bill.

Teaching is a ministry. It wasn't given to me for my individual benefit: it was given to make me a blessing to others. The same is true of the working of miracles and the gifts of healings and of all the ministry gifts.

As we've seen, in First Corinthians 12:29, Paul asks, *"Are all apostles? . . ."* Of course not. *". . . Are all teachers? . . ."* The answer is no. Everyone doesn't have a teaching ministry. I didn't for years. I would teach when I had to, but I didn't have that ministry. Then Paul asks, *". . . are all workers of miracles?"* Well, it is quite obvious that all are not workers of miracles.

Then in verse 30 it says, *"Have all the gifts of healing? . . ."* No, all people do not have the gifts of healings. This scripture refutes the idea that if a person receives healing, he has also automatically received the impartation of the supernatural gifts of healings — a gift of the Spirit to minister healing to others. And this scripture refutes the idea that a person is necessarily always healed by gifts of healings; he could be healed on his own faith in God's Word.

So First Corinthians 12:28 isn't referring to a healing that is given to a person to bless *him*; it is a *ministry* of healing given to bless others.

Any healing from God is a gift, of course. In fact, anything we receive from God — any blessing — would be a gift. But these gifts of the Spirit are supernatural manifestations of the Spirit, and gifts of healings are one such operation manifested to someone through another. Gifts of healings are one way of receiving healing. But as I've said, there are ways of receiving divine healing other than by the manifestation of the gifts of healings.

As a Baptist boy preacher, I would preach on faith and prayer. I wasn't conscious of any kind of anointing or any manifestation of the gifts of the Spirit in operation as I ministered to people. I would just pray for people in faith and God would honor faith because God honors faith in His Word. Therefore, people were healed.

Later I learned that there were others preaching divine healing besides me. They called themselves "Full Gospel." I would fellowship with them, and soon afterwards, I got the baptism of the Holy Ghost and spoke with other tongues.

I continued to pray for the sick by the laying on of hands and by the anointing with oil. In 1938 I accepted the pastorate of a little Full Gospel church in the blackland of north central Texas. While in prayer late one night, the Lord said to me through the Spirit, "I have given thee gifts of healings and have sent you to minister to the sick."

As a pastor, I had been anointing people with oil and praying for them in faith for healing by the laying on of hands. Up to that time, there had been no manifestation of the gifts of healings through me. Many times people would be healed because they got in agreement with me, and we were acting in faith on God's Word.

But after the Lord spoke to me concerning my ministry to the sick, I became conscious of this other "something" working in my ministry, and there would be a manifestation to other people through me. And I really didn't do anything about it except to yield to the Spirit. Then I saw the difference between healing by simply believing God's promises and by the operation of the gifts of healings.

People can be healed directly by believing God for themselves. Many are healed as I was, simply by believing God. But when it comes to the gifts of healings, there is a special manifestation of the Spirit through one person to another person who is in need.

When people ask me to minister to them, all I can say is that I will minister to them with all the ability I have and with all that God gives me. But we don't operate the gifts of the Spirit as we will; it is as *the Spirit* wills.

However, if there is no gift of the Spirit in manifestation, people can always be healed and set free based on the Word of God. The Bible says it is the anointing, or the power of God, that breaks the yoke (Isa. 10:27). The anointing is on the Word of God.

That's why it is so important for believers to be members of a local body — a local church — where the Word of God is preached and where God moves by His Spirit. Also, I have found that when the Spirit of God is moving, it is a whole lot easier to receive whatever it is you need from God than it is at other times.

However, that still does not eliminate receiving healing on your own by simple faith in God's Word because the Bible says, *". . . by whose* [Jesus'] *stripes ye were healed"* (1 Peter 2:24).

Thank God for His Word and for the privilege of believing and acting upon His Word. Thank God, too, for supernatural manifestations and for gifts of

Questions for Study

1. What are *natural* means of healing?

   _____

   _____

2. What are *supernatural* means of healing?

   _____

   _____

3. In the New Testament, there are many examples of what spiritual gift in operation?

   _____

   _____

4. How did Jesus minister while He was on the earth?

   _____

   _____

5. John 3:34 infers that the entire Body of Christ has the same measure of the Spirit
   _____ as Jesus had _____.

6. In the ministry of Jesus, what manner of sickness and disease was healed and why?

   _____

   _____

7. What was Paul talking about in First Corinthians 12:28 when he said, *"And God hath set some in the church . . . ."*?

   _____

   _____

8. What two ideas does First Corinthians 12:30 refute?

   _____

   _____

9. How can people be healed if there is no gift of the Spirit in operation?

   _____

   _____

10. According to Isaiah 10:27, what breaks the yoke?

    _____

    _____

Chapter 18

Gift of Prophecy

But the manifestation of the Spirit is given to every man to profit withal.

For to one is given by the Spirit the word of wisdom; to another the word of knowledge by the same Spirit;

To another faith by the same Spirit; to another the gifts of healing by the same Spirit;

To another the working of miracles; TO ANOTHER PROPHECY; to another discerning of spirits; to another divers kinds of tongues; to another the interpretation of tongues:

But all these worketh that one and the selfsame Spirit, dividing to every man severally as he will.
— 1 Corinthians 12:7-11

As I explained earlier, the simplest way to describe the gifts of the Spirit is to say that three of them *say* something. Three of them *do* something. And three of them *reveal* something.

Three gifts of utterance that *say* something:
Prophecy
Divers kinds of tongues
Interpretation of tongues

Three gifts of power that *do* something:
The gift of faith
The working of miracles
The gifts of healings

Three gifts of revelation that *reveal* something:
The word of wisdom
The word of knowledge
The discerning of spirits

In this lesson, we will begin our discussion of the three gifts of inspiration or utterance. Of these three gifts, prophecy is the most important. Of course, the reason it is the most important is that it takes the other two inspirational gifts — divers kinds of tongues and the interpretation of tongues — to equal this one gift.

The Bible says, *". . . greater is he that prophesieth than he that speaketh with tongues, except he interpret . . ."* (1 Cor. 14:5). This infers that to speak with tongues and to interpret the tongues is equivalent to prophecy. Therefore, prophecy is really the most important of these three gifts of inspiration or utterance in that it does not require another gift to complete it.

Prophecy is supernatural utterance in a *known* tongue.

Divers kinds of tongues is supernatural utterance in an *unknown* tongue.

Interpretation of tongues is a supernatural *showing forth* of that which has been said in an unknown tongue.

The Hebrew meaning of the phrase, "to prophesy" is *to flow forth*. It also carries with it the thought: *to bubble forth like a fountain, to let drop, to lift up, to tumble forth,* and *to spring forth.*

The Greek word that is translated "prophesy" means *to speak for another.* So "prophesy" can mean to speak for God or to be His spokesman.

In First Corinthians 14:1 we read: *"Follow after charity [love], and desire spiritual gifts, but rather that ye may PROPHESY."* We are told to desire spiritual gifts, but especially that we might prophesy. That doesn't mean we are not to desire the other gifts, but we are to especially desire to prophesy.

Again, at the end of First Corinthians chapter 14, Paul repeated, *"Wherefore, brethren, covet to prophesy . . ."* (1 Cor. 14:39). Paul was writing by the inspiration of God. We could say it this way: God through Paul spoke to the Church at Corinth (and it applies to the Church everywhere) to desire spiritual gifts, but rather that we may prophesy (1 Cor. 14:1,39).

Foretelling vs. Forth Telling

The simple gift of prophecy should not be confused with the prophetic office or with prophetic utterance that may come forth in the prophet's ministry. Paul said, *"But he that prophesieth speaketh unto men to EDIFICATION, and EXHORTATION, and COMFORT"* (1 Cor. 14:3).

Thus, we can readily see that in the simple gift of prophecy there is no revelation. The simple gift of prophecy is given for edification, exhortation, and comfort. In the office of the prophet, however we very often find that revelation or *foretelling* does come forth, even through the vehicle of prophecy.

It is also interesting to note the difference between prophecy in the Old Testament and prophecy in the New Testament. In the Old Testament prophecy was essentially *foretelling*, but in the New Testament we see that the gift of prophecy shifts strongly to *forth telling.*

Prophesying Is More Than Preaching

Some people think that "to prophesy" means *to preach*. All inspired utterance *is* prophecy in some form or another, but the spiritual gift of prophecy isn't preaching. Sometimes there is an element of prophecy in preaching when a person is anointed by the Spirit and is inspired to say things spontaneously that come from his spirit rather than his head. But that is only one phase of the operation of the gift of prophecy.

I have heard people say, "I was witnessing to someone about the Lord and I said things to them that were in line with the Word but that were beyond my own thinking. I didn't think it and it didn't come out of my mind. I was just inspired by the Holy Spirit to say it." That is a part of the operation of this gift of prophecy because prophecy is inspired utterance. The gift of prophecy goes beyond speaking by our own reasoning processes and intellect.

"To preach" means *to proclaim, to announce, to cry,* or *to tell.* The scriptural purpose of the gift of prophecy is different from the purpose of preaching.

For example, Jesus didn't say that men would be saved by the foolishness of *prophesying,* but by the foolishness of *preaching* (1 Cor. 1:21). The supernatural gifts of the Spirit are given to arrest people's attention, not to save them. Even on the Day of Pentecost when people were speaking in tongues, none of those standing by listening got saved until Peter got up and *preached* to them (Acts 2:14-41).

The Gift of Prophecy vs. the Office of the Prophet

As we have said, the gift of prophecy should not be confused with the prophetic office. The simple gift of prophecy has no revelation in it. Rather, it speaks unto men for their edification, exhortation, and comfort (1 Cor. 14:3); it is to edify the Church (1 Cor. 14:4).

Notice that in First Corinthians 14:1, Paul was telling the whole Church at Corinth to covet to prophesy and to desire spiritual gifts, "*. . . but rather that ye may prophesy.*" Yet in First Corinthians 12:28, Paul said that all are not prophets. If prophesying made a person a prophet, then Paul would be contradicting himself. In other words, the fact that the gift of simple prophecy operates through a person doesn't make him a prophet.

For example, a rich man has money. Most of us have at least some money, even if it's only a few cents, but that doesn't make us rich. By the same token, a prophet would of course prophesy, but a person who prophesies wouldn't necessarily be a prophet.

Also, a prophet would have more of the gifts of the Spirit in operation than just the gift of prophecy. He would have revelation gifts operating along with prophecy for the simple reason that Paul says in First Corinthians 14:29 and 30, "*Let the prophets speak two or three, and let the other judge. If any thing be REVEALED to another that sitteth by* [that is, another prophet], *let the first hold his peace.*"

Here Paul is talking about revelation. "*If any thing be REVEALED . . .*" (v. 30). Therefore, the prophet would have other revelation gifts operating in his ministry, as well as the gift of prophecy.

To constitute standing in the office of the prophet, a person needs to have at least two of the revelation gifts operating on a continual basis in his life and ministry, plus the gift of prophecy.

In other words, for a person to stand in the office of the prophet, he would need to be called to the five-fold ministry as a preacher or teacher of the Word (Eph. 4:11,12), and have two of the three revelation gifts — the word of wisdom, the word of knowledge, or the discerning of spirits — *plus* prophecy operating consistently in his ministry.

Therefore, we should not confuse the office of the prophet with the simple gift of prophecy which we are all told to covet: "*Wherefore, brethren, covet to prophesy . . .*" (1 Cor. 14:39). We can all have the gift of prophecy because God wouldn't tell us to covet something that wasn't available to us, nor to desire something that we couldn't have (1 Cor. 14:1,5,39). Yet all will not have all the gifts of the Spirit operating in their lives and ministries.

1 CORINTHIANS 14:1,5,39
1 Follow after charity, and desire spiritual gifts, but rather that ye may PROPHESY. . . .
5 I would that ye all spake with tongues, but rather that ye PROPHESIED: for greater is he that PROPHESIETH than he that speaketh with tongues, except he interpret, that the church may receive edifying. . . .
39 Wherefore, brethren, covet to PROPHESY, and forbid not to speak with tongues.

We can all prophesy, but we can't all be prophets. And although we can all prophesy, we must also realize that prophecy through the office of the prophet carries more authority than the simple gift of prophecy would operating through the laity.

New Testament Example of the Gift of Prophecy

In Acts chapter 21, we see a scriptural illustration of some believers who had the gift of prophecy operating in their lives.

ACTS 21:8,9
8 And the next day we that were of Paul's company departed, and came unto Caesarea: and we entered into the house of Philip the evangelist, which was one of the seven; and abode with him.
9 And the same man [Philip] had four daughters, virgins, WHICH DID PROPHESY.

All four of Philip's daughters had this simple gift of prophecy operating in their lives. They must have prophesied in the services held in their house because otherwise Paul and his company would not have known that they prophesied.

Philip's daughters spoke to the whole company to edification, exhortation, and comfort (1 Cor. 14:3). However, when the prophet Agabus came, he had a message from the Holy Spirit on a higher order, which brought revelation.

New Testament Example of the Prophet's Ministry

ACTS 21:10,11
10 And as we tarried there many days, there came down from Judaea a certain prophet, named Agabus.
11 And when he was come unto us, he took Paul's girdle, and bound his own hands and feet, and said, Thus saith the Holy Ghost, So shall the Jews at Jerusalem bind the man that owneth this girdle, and shall deliver him into the hands of the Gentiles.

Agabus wasn't necessarily prophesying here in the sense that we normally think of the gift of simple prophecy. He just had a message from the Holy Ghost. He had a message that had some revelation with it — the word of wisdom.

However, no definite *direction* was given to Paul in this message in the sense that Agabus didn't tell Paul to go or not to go to Jerusalem. That decision was left up to Paul. Agabus just told Paul what was going to happen in the near future *should* he go to Jerusalem.

There are two possible ways of interpreting the word of wisdom that Agabus had for Paul. One, it was a word of wisdom delivered through the vehicle of prophecy. Two, Agabus was just reporting the word of wisdom he already knew by the Spirit of God.

Therefore, we see that the prophet may prophesy, but the message he brings may not be simple prophecy at all. In other words, the message the prophet gives may come *through* the vehicle of prophecy (inspired utterance), but the message may actually be the revelation gifts in operation, such as the word of wisdom or the word of knowledge.

Or the prophet may just speak what he has already previously received from the Lord, reporting, "Thus saith the Lord," and the message may actually be other gifts of the Spirit in operation, such as the word of wisdom.

Therefore, in Acts 21:10,11, one of the revelation gifts — the word of wisdom — may have been manifested through the gift of prophecy. In that case, prophecy would just be the vehicle through which the word of wisdom came.

As I said, the other possibility is that when Agabus gave the word of the Lord to Paul, he was only reporting the word of wisdom he already knew by the Spirit, saying, "Thus saith the Holy Ghost," and was not literally speaking under the unction of prophecy.

Misuses of the Gift of Prophecy

The misuse of the gift of prophecy can cause confusion among believers. If folks would use prophecy as the Scripture teaches, it would be a great blessing to the Body of Christ. But some people hear a minister who operates in the prophet's ministry bring forth revelation and they think they can do that too. So they try to bring forth some *foretelling* instead of just *forth telling*, and they get into trouble.

A woman once told me: "I attend a prayer group where all they do is lay hands on one another and prophesy. But if anything has ever come to pass, I don't know it. They laid hands on me and prophesied that my mother was going to die within six month's time, but it's been longer than that and she hasn't died yet."

The woman continued, "Then they prophesied that my husband was going to leave me within the year, but it's been longer than that and he hasn't left me yet. We have a good marriage. They have prophesied a lot of other things, too, none of which has happened."

These people were misusing whatever gift they may have had. But if people would just stay with the simple gift of prophecy, "speaking unto men to edification, to exhortation and to comfort," they would be fine.

Certainly, there are those who stand in the prophet's ministry who sometimes minister along the line of foretelling or prediction. There are others who operate in other gifts of the Spirit such as a word of wisdom or a word of knowledge, which may also come forth in prophecy.

However, those who operate in the word of knowledge or the word of wisdom through prophecy do not *necessarily* stand in the office of the prophet, because, as we saw earlier, there are other qualifications needed to stand in that office. Also, revelation gifts are ministered more on a continual basis in the office of the prophet.

The Simple Gift of Prophecy Is Not Prediction

Many people think the gift of prophecy is *prediction*. The simple gift of prophecy, however, is not prediction but is speaking unto men *". . . to edification, and exhortation, and comfort"* (1 Cor. 14:3).

When it comes to the gifts of the Spirit, you don't have them when you are born into this world. You must first be born into the Kingdom of God through the new birth (2 Cor. 5:17), and then you must receive the baptism of the Holy Spirit (Acts 2:4).

Then the Bible says the Holy Spirit divides the gifts of the Spirit to every man severally as *He* wills (1 Cor. 12:11). Also, you must then be *in the Spirit* for the gifts of the Spirit to operate; gifts of the Spirit do not operate in the flesh. In other words, you must wait upon the unction of the Holy Spirit for the manifestation of spiritual gifts. That is *not* something we do apart from God.

It is amazing how many people have followed the wrong teaching along this line. But there is no use in backing off from the real and the genuine because of the counterfeit. No, that is all the more reason we need to allow the Holy Spirit to demonstrate the genuine gifts of the Spirit through us and show people from the Word of God what is genuine.

It is unfortunate that even some Christians are misled about spiritual gifts. For example, one fellow told me that before he went to work every morning, he waited for the Lord to give him a word of prophecy to know which tie to wear. God is not interested in which tie you wear! That wasn't a word of prophecy; actually he was opening himself to deception by the devil.

Someone once wrote asking me to prophesy to him which church he should attend. This is unscriptural! Each believer has the Holy Spirit as a Guide and Counselor on the inside (John 16:13). And the primary way God leads His children is by the inward witness (Rom. 8:14), not by someone else prophesying to them.

On another occasion while I was holding a meeting in Colorado, some folks from New York called the owner of the motel where I was staying at 4:00 in the morning and said that it was an emergency and they needed to talk to me.

My wife and I had no phone in the room where we were staying, so the owner came knocking on our door. He said I had a telephone call. I got out of bed and about half awake, I put my shirt on and started out the door to the motel office. My wife called out to me, "Honey, aren't you going to put on your pants?" Only half awake, I hadn't realized that I wasn't wearing them! I went back and put on my pants.

When I answered the phone, the person on the other end said, "Brother Hagin, we are having an all-night prayer meeting and we just got to thinking we would call you and see if you had a word for us." She meant a word of prophecy. Well, I had a word for them, all right, but it wasn't a word of prophecy! And I didn't give it to them because it wouldn't have been from the Lord — it would have been from my flesh!

Sometimes God may use you to give a word to someone, but that doesn't mean you can just turn the gifts of the Spirit on and off whenever you want to. Let's realize that what we have is *from* and *by* the Spirit of God, and let's minister what we have according to the direction and unction of the Spirit of God.

Manifestations of the Holy Spirit in Corporate Worship

We find additional instruction regarding this use of the gift of prophecy in First Corinthians 14:26.

1 CORINTHIANS 14:26
26 How is it then, brethren? when ye come together, every one of you hath a psalm, hath a doctrine, hath a tongue, hath a revelation, hath an interpretation. Let all things be done unto edifying.

This scripture shows us that the Spirit of God is more apt to move when folks come together in the Name of Jesus to worship. The Spirit of God manifests Himself more readily in an atmosphere of worship and praise where God is being glorified.

For example, in my ministry I always get greater results when I pray for people under the anointing. Whether praying for the sick, praying for people to be filled with the Holy Spirit, or praying for the needs of the people, I have found that it is better to pray for the people after the Word has gone forth. Then I am usually more anointed to minister. That is why I pray for people many times at the conclusion of the service.

Some want to rush in and be prayed for right away, but when we come together in the Name of

Jesus, worshipping God and teaching the Word, we are often in a much better spiritual attitude to believe God and to receive from Him. And the gifts are more likely to be manifested in an atmosphere of praise and worship.

The Holy Spirit Manifests Himself as We Seek the Lord

We find another indication about the kind of atmosphere the Holy Ghost manifests Himself in as we read Acts 13:1: *"Now there were in the church that was at Antioch certain prophets and teachers. . . ,"* and it goes on to list the names of five men.

ACTS 13:1-4
1 Now there were in the church that was at Antioch certain prophets and teachers; as Barnabas, and Simeon that was called Niger, and Lucius of Cyrene, and Manaen, which had been brought up with Herod the tetrarch, and Saul.
2 AS THEY MINISTERED TO THE LORD, and fasted, THE HOLY GHOST SAID, Separate me Barnabas and Saul for the work whereunto I have called them.
3 And when they had fasted and prayed, and laid their hands on them, they sent them away.
4 So they, being sent forth by the Holy Ghost, departed. . . .

Notice that it was as they ministered to the Lord and fasted that the Holy Spirit manifested Himself.

But notice in Acts 13:2, the Scripture doesn't say that the Holy Ghost just *witnessed* to the disciples' spirits about separating Barnabas and Saul unto the ministry. It says the Holy Ghost *said* something. He said *". . . Separate me Barnabas and Saul for the work whereunto I have called them"* (Acts 13:2).

The Holy Ghost *said* something through one of the prophets because it is through this ministry gift, the office of the prophet — those who are especially equipped with certain revelation and utterance gifts — that the Holy Ghost normally speaks. Otherwise, the Holy Spirit leads by an inward witness, which every believer has (Rom. 8:14).

Notice something else in this passage. This wasn't when Barnabas and Saul were called to the ministry; they had already received the call to the ministry because the Holy Spirit said, *". . . for the work whereunto I HAVE CALLED THEM"* (v. 2). That's past tense.

Therefore, Barnabas and Saul had already received the call to the ministry from God in their own private lives. In other words, they weren't receiving their call to the ministry through a prophet. The Holy Spirit was merely *confirming* that

call through a prophet.

Caution Needed With Personal Prophecies

Let me stress that we need to be very careful about personal prophecies. Lives have been ruined and many unfortunate things have happened through misuse of personal prophecies.

I have to be very careful myself because God uses me from time to time prophetically in this way. But over the years I have seen so much error in the area of personal prophecy that it almost makes a person want to draw back from the genuine prophetic ministry. I have to watch myself in order not to pull back too far the other way and not yield to the Spirit of God to be used the way He wants to use me.

Simple Prophecy *Edifies*, *Exhorts*, and *Comforts*

1 CORINTHIANS 14:3
3 But he that prophesieth speaketh unto men to edification, and exhortation, and comfort.

If we keep in mind the scriptural use of prophecy, we will not get off doctrinally in this area. The simple gift of prophecy is given to speak to people supernaturally — to *edify* the church: *". . . he that prophesieth edifieth the church"* (1 Cor. 14:4).

This gift of prophecy is also given to edify the Church through exhortation. In the Greek, the word "exhort" in First Corinthians 14:3 means *a calling nearer to God* or *an invitation*.

First Corinthians 14:3 also says the gift of prophecy is given to comfort. Much of what some people call "prophecy" never comforts anyone; rather, it *discomforts* them.

Therefore, it could not be this bona fide gift of the Spirit in operation because the gift of prophecy is given for edification, exhortation, and comfort. We might find, however, that the *revelation* given forth in a prophet's ministry may sometimes be discomforting because it sometimes brings with it correction or conviction of sin. But the simple gift of prophecy only ministers edification, exhortation, and comfort.

For example, once while teaching a faith seminar in Phoenix, Arizona, I discerned an evil spirit in a fellow sitting near the front of the church. I knew he had a wrong spirit and would disrupt the service if given an opportunity.

I tried to keep from pausing in my sermon long enough to give him a chance to break in. However, at the conclusion of the message he leapt to his feet, threw up his hands, and started telling the congregation everything he thought was wrong with them.

This fellow did everything *except* what the scriptural use of the gift of prophecy should do. Instead of edifying the people, he tore them down. Instead of exhorting or calling them nearer to God, he drove them away. Instead of comforting them, he discomforted them.

Realizing that he might be mentally unbalanced, I tried to bear with him somewhat, remembering the following passage of Scripture:

1 THESSALONIANS 5:14-21
14 . . . comfort the feebleminded, support the weak, be patient toward all men.
15 See that none render evil for evil unto any man; but ever follow that which is good, both among yourselves, and to all men.
16 Rejoice evermore.
17 Pray without ceasing.
18 In every thing give thanks: for this is the will of God in Christ Jesus concerning you.
19 Quench not the Spirit.
20 Despise not prophesyings.
21 Prove all things; hold fast that which is good.

It was necessary for Paul to give these instructions because the Church at Thessalonica had so much misuse of the gift of prophecy that these folks almost despised it. Therefore, Paul, writing by the Spirit of God, had to instruct them, *"Despise not prophesyings"* (1 Thess. 5:20).

However, those who go around telling everyone what is wrong with them and tearing people down, supposedly operating in the gift of prophecy as this fellow in my meeting did, are not operating in the bona fide gift of the Spirit of God.

A woman once came to me and thanked me after I corrected her for her misuse of the gift of prophecy. Teachable people like to know when they are wrong and appreciate godly correction. She said, "I can see that I misused what I had. God uses me in prophecy sometimes, but I see now that what I was trying to do was to get everybody in line through prophecy."

She had been trying to regulate people's lives through the gift of prophecy; she was trying to make all women dress as she dressed. But she had some strange ideas about dress and about a number of other things! Comfort, *not correction*, is the purpose of this simple gift of prophecy.

Prophecy in One's Prayer Life

The gift of prophecy, like tongues, has to do with more than just public utterance. Prophecy can be used in one's prayer life too. For example, in the Book of Psalms, prophecy was used in prayer and praise to God. As a matter of fact, the whole Book of Psalms was given by the spirit of prophecy. The Psalms were Israel's prayer and songbook. Some of the psalms are prayers that were given by inspired utterance.

We can see prophecy being used in the believer's prayer life in the New Testament too. For example, in Ephesians 5:19, believers are encouraged to speak to themselves *". . . in psalms and hymns and spiritual songs, singing and making melody in your heart to the Lord."* That is the gift of prophecy in operation.

Many times while praying, a person can speak in tongues and then speak out things by the Spirit of God. Speaking with tongues is the beginning of the things of the Spirit, because speaking with tongues is the door into the supernatural. And we know that the gift of tongues is given to every Spirit-filled believer as the evidence of the infilling of the Holy Spirit.

Also, Jesus didn't say that just a few disciples should speak with tongues. He said that *all* believers should speak with tongues: *"And these signs shall follow them that believe . . . they shall speak with new tongues"* (Mark 16:17).

But God wants every Spirit-filled believer to do more than speak with tongues. He wants us to be able to interpret what we pray in tongues, as the Spirit leads. *"Wherefore let him that speaketh in an unknown tongue pray that he may interpret"* (1 Cor. 14:13). God wouldn't tell us to pray for something we couldn't have. Of course, it is not necessary to interpret everything we pray in the Spirit in our own private prayer life.

And then, of course, there is also the public use of the gift of interpretation of tongues. That is to be used in the local assembly: *"If any man speak in an unknown tongue, let it be by two, or at the most by three, and that by course; and let one interpret"* (1 Cor. 14:27). Not every believer will have this gift; not every believer will minister publicly in the gift of interpretation of tongues.

And God also wants us to prophesy in order to bring comfort and encouragement to the Body of Christ because the Bible plainly says, *". . . desire spiritual gifts, but rather that ye may prophesy . . . he that prophesieth edifieth the church"* (1 Cor. 14:1,4). Through this gift of prophecy we can speak supernaturally, not only unto believers and for our own personal benefit, but we can also speak supernaturally unto God (Eph. 5:19; Col. 3:16).

Prophesying in your own personal prayer life

begins with speaking in other tongues (1 Cor. 14:2). In my own experience, for example, as I pray in other tongues, my spirit is in direct contact with God, yet I am communicating with Him in a tongue that is unknown to me.

When you are speaking in tongues, that is a supernatural utterance in an unknown tongue. Paul said when we pray in an unknown tongue, our understanding is unfruitful, unless we interpret what we are praying (1 Cor. 14:14,15). In other words, we don't always know what we are praying about when we pray in other tongues. However, when you pray with prophecy, you can listen to yourself speak in a known tongue and, therefore, you can know what you are saying.

Very often praying in tongues is a springboard to go into prophecy in prayer. Remember, prophecy in its broadest sense is inspired utterance. For example, sometimes I pray about certain things with my own understanding, which may not necessarily be inspired utterance at all. I may just be praying as well as I know how to about the situation in my own understanding — in my own native language. (Of course, one can also pray in one's understanding in his own language *in the Spirit*; that is, inspired and directed by the Holy Spirit.)

Then as I pray about the situation awhile in tongues, many times I move over into prophecy — inspired utterance. Then as I pray by inspired utterance, I can actually be praying out the plan of God by inspired utterance as the word of wisdom (John 16:13; Cor. 14:1-5 *Amplified*) manifests through the gift of prophecy in my private prayer life. This can happen in the private prayer life of any Spirit-filled believer.

Praying in prophecy can carry with it a more authoritative anointing because you can actually be praying out the word of wisdom in prayer through the vehicle of prophecy. Praying out the word of wisdom through prophecy lifts you above where you were before in prayer and many times reveals to you a part or a fragment of the plan of God — a "word" of wisdom. You are actually praying out the plan and purpose of God for your own life in prayer (John 16:13,14).

However, a distinction must be made between praying out the plan of God in one's own *private* prayer life by the word of wisdom through the vehicle of prophecy, and in the word of wisdom manifesting through a believer in prophecy in *public* ministry.

Any believer can pray out the plan of God for his own life (John 16:13,14) either in tongues or as the Spirit wills, in prophecy. But that is distinct and separate from public ministry. Because the Holy Spirit may show the believer things to come in private times of prayer, does not necessarily mean that the word of wisdom will operate through the believer *publicly*.

Also, we must realize that the word of knowledge or the word of wisdom may operate in the believer's life in prayer, but that doesn't make him a prophet. There is a difference between the believer who may operate in these spiritual gifts in his own private prayer life, and one who stands in a fivefold office (such as the prophet) through whom the Holy Spirit manifests spiritual gifts in *public* ministry.

Psalms, Hymns, and Spiritual Songs By the Gift of Prophecy

Paul said, *"And be not drunk with wine, wherein is excess; but be filled with the Spirit"* (Eph. 5:18). Then in the next verse he said, *"Speaking to yourselves in psalms and hymns and spiritual songs, singing and making melody in your heart to the Lord."*

We read in Acts chapter 13 that the disciples ministered to the Lord. This was perhaps one way that they ministered to the Lord — by singing and making melody in their hearts to Him.

Psalms, hymns, and spiritual songs are not songs that are sung out of a songbook. They are songs given by the inspiration of the Spirit of God. A psalm is a spiritual poem or an ode. It can be recited or chanted or sung. The hymn and the spiritual song are, of course, sung. One who is given more to singing would probably *sing* the psalms and hymns given to him by inspiration of the Spirit.

Psalms and hymns come through the spirit of prophecy as an inspired utterance, and therefore could also come through the vehicle of tongues and interpretation.

I am not a singer. Therefore, when I get psalms, particularly during times of stress or strain or when I am going through a crisis, I just recite them. Sometimes I will speak in psalms all night long to myself and to the Lord, one right after another.

These psalms, hymns, and spiritual songs are given spontaneously by the inspiration of the Spirit. They are a demonstration of the gift of prophecy or its equivalent tongues and interpretation in manifestation. These psalms, hymns, and spiritual songs can be used to comfort us in times of tests or trials.

Paul writing to the Church at Colossae even further said, *"Let the word of Christ dwell in you richly in all wisdom; teaching and admonishing one another in psalms and hymns and spiritual songs . . ."* (Col. 3:16).

Another interesting thing to note is that the order of the services in the Early Church evidently differed from ours in that believers went to church because they *had* something, not just to *get* something.

1 CORINTHIANS 14:26
26 How is it then, brethren? when ye come together, every one of you hath a psalm, hath a doctrine, hath a tongue, hath a revelation, hath an interpretation. . . .

Why did they have a psalm they could share with one another? Because they had been speaking in psalms to the Lord; they had been edifying themselves at home.

The Book of Psalms in the Old Testament were not written *to* us in the same way the Epistles were written directly to us — the Church. We read the psalms and they bless us and encourage us because they are inspired by the Spirit. There is some revelation in some of these psalms concerning prophecy of the coming Christ and of things pertaining to the future and to the Church. But many of the psalms were given to David, for example, when he was going through a certain test or trial in his life.

For instance, one time Saul sought to kill David. While hiding in a cave, David got a psalm by the spirit of prophecy, and it was given to him personally to encourage him. It encouraged him then, and those psalms encourage us, too, when we are facing tests and trials in life.

So we can see why Paul said to the members of the Church at Corinth, and to Christians everywhere, to covet to prophesy, for in this way they can talk to God supernaturally and to themselves in a known language. There is a fellowship in the Spirit that comes through using prophecy in prayer that is beyond what we've previously experienced.

God's Word teaches that all Spirit-filled believers should not only speak with tongues when they are initially filled with the Spirit, but they should continue to speak with tongues as a continual experience, after they are filled with the Spirit. The Word also teaches that all Spirit-filled believers should be speaking to themselves in psalms, hymns, and spiritual songs.

If we follow Paul's admonition today and covet to prophesy, we, too, can speak to ourselves in psalms, hymns, and spiritual songs. Begin to covet to prophesy because the Word of God encourages believers to do so.

First Corinthians 12:31 says, *". . . covet earnestly the best gifts. . . ."* As you do, then you will be able to speak supernaturally to the Body of Christ God's words of edification, exhortation, and comfort as the Spirit wills. You will also be able to speak supernaturally through the gift of prophecy in your private prayer life, edifying yourself and worshipping God in psalms, hymns, and spiritual songs.

Questions for Study

1. Why is the gift of prophecy the most important gift of utterance?

   _____

   _____

2. What is prophecy?

   _____

   _____

3. The simple gift of prophecy should not be confused with what?

   _____

   _____

4. We can readily see that in the simple gift of prophecy there is no _____.

5. In the Old Testament, prophecy was essentially _____, but in the New Testament, we see that the gift of prophecy shifts strongly to _____ _____.

6. What does "to preach" mean?

   _____

   _____

7. Give a New Testament example of the gift of prophecy.

   _____

   _____

8. Give a New Testament example of the prophet's ministry.

   _____

   _____

9. In what kind of atmosphere does the Spirit of God more readily manifest Himself?

   _____

   _____

10. What kind of prophecies do we need to be very careful about?

    _____

    _____

Chapter 19

The Gift of Divers Kinds of Tongues

But the manifestation of the Spirit is given to every man to profit withal.

For to one is given by the Spirit the word of wisdom; to another the word of knowledge by the same Spirit;

To another faith by the same Spirit; to another the gifts of healing by the same Spirit;

To another the working of miracles; to another prophecy; to another discerning of spirits; TO ANOTHER DIVERS KINDS OF TONGUES; to another the interpretation of tongues:

But all these worketh that one and the selfsame Spirit, dividing to every man severally as he will.
— 1 Corinthians 12:7-11

In our study of the gifts of the Spirit, we come to the subject of divers kinds of tongues. The word "divers" in First Corinthians 12:10 is italicized, which means that it was added by the translator.

Actually, this verse reads, ". . . to another, kinds of tongues. . . ." However, in another scripture, Paul said that God set in the Church diversities of tongues (1 Cor. 12:28); therefore, we would not be out of line scripturally to say "divers" kinds of tongues, or different kinds of tongues.

This utterance gift of tongues is an important gift in that tongues is the door into the supernatural. This doesn't necessarily mean the gift of tongues is the best gift, for as we indicated previously, the best gift is the gift needed at the moment.

Tongues: the Most Prominent Gift

Of the three vocal gifts, or as they are sometimes called, the gifts of utterance or inspiration — the gift of prophecy, divers kinds of tongues and the interpretation of tongues — the gift of tongues is the most prominent.

A question often asked by those in denominations is, "Why do Full Gospel people place such emphasis on tongues?" The answer is, "We do not." There are several reasons why it may *seem* that we do.

First, we are often questioned about tongues and are therefore drawn into discussions about tongues.

Second, speaking in tongues is the initial physical evidence when people are baptized in the Holy Ghost.

Third, utterance in tongues in public assembly is the most frequently manifested gift of the Spirit.

Fourth, tongues and interpretation of tongues are distinctive to the Church Age. Therefore, they are more in operation.

We see all the other gifts of the Spirit in operation in the Old Testament — the word of wisdom, the word of knowledge, special faith, gifts of healings, working of miracles, prophecy, and discerning of spirits — all the gifts of the Spirit except for tongues and interpretation of tongues.

And in the ministry of Jesus, too, we see all the gifts of the Spirit in operation except for tongues and interpretation of tongues; you won't find tongues and interpretation of tongues in operation in His ministry.

The fifth reason why it seems that Full Gospel people emphasize tongues so much is that Paul gave prominence to tongues. One reason he did was that then, just as now, speaking in tongues was widely misunderstood.

The Gift of Tongues Is a Supernatural Sign

Divers kinds of tongues is supernatural utterance by the Holy Spirit in languages never learned by the speaker, nor understood by the speaker, nor necessarily always understood by the hearer. Speaking with tongues has nothing whatsoever to do with linguistic ability; it has nothing to do with the mind or the intellect of man. It is a vocal miracle of the Holy Spirit.

We might ask, "What is the good of speaking with tongues?" Jesus said in Mark 16:17, ". . . *these signs shall follow them that believe . . . they shall speak with new tongues.*"

One preacher, endeavoring to explain that, said, "This just means that a fellow who used to curse and tell lies and vulgar jokes doesn't do that anymore; he speaks with a new tongue." This argument, however, is a little thin because in reading the entire context of the following passage of Scripture, we see that every one of these signs is supernatural.

MARK 16:15-18
15 . . . Go ye into all the world, and preach the gospel to every creature.
16 He that believeth and is baptized shall be saved; but he that believeth not shall be damned.
17 And these signs shall follow them that believe; In my name shall they cast out devils [exercise authority over demons and evil spirits in His name]; **they shall speak with new tongues;**
18 They shall take up serpents [meaning believers won't be harmed if they do so accidentally, as Paul did on the island of Melita]; **and if they drink any deadly thing** [accidentally], **it shall not hurt them; they shall lay hands on the sick, and they shall recover.**

Any thinking person could see that if the other four of these signs — casting out devils, taking up serpents, drinking any deadly thing without suffering harm, and laying hands on the sick — are supernatural, surely the fifth sign, speaking in tongues, is also supernatural.

Therefore, one reason we speak in tongues is that Jesus said this is one sign which should follow believers. Also, tongues is the scriptural, initial evidence also of the baptism in the Holy Ghost (Acts 2:4).

The Gift of Tongues Is Unique to This Dispensation

One preacher disagreed with speaking in tongues, saying, "John the Baptist had the Holy Ghost and he didn't speak with tongues. Prophets of the Old Testament had the Holy Ghost, but they never spoke in tongues. So why do we need to speak in tongues?"

But we must remember that John the Baptist ministered as a prophet under the Old Covenant. Prophets under the Old Covenant had not been born again. They did not have a recreated human spirit; they had never been made a new creature in Christ (2 Cor. 5:17) because Jesus had not yet come in His death, burial, and resurrection to redeem mankind.

Therefore, prophets under the Old Covenant did not have the infilling of the Holy Spirit in the same way that a born-again, Spirit-filled believer does living under the New Covenant.

Under the Old Covenant, the Holy Spirit *came upon* those who stood in the offices of the prophet, priest, and king to enable them to fulfill their offices or ministries, but He did not *indwell* and *infill* them in the same sense that He does the born-again, Spirit-filled believer living under the New Covenant.

We are not living under the Old Covenant. What happened under the Old Covenant was written as an example for us now, but that doesn't mean we are to try to live like they did under the Old Covenant. We want the Holy Ghost and His gifts manifested in our lives according to the dispensation in which *we* live. And the gift of tongues and interpretation of tongues are unique to the dispensation of the Church Age.

John the Baptist was still under the Old Covenant. He was a prophet under the Old Covenant. Jesus Himself said concerning John the Baptist, "*. . . Among them that are born of women there hath not risen a greater than John the Baptist: notwithstanding he that is least in the kingdom of heaven is greater than he*" (Matt. 11:11).

Therefore, we have to start with the Acts of the Apostles. We can't go back to the Old Covenant to pattern our lives because we are not living under that covenant.

We have a better covenant established on better promises (Heb. 8:6), particularly in the area of the promise of the Holy Spirit.

Tongues Is the Evidence of Being Filled With the Spirit

Having been taught in a denominational church that when one is born again he receives the Holy Ghost, and that is all of the Holy Ghost there is to receive, I decided as a young boy pastor to find out about this for myself. I went to the Bible for my answer.

I believed that I was preaching in my church the same new birth that they preached and experienced in the Acts of the Apostles. I believed and still do believe that I was preaching the same water baptism that they preached and practiced in the Acts of the Apostles. I believed and still do believe that I was teaching and observing the Lord's Supper or Holy Communion just as the Early Church did.

I wanted to be scripturally based and New Testament taught and follow biblical doctrinal practices, so I simply went to the Acts of the Apostles to satisfy my own mind.

As I examined the scriptures closely in the Book of Acts, I found that there are five recorded instances where believers received the Holy Spirit.

These five instances, discussed in Chapter 8, are sufficient to show us a pattern of the Holy Spirit's dealing in the Early Church: people were saved and subsequently filled with the Holy Spirit with the evidence of speaking in tongues. This is a pattern for us living under the *same* covenant today. God desires that *every* believer be filled with the Holy Spirit — the enduement of power from on High (Luke 24:49). Let's review these five instances once more.

1. Acts 2:1-4

   The 120 on the Day of Pentecost: These were men *and* women, including Mary, the mother of Jesus. Gathered in the Upper Room on the Day of Pentecost, they were filled with the Holy Ghost and spoke in tongues as the Spirit gave them utterance.

2. Acts 8:5-17

   The Samaritans: Saved under Philip's ministry, they received the Holy Spirit when Peter and John laid hands on them. Simon *saw* physical evidence of the infilling of the Holy Spirit, which was probably speaking in tongues.

3. **Acts 9:3-18**

   Saul (later called Paul): When Ananias laid hands on him, Paul received the Holy Spirit. We know Paul spoke in tongues because later he wrote to the Church at Corinth, *"I thank my God, I speak with tongues more than ye all"* (1 Cor. 14:18).

4. **Acts 10:44-46**

   Cornelius and his household: This incident occurred years after the Day of Pentecost. As Peter was preaching the gospel to these first Gentile converts, they were all saved (Acts 11:14) and filled with the Holy Spirit, and spoke with other tongues.

5. **Acts 19:1-7**

   The Ephesian disciples: This incident occurred many years after the Day of Pentecost. These Ephesian disciples were saved and baptized in the Name of Jesus after Paul explained the gospel to them. Then when Paul laid hands on them, they were immediately filled with the Holy Spirit and they spoke with other tongues.

Thus, in the Bible in the Acts of the Apostles, we see that over many years there are three recorded incidents of believers receiving the Holy Ghost with the evidence of speaking with tongues. And twice it is *inferred* that the evidence for believers receiving the Holy Spirit was speaking in tongues. We should expect to have the same witness of the baptism of the Holy Spirit in evidence today.

Purposes of Speaking in Tongues

We talked in detail in Chapter 8 about the reasons for speaking in tongues. Let's briefly go over a few of those reasons again.

Initial Evidence of Receiving the Holy Spirit

Speaking in tongues is the initial evidence or sign of the Holy Spirit's infilling Presence (Acts 2:4). I believe, of course, that there are other evidences that will follow, but this is the first or initial physical evidence.

Speaking Mysteries Supernaturally to God

Paul gives another reason for speaking with tongues in First Corinthians 14:2: *"For he that speaketh in an unknown tongue speaketh not unto men, but UNTO GOD: for no man understandeth him; howbeit IN THE SPIRIT HE SPEAKETH MYSTERIES"* (1 Cor. 14:2).

Moffatt's translation reads, ". . . he is talking of divine secrets. . . ." Therefore, one reason for speaking with tongues is so that men may speak mysteries supernaturally to God: *". . . he . . . speaketh not unto men, but UNTO GOD . . ."* (1 Cor. 14:2).

I remember as a young Baptist pastor, my heart longed to fellowship supernaturally with God. I sometimes prayed several hours at a time, but I always went away feeling somewhat cheated in my spirit. My spirit hadn't said what it wanted to because I was praying mostly out of my head — my own understanding — and I was not able to fully express my heart supernaturally to God that way.

One of the great benefits of being filled with the Spirit and speaking with other tongues is that we can talk to God *supernaturally*. It is your spirit, by the Holy Spirit within you, talking to God: *"For if I pray in an unknown tongue, my spirit prayeth, but my understanding is unfruitful"* (1 Cor. 14:14). *The Amplified Bible* says, ". . . my spirit [by the Holy Spirit within me] prays . . ." (1 Cor. 14:14).

Magnifying God

Another scriptural purpose of speaking in tongues is to magnify God.

ACTS 10:45,46
45 And they of the circumcision which believed were astonished . . . because that on the Gentiles also was poured out the gift of the Holy Ghost.
46 For they heard them SPEAK WITH TONGUES, AND MAGNIFY GOD. . . .

So, you see, speaking in tongues is a means of magnifying God.

Edifying Ourselves

Still another scriptural purpose for speaking with tongues is to edify ourselves. In First Corinthians 14:4, Paul makes the statement that *"He that speaketh in an unknown tongue EDIFIETH HIMSELF. . . ."* To edify means *to build oneself up.*

Then in verse 18, Paul said, *"I thank my God, I speak with tongues more than ye all."* In other words he said, "I thank God I edify myself more than ye all." If Paul needed this edification, we need it too.

Jude also links praying in tongues with spiritual edification.

JUDE 20
20 But ye, beloved, BUILDING UP YOURSELVES on your most holy faith, PRAYING IN THE HOLY GHOST.

Praying in the Spirit

Jude instructs believers to "pray in the Holy Ghost." Paul uses a similar phrase in his letters. Writing to the Church at Ephesus, Paul said, *"Praying always with all prayer and supplication IN THE SPIRIT . . ."* (Eph. 6:18). What does it mean to "pray in the Spirit"?

One meaning of "praying in the Spirit" is found in First Corinthians 14:2, where Paul says, *"For he that speaketh in an UNKNOWN TONGUE speaketh not unto men, but unto God . . . howbeit IN THE SPIRIT he speaketh mysteries."* As I mentioned earlier, praying in the Spirit also can mean praying in your understanding as the Holy Spirit inspires you.

Be *Being* Filled With the Spirit

Paul also encouraged the saints at Ephesus to edify themselves, for in Ephesians 5:18 he says, *"And be not drunk with wine, wherein is excess; but BE FILLED WITH THE SPIRIT."*

Remember that this letter was written to Spirit-filled believers, because we read in Acts chapter 19 that Paul came to Ephesus, and there he found these disciples and laid hands on them. The Holy Ghost came on them and they spoke with tongues (Acts 19:1-6). In Ephesians 5:18, Paul is later writing a letter to that same church, and he said, *"And be not drunk with wine, wherein is excess; but be filled with the Spirit"* (Eph. 5:18).

Greek scholars tell us that a more literal translation would be, "Be *being* filled." In other words, we should *maintain* a continuous experience of being filled up to overflowing with the Holy Spirit. It is one thing to *be* filled with the Holy Ghost initially; it is another thing to *stay* continually filled with the Holy Ghost.

Beginning in verse 19, Paul lists the characteristics of the Spirit-filled life.

EPHESIANS 5:19-21
19 Speaking to yourselves in psalms and hymns and spiritual songs, SINGING AND MAKING MELODY IN YOUR HEART TO THE LORD;
20 GIVING THANKS ALWAYS for all things unto God and the Father in the name of our Lord Jesus Christ;
21 SUBMITTING YOURSELVES ONE TO ANOTHER in the fear of God.

Those believers who are continually being filled with the Holy Spirit have a song in their heart; they are always giving thanks to God; and they have a submissive attitude. They sing and make melody in their hearts to the Lord continually.

As we discussed in Chapter 18, the Lord wants us to maintain a continual experience of being filled with the Holy Spirit. One way the believer does that is by speaking to himself in psalms, hymns, and spiritual songs, singing and making melody in his heart to the Lord.

These psalms, hymns, and spiritual songs are given by the inspiration of the Spirit of God. They come through the spirit of prophecy (Rev. 19:10), which may include tongues and interpretation.

Allowing Our Spirits Contact With the Father of Spirits

Another scriptural purpose for speaking with tongues is so that our spirits (as distinct from our minds or our own understanding) might pray. God is a Spirit, and He has provided a supernatural means whereby the human spirit can be in direct contact with the Father of spirits (Heb. 12:9).

Paul said, *"For if I pray in an unknown tongue, MY SPIRIT PRAYETH, but my understanding is unfruitful"* (1 Cor. 14:14).

Paul also made reference to this in Romans 8:26: *"Likewise the Spirit also helpeth our infirmities: for we know not what we should pray for as we ought: but the Spirit itself maketh intercession for us with groanings which cannot be uttered."*

A more correct translation would be, ". . . with groanings which cannot be uttered in articulate speech." Therefore, praying in the Spirit provides a way whereby the Holy Spirit enables our spirit, apart from our understanding, to pray to God and commune with Him.

Spiritual Refreshing

Isaiah prophesied not only about the coming Messiah and the great plan of redemption which Jesus would consummate, but also about the Holy Ghost and speaking in other tongues.

ISAIAH 28:11,12
11 For with stammering lips and ANOTHER TONGUE will he speak to this people.
12 To whom he said, THIS IS THE REST wherewith ye may cause the weary to rest; and THIS IS THE REFRESHING. . . .

There is a very real spiritual *rest* and a spiritual *refreshing* in communicating with God our Father, as our spirits pray distinct and separate from our understanding.

Interpreting Tongues in Our Private Prayer Life

Let us notice something else in this scripture in First Corinthians 14:14,15.

1 CORINTHIANS 14:14,15
14 For if I pray in an unknown tongue, my spirit prayeth, but my understanding is unfruitful.
15 What is it then? I will pray with the spirit, and I will pray with the understanding also. . . .

Paul had just stated in First Corinthians 14:13, "*. . . let him that speaketh in an unknown tongue pray that he may interpret.*"

Through the gift of interpretation of tongues, we may know by our understanding, as the Spirit wills, what our spirit prays. This is not always necessary, but it is available to us through a gift of the Spirit, the interpretation of tongues.

Years ago when I was filled with the Holy Ghost, I took First Corinthians 14:13 literally. After I was filled with the Spirit, although no one told me to, I found that I received spiritual blessing by continuing to pray in other tongues. Later as I studied the Word of God, I learned that this was scriptural.

Then when I read, "*. . . let him that speaketh in an unknown tongue pray that he may interpret*" (1 Cor. 14:13), I began to pray that I might interpret what I was praying about. I was sure God wouldn't tell us to pray for something we couldn't have.

That is when I first started moving in the gift of interpretation of tongues — in my own prayer life. As I interpreted some of the things I prayed, I began to know in my *understanding* what I had prayed about.

I am convinced that all believers, as the Spirit wills, can interpret their prayers. They may never be used, however, to interpret tongues in a church service because one use of interpretation of tongues is for *private* benefit, and another use of interpretation of tongues is for *public* ministry.

Tongues Is Primarily a Devotional Gift

In talking about the subject of tongues in general, let me say that tongues is primarily a devotional gift. We need to put emphasis on tongues where the emphasis belongs. That is what Paul was trying to do with the Church at Corinth by saying to them, "*I thank my God, I speak with tongues more than ye all*" (1 Cor. 14:18).

Paul was telling the Corinthians the purpose of speaking in tongues and what praying in tongues would do for them. Tongues is primarily a devotional gift to be used in one's prayer life for praising and worshipping God, for speaking mysteries to God, and for building oneself up on his most holy faith.

We should not be as concerned about ministering in tongues and interpreting tongues publicly as we should be about maintaining the blessing tongues produces in our personal prayer lives. However, as we are faithful to pray in tongues in our own personal prayer lives, that allows us to be sensitive to the Holy Spirit should He desire to use us in tongues and interpretation in the local church.

As mentioned earlier, Howard Carter spoke of the continual blessing that tongues are meant to be to believers in their individual prayer life:

> We must not forget that speaking in other tongues is not only an initial evidence or sign of the Holy Spirit's indwelling, but it is also an experience for the rest of one's life to assist in the worship of God. It is a flowing stream that should never dry up, but will enrich your life spiritually. [1]

The Gift of Tongues in Public Ministry

In addition to praying in tongues in one's individual prayer life, it is also true that there is a public side to speaking in tongues. Paul said that not everyone would be used in what we call the public ministry of tongues, for he said in First Corinthians 12:30, "*. . . do all speak with tongues? . . .*"

The obvious answer is no because in this verse Paul is talking about the *public ministry* of diversities of tongues which is a ministry gift denoting more the prophetic office, *not* the devotional gift of tongues.

Some take First Corinthians 12:30 out of its context and conclude that Paul was saying, "Speaking in tongues isn't for everyone. Therefore, you can be filled with the Spirit without speaking with tongues."

However, again, we must remember that here Paul is talking about the *ministry gift of tongues,* for he began by saying, "*AND GOD HATH SET SOME IN THE CHURCH, first apostles, secondarily prophets, thirdly teachers, after that miracles, then gifts of healings, helps, governments, DIVERSITIES OF TONGUES*" (1 Cor. 12:28). Ministry gifts or *offices* are "set" in the Church by God; they are people called to the fivefold ministry.

Then he asked the question in First Corinthians 12:29 and 30, "*Are all apostles? . . .* [No, all are not apostles.] *. . . are all prophets? . . .* [No, all are not prophets.] *. . . are all teachers? are all workers of miracles? Have all the gifts of healing? . . .*" Of course, the answer is no.

Let's look a little further in verse 30: *". . . do all speak with tongues? . . ."* The obvious answer is no. Paul was talking here about fivefold ministry gifts, just as he was talking about fivefold ministry gifts when he asked, *"Are all apostles? . . ."* (v. 29), and so forth.

Paul was again talking about the public ministry of tongues in First Corinthians 14:27 and 28: *"If any man speak in an unknown tongue, let it be by two, or at the most by three, and that by course; and let one interpret. But if there be no interpreter, let him keep silence in the church; and let him speak to himself, and to God."*

In the Greek, the words "two" and "three" are personal pronouns and refer to people. Paul was simply saying that not more than two or three people should speak in a service.

In the next verse he said, *"Let the prophets speak two or three . . ."* (1 Cor. 14:29). There may be more prophets who could speak in the assembly, but in any one particular service, this verse says only two or three of them should do the talking.

This administration was given to prevent competitive utterances in the local body. The Bible gives us these instructions regarding the public ministry of the utterance gifts in order that *". . . all things be done decently and in order"* (1 Cor. 14:40).

Prophecy Is Equivalent to
Tongues and Interpretation

The church is edified when someone speaks with other tongues in the public assembly *and* there is an interpretation. Paul plainly stated that to prophesy — which is the equivalent of tongues and interpretation — is to speak unto men *". . . to edification, and exhortation, and comfort"* (1 Cor. 14:3).

Paul also said, *". . . greater is he that prophesieth than he that speaketh with tongues, EXCEPT HE INTERPRET . . ."* (1 Cor. 14:5). Paul was saying that if someone interprets what he gives forth in tongues, then the one who prophesies is *not* greater than the one who gives forth a tongue *and* interpretation. Paul was also saying in this passage that tongues with interpretation is equivalent to prophecy.

To illustrate this point, it takes two nickels to make a dime. Two nickels are not a dime, but they are equivalent to a dime. Paul was saying in effect that prophecy is like the dime, and tongues and interpretation are like the two nickels. In other words, they are equivalent.

Naturally, it would be better to have the "dime" (prophecy) than to have just the "nickel" (speaking with tongues) in the public assembly. But if interpretation went along with the tongues, then the two of them together would be equivalent to prophecy, the "dime."

As I said before, prophesying is not preaching per se. Certainly, there can be an element of prophecy in preaching sometimes because prophecy is inspired utterance. But in the specific sense prophecy is a supernatural gift that is manifested spontaneously as the Spirit wills.

If prophesying were *just* preaching, then you wouldn't have to make any preparation to preach. But you have to study in order to preach effectively. Paul said, *"STUDY to shew thyself approved unto God, a workman that needeth not to be ashamed . . ."* (2 Tim. 2:15).

You don't have to study to speak with tongues or to interpret tongues. You don't have to study to prophesy. That comes by inspiration of the Spirit.

Of course, when one is preaching under the anointing and suddenly he says something he hadn't previously thought of, that is the inspiration of the Holy Spirit. And that kind of supernatural speaking has an element of prophecy to it because it is given by the inspiration of the Spirit.

When someone speaks with tongues and interprets the tongues, the church is edified. When used in line with the Word of God, speaking with tongues with the interpretation of tongues can convince any unbelieverss who are present of the reality of the Presence of God, and that often causes them to turn to God and be saved (1 Cor. 14:22).

Speaking in Tongues in a Public Setting

Is there ever a time when it is appropriate to speak with other tongues in a public setting? We find a clue to the answer in Mark 16:17 and 18.

MARK 16:17,18
17 And these signs shall follow them that believe; In my name shall they cast out devils; they shall speak with new tongues;
18 They shall take up serpents; and if they drink any deadly thing, it shall not hurt them; they shall lay hands on the sick, and they shall recover.

First let's look at verse 17. Jesus said, *"And these signs shall follow them that believe; In my name shall they cast out devils . . ."* (Mark 16:17). Casting out devils can be done privately or, if necessary, publicly (although wisdom must be exercised if it is done publicly).

That same passage of Scripture continues, *". . . they shall lay hands on the sick, and they shall recover"* (Mark 16:18). Laying hands on the sick can also be done privately or publicly.

Another sign that will follow those who believe is also stated: *". . . they shall SPEAK WITH NEW TONGUES"* (Mark 16:17). As with the other two signs, speaking in tongues can be done publicly at times, as well as privately.

Of course, we don't want to have prolonged praying in tongues in public services because unless there is an interpretation, folks don't know what is being said and they won't be edified. However, it is all right to pray in tongues quietly at the altar as long as you desire, because you go there to get edified.

Also, if everyone in a service is worshipping God and praying in tongues, then it is all right for you to pray in tongues at that time too. As the congregation prays and worships God in tongues, I join in and pray that way too.

But when the congregation ceases praying, I cease praying. The congregation wouldn't be edified if I went on and on praying aloud in tongues. So we do need to know how to use what we have to the greatest advantage so that people are blessed and edified.

Private vs. Public Operation of the Gift of Tongues

1 CORINTHIANS 14:18,19
18 I thank my God, I speak with tongues more than ye all:
19 YET IN THE CHURCH I had rather speak five words with my understanding, that by my voice I might teach others also, than ten thousand words in an unknown tongue.

In this passage, Paul was explaining the difference between tongues used as a devotional gift: *". . . I speak with tongues more than ye all"* (v. 18), and tongues used in public ministry: *"Yet IN THE CHURCH I had rather speak five words with my understanding, that . . . I might teach others . . ."* (v. 19).

Tongues is not a teaching gift or a preaching gift. This is not the purpose of tongues. For example, if I were to speak in tongues from the pulpit instead of teaching or preaching from the pulpit, it wouldn't edify the congregation at all. It would edify me, but not the hearers. Therefore, it is more profitable that I teach the congregation, not speak to the congregation in tongues.

Paul was not belittling tongues when he said, *". . . I had rather speak five words with my understanding . . ."* (1 Cor. 14:19). He merely divided it as it should be divided. He said, *". . . I HAD RATHER speak five words with my understanding, that by my voice I might teach others also, than ten thousand words in an unknown tongue"* (1 Cor. 14:19).

In other words, he was saying, "The congregation would get more good out of just those five words spoken in their own language than ten thousand words that I could speak in other tongues."

Every believer can pray to interpret his tongues in his own private devotions (1 Cor. 14:13). However, God will not use every believer in *public* utterance in tongues, for that is a gift and is not given to everyone: *"But all these [spiritual gifts] worketh that one and the selfsame Spirit, DIVIDING TO EVERY MAN SEVERALLY AS HE WILL"* (1 Cor. 12:11).

As with every gift of the Spirit, the gift of tongues operates only *as the Spirit wills*. No one should *try* to operate this gift in the public assembly without the unction of the Holy Spirit. This is the mistake the Corinthians were making, and this is where many believers today often make a mistake.

As we have seen, God has given us instruction in the public use and operation of the gift of divers kinds of tongues. We need to obey those instructions. But most of all we need to exercise devotional tongues in our private prayer life on a consistent basis. As we do so, our spirits will be edified as we speak mysteries supernaturally to God.

Then we as a body of believers should covet the spiritual gifts earnestly, and as the Spirit wills, God will bring forth His messages to His people through the gifts of tongues and interpretation of tongues.

---

[1] Howard Carter, *Questions and Answers on Spiritual Gifts*, (Tulsa, Oklahoma: Harrison House, Inc., 1976), p. 120.

Questions for Study

1. Of the three vocal gifts — the gifts of utterance or inspiration — which is the most prominent?

2. Name the five reasons listed in this chapter why it seems that Full Gospel people place such an emphasis on tongues.

3. Define "divers kinds of tongues."

4. Name the five recorded instances in the Book of Acts where believers received the Holy Spirit.

5. Name the eight purposes for speaking in tongues listed in this chapter.

6. What kind of gift is tongues and how is it primarily used?

7. Speaking in tongues with the interpretation of tongues can convince unbelievers who are present of what?

8. Why isn't it good to have prolonged praying in tongues in public services?

9. Tongues is not a _____ gift or a _____ gift.

10. According to First Corinthians 12:11, how does the gift of tongues operate?

Chapter 20

The Gift of Interpretation of Tongues

But the manifestation of the Spirit is given to every man to profit withal.

For to one is given by the Spirit the word of wisdom; to another the word of knowledge by the same Spirit;

To another faith by the same Spirit; to another the gifts of healing by the same Spirit;

To another the working of miracles; to another prophecy; to another discerning of spirits; to another divers kinds of tongues; TO ANOTHER THE INTERPRETATION OF TONGUES:

But all these worketh that one and the selfsame Spirit, dividing to every man severally as he will.
— 1 Corinthians 12:7-11

In studying these gifts of the Spirit, we have come to the end of the list: the gift of interpretation of tongues. First, we covered the three gifts of revelation or the three gifts that *reveal* something: the word of wisdom, the word of knowledge, and the discerning of spirits.

Then we studied the three gifts that *do* something, or the three power gifts: the gift of faith, the gifts of healings, and the working of miracles.

Now we will finish our study of the three utterance gifts or the three inspirational gifts, the three gifts that *say* something: prophecy, divers kinds of tongues, and interpretation of tongues.

There has been a great deal of misunderstanding about the gifts of the Spirit. That is the reason Paul said, *"Now concerning spiritual gifts, brethren, I WOULD NOT HAVE YOU IGNORANT"* (1 Cor. 12:1). As I said before, if God didn't want His people to be ignorant in the days of the Early Church, He certainly doesn't want His people to be ignorant today. Yet it is amazing the ignorance that exists among people of God concerning spiritual things.

Many people do not believe that any of the gifts of the Spirit are for us today. Some people believe that a few of the gifts are for us, but not all of them. However, if any of them are for us today, then *all* of them are for us today.

Also, the Bible says that the Holy Spirit gives these gifts to every man to *profit* (1 Cor. 12:7). God wants us to *profit* and spiritual gifts are one means whereby we may profit. I have never read anywhere in the Bible that He took them away from the Church. These gifts are rightfully ours today, and

ignorance concerning them exists only because people do not understand what the Bible says about spiritual gifts.

The three utterance gifts — prophecy, divers kinds of tongues, and interpretation of tongues — are very closely associated. In fact, as I've said, the Bible plainly tells us that tongues with interpretation is equal to prophecy: *". . . greater is he that prophesieth than he that speaketh with tongues, except he interpret . . ."* (1 Cor. 14:5). Although spiritual gifts can be closely associated, we differentiate between them and list them separately so we can better define and understand them.

As we begin our study of the last of the three vocal or inspirational gifts, let us first define them.

Prophecy is *supernatural utterance in a known tongue.*

Divers kinds of tongues is *supernatural utterance in an unknown tongue.*

The interpretation of tongues is *the supernatural showing forth by the Spirit the meaning of an utterance in other tongues.* Also, it is not *translation* of tongues; it is the *interpretation* of tongues.

The Gift of Interpretation of Tongues

The gift of interpretation of tongues is the least gift of all of the gifts of the Spirit because it depends upon another gift — divers kinds of tongues — in order to operate. It does not operate unless tongues have been in operation.

The purpose of the gift of interpretation of tongues is to render the gift of tongues understandable to the hearers so that the whole church congregation, as well as the one who gave the utterance in an unknown tongue, may know what has been said and may be edified thereby. Paul said, *". . . greater is he that prophesieth than he that speaketh with tongues, except he interpret, THAT THE CHURCH MAY RECEIVE EDIFYING"* (1 Cor. 14:5).

But can't God speak to us in some other way in the public assembly? Yes, He can and does. We have other public messages given by the Spirit of God that are not interpretation of tongues; they are a manifestation of the gift of prophecy. For example, psalms, hymns, and spiritual songs are also given by the Holy Spirit through the gift of prophecy (we discussed this in chapter 18).

All these gifts operate by faith, but it takes more faith to operate in the gift of prophecy than tongues or interpretation of tongues. That is because those who operate in the gift of tongues and interpretation of tongues have another person to lean on to complete the utterance. The person with the gift of tongues can lean on the one with the gift of interpretation of tongues, and vice versa. However, the one who has the gift of prophecy must have enough faith just to start giving what he has received (Rom. 12:6).

The Gift of Interpretation of Tongues in Our Private Prayer Life

In private prayer it is not necessary that everything we utter in other tongues be clear to our understanding, because Paul said, *"For if I pray in an unknown tongue, my spirit prayeth, but my understanding is unfruitful"* (1 Cor. 14:14).

Therefore, it isn't necessary that everything I pray in tongues be clear to my understanding or be interpreted because I am not talking to myself, I am talking to God. What I pray in tongues is clear to God and that is sufficient: *"For he that speaketh in an unknown tongue speaketh not unto men, BUT UNTO GOD: for no man understandeth him; howbeit in the spirit HE SPEAKETH MYSTERIES"* (1 Cor. 14:2).

Yet on some occasions God may desire that we interpret our prayers. Paul suggests this in First Corinthians 14:13: *"Wherefore let him that speaketh in an unknown tongue pray that he may interpret."*

There may be times, if it is as the Spirit of God wills, that we know what we are praying about in tongues in our personal devotions, and God will give us the interpretation. That is the way I first started interpreting tongues — in my private prayer life. I was simply praying in other tongues when suddenly I realized I was speaking in English, and I understood that I was interpreting what I had been praying about.

God knows what we are praying about because when we are praying in other tongues, we are talking to Him. But sometimes He wants us to know what we are praying about too.

For example, once before I was married, I was praying in the Spirit. I wasn't even thinking about getting married. I had been praying two or three hours in the Spirit when suddenly I began to interpret part of my prayer. I realized then that I was talking to God about a wife, although from the natural standpoint, I hadn't been thinking or praying

with my understanding along that line. I wasn't even concerned about getting married at that time.

I prayed in English, interpreting what I had been praying in tongues. As I did, by interpretation of tongues I knew in the Spirit that I would be married. I knew who the girl was that I was going to marry, although at this time I had only had one or two dates with her. I also knew by interpretation that we would have two children; the first child would be a boy and the second would be a girl.

Naturally, after we were married and were expecting our first child, I told my wife, "It's a boy." We only picked out a boy's name. We didn't select any girls' names. Then when we were expecting our second child, I said, "This one is a girl." This is what I had learned in the Spirit even before we had been sweethearts.

So we see that there is a private side to the gift of interpretation of tongues that is of great importance to us personally.

There is also a public side to the manifestation of this gift. But not all of us will be used in this way. That will occur only as the Lord wills.

The Gift of Interpretation of Tongues In Public Ministry

1 CORINTHIANS 14:27
27 If any man speak in an unknown tongue, LET IT BE BY TWO, OR AT THE MOST BY THREE, and that by course; and LET ONE INTERPRET.

In ministering publicly in tongues in any one service, Paul is saying here that it should be done by two or at the most by three people. In other words, only two or three people at the most should participate.

The meaning of this passage is made clearer in the *New International Version*.

1 CORINTHIANS 14:27 (*NIV*)
27 If anyone speaks in a tongue, two — or at the most three — should speak, one at a time, and someone must interpret.

Some have asked the question, "Does that refer to three *messages*?" Actually we do not find the expression "messages in tongues" anywhere in the Bible. This is just a phrase that man has coined to try to explain this verse. A better term would be *"utterance* in tongues."

But this particular verse is talking about *people,* not messages or utterances: *"If any MAN speak* [not necessarily referring to the male gender but to any human being] . . . *let it be by two, or at the most by three . . .*" (1 Cor. 14:27).

Paul didn't actually say *how much* they were to speak or not to speak. He just said to let two or three people speak and let it be *by course* or in succession. This implies that they shouldn't all speak at once. And it also implies that the same person might speak more than once.

Based on these scriptures, my suggestion to any congregation is that if three people have already spoken publicly in tongues, a fourth one should not join in and give out an utterance in tongues. If something else needs to be said, one of those who has already spoken should say it. That maintains good order and is consistent with this passage of Scripture where Paul was laying down principles of proper order for supernatural utterances in the local assembly.

Notice that Paul said, "*. . . let one interpret*" (1 Cor. 14:27). There is nothing in the Scriptures that would negate the thought that a person may speak with tongues and interpret the utterance himself.

In fact, one of those who is giving the message in tongues may certainly interpret it himself. Or there may be more than one person who could interpret it.

According to First Corinthians 14:13, those who speak in other tongues are instructed to pray for the gift of interpretation: "*Wherefore let him that speaketh in an unknown tongue pray that he may interpret.*"

What Paul was saying here was that the reason a person is to seek for the gift of interpretation is not necessarily so that he can interpret publicly, but so that he can interpret his own prayers privately if God so wills. That would mean a great deal to his spiritual edification. Then if God did will to use him publicly, he would be equipped to operate in that realm as well.

Actually, in First Corinthians 14:27 when Paul said, "*. . . let ONE interpret,*" he was admonishing us not to have competitive interpretations; that is, two or three people trying to outdo one another by interpreting an utterance. So there is nothing wrong with someone giving an utterance in tongues and interpreting it himself. That would not be unscriptural.

When someone is speaking with tongues, a person who is used often in the gift of interpretation of tongues should immediately begin to be sensitive to the Holy Spirit's moving, if he is not already in tune with what the Holy Ghost is doing in the service. He should make himself available and be ready for the Lord to use him in the operation of that gift.

Sometimes I have waited on someone else to interpret, but they were waiting on me. Either one of us could have interpreted the message given in tongues, but we lost it because we didn't tune in to the Holy Spirit; we were waiting for the other one to do it. Of course, we are not going to get things from God unless we are sensitive to Him.

This is the reason that sometimes we don't have an interpretation of a message when we should have. Sometimes when I have missed it, I've said to the person who had the message in tongues, "Please give that again and I will interpret it." Then when they started speaking, the unction came on me again — I got into the Spirit again — and God gave me the interpretation.

The Gift of *Interpretation* — Not Translation

As we mentioned earlier, the *interpretation* of tongues is not a *translation*. I am sometimes asked why it is that when someone speaks at length in tongues, an interpreter will occasionally give only a short message.

The reason for that is the interpretation is simply showing forth supernaturally by the Spirit of God the meaning of what was said in tongues, and it may not take as many words to declare what was said.

For example, someone may speak a short utterance in tongues and another will speak at length in interpretation. It may take longer to give the interpretation in order to show the meaning clearly. Therefore, we can see why this gift is called the *interpretation* of tongues and not the *translation* of tongues.

Also, very often when one is interpreting tongues, if that person is also used in prophecy, he may finish that interpretation and go into prophecy. I do this quite often.

Most people who are keen in the Spirit can recognize the difference because the minute prophecy begins, there is a little higher authority that can sometimes come with it. In other words, the words in prophecy can sometimes take on more authority and have a greater anointing. There can be more inspiration to it and people are blessed in a greater measure.

Maintaining Good Order in The Public Use of Utterance Gifts

Paul devotes the entire chapter of First Corinthians 14 to the gifts of prophecy, and tongues and interpretation of tongues. In verse 33, he says, *". . . God is not the author of confusion . . ."* (1 Cor. 14:33).

Paul was saying that in the use, or rather the misuse, of prophecy, and tongues and interpretation of tongues there is sometimes confusion. I have been in some services where I have seen the misuse of these gifts and it has brought confusion to a congregation. (These were not my own services, as I usually try to bring out any errors and explain them to the people so they won't go home confused.)

This doesn't mean that the devil was necessarily working in the service. It just means that people can get things mixed up. If we will learn to stay in the Spirit and walk according to the Word, however, we will not operate in these gifts in confusion. God is not the author of confusion.

In this chapter we see such statements as *". . . God is not the author of confusion . . ."* (1 Cor. 14:33) and *"Let all things be done decently and in order"* (v. 40).

We know these verses refer to public services in the church because it said, *"If any man speak in an unknown tongue, let it be by two, or at the most by three, and that by course; and let one interpret. But if there be no interpreter, let him keep silence in the church; and let him speak to himself, and to God"* (1 Cor. 14:27,28). One wouldn't be disturbing the service by just sitting there and talking quietly to God in tongues, but he would be edifying himself.

Sometimes we just need practical advice concerning these manifestations to help us maintain good order. Then even folks who come in to the service who aren't saved or who aren't familiar with the operation of these gifts would understand and be impressed by the good order. More importantly, we would not grieve the Spirit of God. The Bible says, *"And grieve not the holy Spirit of God . . ."* (Eph. 4:30).

The Holy Spirit has been grieved at times in some of our church services. He has been grieved because He wanted to manifest Himself and wasn't permitted to do so. And it grieves the Holy Spirit by the way some folks misuse the gifts of the Spirit and bring confusion to others.

All Things Done Unto Edifying

A final point I want to stress about tongues and interpretation of tongues is that Paul said, *". . . Let all things be done unto edifying"* (1 Cor. 14:26).

When the gift of tongues and interpretation of tongues is manifested by the Spirit of God (and this is one way to judge if it is by the Holy Spirit or not), the utterance will be edifying, inspiring, and a blessing. Of course, if we ourselves are out of tune with the Spirit, we will not always be in a position to judge.

For example, once when I was a pastor, our church was participating with several other churches in a service nearby. I had been particularly busy all that day. I had been on the go all day long, and I hardly had time to pray at all. Then I just ran in, got ready for the service, and hurriedly drove to the church meeting. I was exhausted when I finally got there and sort of just sank into a pew.

God moved in a wonderful way in that service, but I couldn't enter into the blessing; I was just too tired. I knew that what was going on was right and that it was a blessing, but if I had been going to judge the moving of the Spirit that night, I would probably have said, "Boy, they are all out of tune but me." The truth was that *I* was out of tune with the *Holy Spirit* and with *them*.

So it won't always be easy to judge spiritual things if you are out of tune with the Holy Spirit. This doesn't mean you are backslidden, but just that you are not able to enter into the moving of the Holy Spirit and of worship at that particular time.

Spiritual manifestations do need to be judged, however. And we do judge them, whether we do it publicly or not, because we either accept them or reject them. We can't always accept just any man's judgment, however; we only accept those who know the Word of God and who are sensitive to the moving of the Spirit.

We need to be very careful how we regard the gifts of the Holy Spirit in walking before the Lord. We need to stay open to the Spirit of God and to the move of God as we walk meekly, honorably, and reverently before the Lord.

Certainly, we need to invite the operation of the Spirit of God among us, but we need to reverence God and the things of the Spirit of God, and allow God to use whom He will to manifest Himself in our midst through the gifts of the Spirit. Then when God moves, we will be open to Him and ready to receive whatever He has for us.

Questions for Study

1. Define "interpretation of tongues."

   _____

   _____

2. Why is the gift of interpretation of tongues the least of all the gifts?

   _____

   _____

3. What is the purpose of the gift of interpretation of tongues?

   _____

   _____

4. Why does it take more faith to operate in the gift of prophecy than tongues or interpretation of tongues?

   _____

   _____

5. Why isn't it necessary that everything you pray in tongues be clear to your understanding?

   _____

   _____

6. In First Corinthians 14:27, how many people did Paul say should participate in ministering publicly in tongues in any one service?

   _____

   _____

7. In First Corinthians 14:13, what did Paul say was the reason a person is to seek the gift of interpretation?

   _____

   _____

8. In First Corinthians 14:27, when Paul said, "*. . . let ONE interpret,*" what was he doing?

   _____

   _____

9. When someone speaks at length in tongues, why does an interpreter occasionally give only a short message?

   _____

   _____

10. What is one way to judge whether the gift of tongues and interpretation of tongues is by the Holy Spirit or not?

   _____

   _____

STUDY GUIDES AVAILABLE

BY KENNETH E. HAGIN

Baptism in the Holy Spirit

This important study guide, which focuses on the baptism in the Holy Spirit and speaking in other tongues, teaches believers how to draw from the ever present source of power within them—the Holy Spirit.
Item No. BM063
ISBN-10: 0-89276-063-X / ISBN-13: 978-0-89276-063-3
Saddle bound—5.5" x 8.5"/ 66 pages

Biblical Ways to Receive Healing

There is no set way by which people may receive healing. And in this new study guide, you will discover various methods for receiving healing as recorded in the Word of God.
Item No. BM074
ISBN-10: 0-89276-074-5 / ISBN-13: 978-0-89276-074-9
Saddle bound—5.5" x 8.5"/ 71 pages

Foundations for Faith

Faith makes the difference between defeat and victory in a Christian's life. And this study guide explains why receiving from God is dependent upon the faith of the believer.
Item No. BM067
ISBN-10: 0-89276-067-2 / ISBN-13: 978-0-89276-067-1
Saddle bound—5.5" x 8.5"/ 64 pages

Gifts of the Holy Spirit

The lessons in this valuable study guide closely examine the gifts of the Holy Spirit, their operations, and their practical uses.
Item No. BM064
ISBN-10: 0-89276-064-8 / ISBN-13: 978-0-89276-064-0
Saddle bound—5.5" x 8.5" / 69 pages

God's Word on Divine Healing

This dynamic study guide gives convincing scriptural proof that it is God's will to heal!
Item No. BM069
ISBN-10: 0-89276-069-9 / ISBN-13: 978-0-89276-069-5
Saddle bound—5.5" x 8.5" / 77 pages

The Ministry Gifts

This informative, in-depth study guide discusses the biblical characteristics of the ministry gifts—apostle, prophet, evangelist, pastor, teacher—and their roles in the Body of Christ.
Item No. BM073
ISBN-10: 0-89276-073-7 / ISBN-13: 978-0-89276-073-2
Saddle bound—5.5" x 8.5" / 120 pages

Steps to Answered Prayer

Steps to Answered Prayer reveals step-by-step guidelines that, when faithfully followed in prayer, assure the believer of an answer.
Item No. BM065
ISBN-10: 0-89276-065-6
ISBN-13: 978-0-89276-065-7
Saddle bound—5.5" x 8.5" / 67 pages

Walking by Faith

Each lesson in this comprehensive study guide will help the believer achieve a workable operation of faith in his life—a faith that works.
Item No. BM068
ISBN-10: 0-89276-068-0
ISBN-13: 978-0-89276-068-8
Saddle bound—5.5" x 8.5"/ 67 pages

The Will of God in Prayer

This study guide will instruct believers on how to use the Word of God in prayer and get results.
Item No. BM066
ISBN-10: 0-89276-066-4
ISBN-13: 978-0-89276-066-4
Saddle bound—5.5" x 8.5" / 64 pages

Why should you consider attending
RHEMA
Bible Training Center?

Here are a few good reasons:

- Training at one of the top Spirit-filled Bible schools anywhere

- Teaching based on steadfast faith in God's Word

- Growth in your spiritual walk coupled with practical training in effective ministry

- Specialization in the area of your choosing: Youth or Children's Ministry, Evangelism, Pastoral Care, Missions, Biblical Studies, or Supportive Ministry

- Optional intensive third-year programs: School of Worship, School of Pastoral Ministry, School of World Missions, and General Extended Studies

- Worldwide ministry opportunities—while you're in school

- An established network of churches and ministries around the world who depend on RHEMA to supply full-time staff and support ministers

- A two-year evening school taught entirely in Spanish is also available. Log on to **www.cebrhema.org** for more information.

Call today for information or application material.
1-888-28-FAITH (1-888-283-2484)
www.rbtc.org

RHEMA Bible Training Center admits students of any race, color, or ethnic origin.

OFFER CODE—BKORD:PRMDRBTC

Always on.

For the latest news and information on products, media, podcasts, study resources, and special offers, visit us online 24 hours a day.

www.rhema.org

Free Subscription!

Call now to receive a free subscription to *The Word of Faith* magazine from Kenneth Hagin Ministries. Receive encouragement and spiritual refreshment from . . .

- *Faith-building articles from Kenneth W. Hagin, Lynette Hagin, and others*

- *"Timeless Teaching" from the archives of Kenneth E. Hagin*

- *Feature articles on prayer and healing*

- *Testimonies of salvation, healing, and deliverance*

- *Children's activity page*

- *Updates on RHEMA Bible Training Center, RHEMA Bible Church, and other outreaches of Kenneth Hagin Ministries*

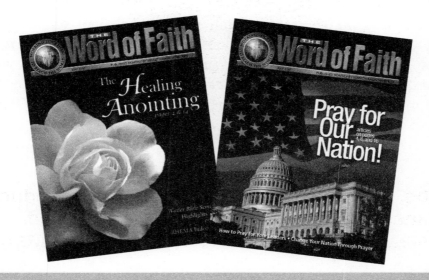

Subscribe today for your free *Word of Faith*!

1-888-28-FAITH (1-888-283-2484)

www.rhema.org/wof

Notes:

Notes:

Notes:

Notes: